The Road to Roussillon

The Road to Roussillon

UPHILL ALL THE WAY

Paul P Torr

ISBN: 1546666664
ISBN 13: 9781546666660

Prologue

THE ARMY IS A STRANGE and unique organisation which affects and influences people's behaviour more than any other organisation, sometimes for better but quite often for worse. It can bring out the best in many people but often it has the opposite effect and makes monsters out of babies. This is particularly the case for anybody who is a thoroughly nasty bastard as the Army can be the perfect environment in which they can apply their nastiness. This may be partly in favour of the need to create aggressive and hostile soldiers who can kill without hesitation or compassion. After all the common basic soldier's training involves firearms and activities which have no purpose other than to incapacitate or kill. In the absence of a hostile and aggressive enemy there may be no option for some people other than to direct this aggression and lack of compassion at the easiest and most convenient target, the subordinate; in rank colleague. It is also the case that soldiers doing what they are trained to do, fight; in peacetime environments attracts so much criticism. It generates loyalty often misguided, alters perception and strengthens stubborn attitudes.

For many it is something akin to a surrogate family sadly minus the care and affection but inclusive of anger, mischief, deceit and treachery.

When I set out to write this book I wanted to share my memories and experiences, both good and bad and to capture some of the history that made my life and that of many others so different from what it would have been in any other organisation.

What sets us apart as humans, is that we can think about our past and segregate the good times from the bad, in addition we can set aside the painful memories and focus on the times and events that we want to remember.

In my post service career I have learned a good deal more about people than I ever did in the Army and in particular that although we can disguise unpleasant and painful memories of bad experiences they never disappear and that the consequences of the service lifestyle remain intact.

Some of the effects stay hidden in our subconscious waiting to emerge when we may be at a low ebb and this may present some pretty awful and depressing feelings.

Some years ago I was stricken with a strain of Meningitis which remained undiagnosed for several weeks. I was also suffering what amounted to post traumatic stress and for literally days on end unable to sleep, unable to reason and in considerable pain. I was also struggling to cope in my mind with tasks that I had been dealing with in the Army over 20 years earlier which had returned to haunt me.

These hallucinatory matters were at the time very real even though all those years ago they did not present so much of a challenge. Coming back to bite me they prompted me to imagine that I was heading for insanity.

A smart and persistent GP, a few days and some invasive and painful procedures in hospital identified the mischievous bug and with some extra care from my wife and children I slowly found my way back to reality.

I have during the past twenty years been involved with a number of social interactive processes including, protective behaviours, restorative and victim interventions, mediation and counselling.

There is a common thread that involves sharing and talking about memories and experiences that are painful and regrettable and which persistently haunt us.

There is virtually nothing that is so bad or awful that can't be shared or talked about.

Part of my reasons for writing this book is to share, not only mine but memories of others, clear out the pain and let in the sunshine.

I have reached the conclusion that the Army contains two distinct groups of individuals, the givers and the takers. In most cases the givers work hard and with the objective of doing all that they can for the service, their colleagues and often their bosses. They do this not for personal gain or glory but out of a sense of honour, loyalty and team spirit. The takers contribute little more than is necessary to comply with any disciplinary obligation whilst making every effort to enhance or project their own image and in particular to take advantage of any other individual's efforts.

It always seemed to me that I was constantly being required to leap through hoops of burning fire in order to make any positive gain whilst others were freely cruising along and reaping benefits.

For some children born of serving soldiers into the army regime who go on to themselves become soldiers the army becomes the heart and soul of their existence.

I actually believe that the relations with the service, regiment or corps becomes for some soldiers far more personal and intimate than any partner or family association and this leads to a high incidence of failed marriages.

Many soldiers are part of a family heritage stretching back for several generations.

This is particularly the case for commissioned ranks but also for enlisted men who often follow their fathers in to a Regiment or Corps.

It is only after leaving the service and with the benefit of hindsight that it is possible to appreciate and understand how the Army creates a dependency from which many soldiers of all ranks struggle to escape. Life after life is never the same.

I think that for career soldiers who complete several years there will always be a feeling of loss when leaving the army regardless of whatever new life they pursue.

Many soldiers particularly those with Military Police service are attached by an umbilical of geography close to the Regimental base or to the traditional home of the Army in Aldershot.

The need of some former soldiers to hang on to their history has resulted in a thriving regimental association organisation clinging to the past, swapping stories and holding tight to past memories. The modern phenomenon of social media may have usurped many other contact mediums.

I have heard many accounts of soldiers struggling to survive on the outside and sadly several accounts of those who have found themselves alone in poor health and in death.

More recently during my second and third career and almost thirty years after leaving the service I have identified just how many "veterans" have been unable to reintegrate into civilian life and who now almost unbelievably account for 8% of the United Kingdom prison population.

Until 2007, thirty years after leaving the Army I had not taken part in any Army/RMP reunion. This had not been a conscious or deliberate avoidance, it was simply the consequence of having a new career and having lost all contact.

In 2008 thanks to one of my old Osnabruck colleagues Ronnie Mac, I took part in the Osnabruck "Last Fling" my very first reunion. I met a load of my former Osnabruck colleagues, none of whom I had seen since March 1968. I am now part of the Osnabruckers annual reunion group.

Sadly since leaving the Army many of my former colleagues have passed away and our annual reunion pilgrimage serves to share memories, good and bad.

Without any sense of pleasure or revenge it is a sad fact that the three officers under whom I served at different times and who were to a large degree responsible for compromising my career, one of whom was personally responsible for causing me a great deal of trauma and depression close to breakdown have died in the past ten years. Each entry into the obituary register represents a small part lost from my own history.

Under different circumstances it may have been the case that the very same men might have provided me with a more positive appraisal in common with those of some of my contemporaries who subsequently achieved high rank and who were most certainly at least in my view far less able than me.

One of the lessons that I should have learned from bad experience yet made the mistake over and over again was; NEVER take over a crock of junk and do a good job.

Take it over, sort it out and hand it over for your successor to take the credit. Additionally a newly arrived commander takes a look and assumes that it has always been that good and then usurps the credit for having such a good infrastructure in place.

Prior to 1970 the Military Police formations were identified according to the Military formation which they supported, this was the case for example with Osnabruck, 12th Infantry Brigade Provost Unit and 2nd Division Provost company.

The establishments were similar in some aspects but different in others. For operational purposes the Provost Company was commanded by a Major rank officer with a Warrant Officer 1 RSM as senior enlisted man. The Provost unit was commanded by a Captain officer rank with a Warrant officer 2 CSM as senior enlisted. The remainder of the men were organised into military police sections of thirteen juniors commanded by a section sergeant and divided into subsections under the subordinate command of a full corporal. Staff sergeants had no direct personnel management remit but were generally employed as training officer or CQMS.

For enlisted men there were differences in pay structures, single men living in barrack accommodation received a flat rate of daily pay, they did not pay for their accommodation or food. Married men however had to pay for their service married quarters and in addition they were paid a daily rate of ration allowance.

In cases where married men were deployed on any operational field exercise or formal training when they were effectively "fed" at Army expense they had part of their ration allowance deducted from their pay. This was a very unpopular action which could be a substantial amount.

In 1970 the Government introduced the Military salary concept, in addition to a fairly decent overall pay increase the ration allowance for married men was abolished and single men in barracks were charged for their accommodation and food.

Married or single was the same pay rate.

This period also saw changes in the structure and title of Military Police formations and these became numerically titled. To begin with in BAOR 111

Provost Company, 112, 113, 114,115. Berlin not strategically part of BAOR remained as 247 Provost Company and some others such as Hong Kong and Cyprus retained their original titles.

Later reorganisation resulted in the creation of 110 Provost Company commanded by the late Major Richard (Dickie) Poole at Sennelager which had under the original restructuring been a detachment of another Provost Company.

Northern Ireland had become a major destination during the escalation of the troubles and the Army had reorganised the Royal Military Police into a Corps with Regiments, thus the birth of 1 Regiment and 2 Regiment RMP. These changes projected RMP into the higher priorities echelon for obtaining increased manpower and resources to undertake the increased and much changed RMP roles in NI.

Several new Provost companies were created in Northern Ireland 174,175,176,177,178 and 179.

The structure of the new provost companies also involved the introduction of the RMP platoon commanded by a SSGT and divided into two sections each commanded by a SGT.

These changes of course generated not only a massive increase in manpower deployed to Northern Ireland but also created many more ranking appointments for officers as well as bigger opportunities for enlisted men.

I often think about what we do with our lives and what if anything is determined by destiny, chance or just luck either good or bad! I have probably spent far too much time wondering if there was anything else that I might have done to have changed things for me and for the better. The answer will be yes; but only in the case of actions and decisions over which I would have had control. It will never be possible to dictate the thoughts and motives of others and whatever actions they might put in motion, the reality is that much of what we do is in response to behaviour and actions of others.

Of course such reflections are only generated as a result of unwelcome outcomes, when things happen that we like we just accept these without any concern.

Good fortune will always be welcome.

My early days

I HAD A REASONABLY GOOD primary education which provided me with the basic skills required to navigate primary age life.

Rather egotistically I can recall being identified as a prolific and competent reader and being recognised for my reading and writing skills. When aged around seven years I had effectively completed the class reading targets way ahead of my classroom contemporaries and was creating and writing scruffy but meaningful stories to reflect my out of school activities.

Sadly; it seems that these skills were not developed as they might have been and it's anybody's guess what a higher education might have produced.

The consequence of my success was the decision by the school head teacher to elevate me from the first year to the second where it was considered I would find the work to be more suited to my abilities and more challenging. I regret to say however that I failed to gain a scholarship when I apparently failed the 11+ although I still don't believe this to be the case and suspect some kind of subterfuge or conspiracy. My suspicion is that my Parents unilaterally rejected the pass and place offer because of the financial implications.

Despite this minor setback my secondary education never the less got off to a good start and I found myself in the cream of the first year. Once again my pet subjects, English, History and Geography were to be my refuge but mathematics and science my Achilles heel. This difficulty with numbers and calculations was made even worse due to my form teacher also being head of maths. Perhaps he had honed his aggressive attitude during military service. I then sort of lost interest and wasted the rest of my education. The evidence of that is that I managed to leave school at fourteen without a single documented qualification.

I may have lacked or failed to exhibit any real ambition and motivation as well as having a serious laid back attitude to life in general.

I clearly remember an otherwise excellent school report with a great write up for my favourite topic, English literature and the English master adding "Talent squandered by sheer laziness"

I just didn't get it and nobody ever bothered to explain.

I suspect that from then on a series of decisions some of which were totally beyond my control would set in motion a sequence of events which would help to determine my future.

Around the age of twelve years my father decided for reasons not clear to me that our family was to move house from the suburbs of a large town and take up residence in a house some six miles away to a village that I had never heard of.

This rather unpopular decision had been made without any debate, discussion or explanation and his reasons, whatever they might have been would seem to have been totally selfish. There was no obvious advantage and in fact it seemed to me that he must have been totally bonkers. He would now have to bus to work rather than a ten minute walk and in a rural setting just about everything is more expensive.

There was little to be gained from any objection or argument so I simply had to get on with the situation with which I was presented. Legally I would have to change senior school following the summer break and more concerning was the fact that all of my friends lived close to the area from which we were moving. The house move actually took place during the summer holiday and on return to school I kept quiet about the change of address but had to suffer the physical effort of a six mile cycle ride to school each day. I should have requested permission to bring my bicycle into school but failed to do so. Such a disclosure would have meant I would have to change school and that was something I did not want. I had given little thought to what I would do post school other than realising that any professional career was beyond any expectations. I had not identified any particular talent, I had no real skills and I had never received any advice or counselling as regards any future career.

During the two summers prior to my leaving school I had managed to secure a holiday job on a local farm. When I left school I was able to continue with this work and eventually I was invited to apply to remain on full time. I had nothing else to do and so it made some sense, it was a job and I was getting very well paid each week.

During the next three years under the auspices of a formal government sponsored agricultural apprenticeship I remained in my farming occupation. As part of the programme I undertook some study at a local college and actually acquired a fairly extensive knowledge of veterinary science, animal husbandry, stock breeding and animal deceases and treatments. I also managed to pass several City and Guilds examinations which represented my first ever formal qualifications.

An added benefit to this occupation was the fact that I also learned to drive every type and class of road vehicle, sometimes under somewhat questionable circumstances, this practical experience would prove to be of considerable benefit during my military service.

I had even procured my own personal set of the implements used to undertake some of the minor routine livestock "operations" and in a moment of over ambitious day dreaming had the idea that I might even secure myself a professional career in veterinary medicine.

I eventually realised that although not impossible; the idea was highly improbable without some long term serious study, financial assistance and a dedicated sponsor.

I was without hope in all three categories.

Time for a Change

IT IS AT THIS POINT in my life, summer 1964 that "fate " intervened. During a late night train journey home I had a chance encounter with a gentleman who impressed me with a fascinating account of his life after leaving a small rural community in the Irish Republic. Just like me he had been stuck in a going nowhere job but had moved to England for his National Service in the Royal Air Force.

As a result of a malicious prank which left him with badly scarred arms he was discharged from the service and as a consequence he had found himself homeless, jobless and broke.

By this time he was literally desperate and as a result of his dire situation he enlisted into the merchant navy as the lowest level deck-hand. During the next 20 years he travelled the world in a variety of commercial ships. He was eventually promoted into senior and well paid positions, had a great deal of fun, made and spent a load of money and enjoyed the company and benefits of girls around the world. At the time of our meeting he was in between ships and had recently returned to the United Kingdom after several years working around Japan and the Far East.

At this point I knew that it might be time for me to make a change. I was eighteen years old with a boring monotonous job and no prospects of any kind of advancement or promotion. Without the slightest idea what I was doing a few days later I took a week off from work and rather excitedly headed for London and the Merchant Navy recruitment office. Wisely perhaps I made no mention of my plans to any of my work colleagues.

The staff at the Merchant Navy office must have thought that I was a bit of a dummy, I had no nautical experience or knowledge, I had no particular skills or any idea what I wanted to do on board ship and my geography was not so hot. On the positive side I was fairly fit, I was physically much stronger than the average eighteen year old and well able to take on and cope with any amount of hard physical work.

Whatever impression I may have made, I came away from the office with a pile of papers and forms to be completed as well as an appointment for me to return some days later with forms completed, passport application, registration fee and Birth certificate. I was sort of on my way.

Here again fate intervened, for some unexplained reason that I can't recall, after leaving the train from London I took a route that I would not normally use and as a result found myself walking past the Army Recruiting Office. I had never even thought about the Army as a job option yet here I was standing outside, reading the notices and looking enviously at the posters of Army Paratroopers enjoying life in tropical surroundings.

On an impulse I went inside and after talking to the recruiting sergeant I completed a short test, filled in a few forms, arranged for a medical the following week and unbelievably compared to modern procedures that was virtually it. I had a bit of a surprise when my Farmer employer told me just a few days later that he had received a form from the Army and that he had already completed and sent it back. A few weeks later I signed on took my day's pay and new testament and I was in the Army.

Launched

THIS BOOK IS A PERSONAL biography which focuses primarily on my own military service career from the date of my "attestation" on 2nd December 1964 and which lasted almost 23 years until I resigned in August 1987.

I have included some local geographical background and military history but it has not been my intention to present a definitive history of any of the towns and cities or any of the Military formations of which the RMP units in which I have served.

I have included some of the more notable moments in just the same way as they are shared at reunions. I know that there are thousands of memories and stories out there but it would be a mammoth task and well beyond the scope of this book to record and share them all.

I have purposely and perhaps mischievously not kept strictly to any chronological sequence except for the postings rotation; from my very first in Osnabruck to my last at Headquarters Rheindahlen Garrison.

Germany and in particular the western Rheineland region is where it had always been my hope and intention to live after the Army. After just a few months into my last posting at Rheindahlen I found myself in an impossible situation where enough was enough, the job was dull and boring, devoid of any form of challenge and despite my rank, length of service and skills base I was treated like a mere novice. From that point it became a matter of pride and I simply had to choose the fastest and most direct exit. Perhaps the only redeeming fact was that it was not an RMP officer that precipitated the end of my service career.

After leaving the Army and although I had a new career in place I found that life as a civilian was never going to be the same combination of mental and physical challenge that the previous 23 years had provided. Although I joined the local British Legion Branch and went through the formal joining induction I never returned, judgementally I was dismayed that the whole branch was full of old men. I took another route and offered my services to the local Army Cadet Force, this was a bit more interesting but again I realised some of the policies including that of appointing civilians with no actual military experience to senior command roles did not suit me. This might have been partly ego on my part because I would have had some difficulty in adopting a subordinate role.

Apart from these two unsuccessful interludes I had no contact whatever with any of my previous colleagues or any military or reunion organisation.

There are more than enough definitive studies of the Royal Military Police already published which testify to the great achievements of certain individuals both in terms of rank and honours and awards, my service career did not recognise me as having met the criteria for any outstanding honour and sadly my service achievements failed to elevate me to the rank and role that I coveted and which in all honesty I believe that I was cruelly denied.

There are probably hundreds of other servicemen who's efforts and contributions were much like mine. They may have been overlooked or in some way hijacked for the good and benefit of someone else or in my case have fallen victim of a bad deal.

I also wanted to include how it was possible for many of us to have missed opportunities, never to be repeated, never offered to everybody but which could have improved the outcome for me and many others.

I have reluctantly come to appreciate that in spite of the fact that I had some quite specific opportunities throughout my service I may not have made best use of them, my only real failings; certainly in my early days I think were being young and naïve and not particularly ambitious.

I would only really appreciate these shortcomings in later years and when I found myself in a position of sufficient authority I was determined that the men under my command did not make the same mistakes and would make the best of every opportunity even if sometimes they did not appreciate what I was doing.

This biography is not an assault on the Army and specifically not the Royal Military Police. However, I am certainly a critic of an organisation that gave me so much but took even more including the best years of my life.

I am ever mindful of how much I owe, it is possible and even probable that without the Army I may have never flown in an aircraft or travelled overseas.

I would never have met my wife and who knows what I might have become.

Life Inside

THE ARMY MUCH LIKE ANY other organisation has; or at least during my years of service had more than it's fair share of two faced, backstabbing and butt kissing individuals and yes men who generally appeared to lead a charmed life immune to most un-pleasantries. Many of these individuals somehow managed to avoid real work and even as seniors had little or no concept of managing men and resources in order to fulfil either of the dual roles of the RMP. Military Police had two separate roles and undertook peacetime garrison policing as well as operational which from day 1 in the Corps we were told was the primary role of assisting the Army in training for war.

Is it really possible? for a member of the RMP as an NCO to be employed as a clerk throughout his career, speeding from one promotion to another with consecutive outstanding confidential reports and then to be commissioned into command having little or no operational or static police duty experience?

Within a military organisation and what is effectively a totally authoritarian and of necessity autocratic regime with virtually unchallenged and absolute power many of these "immune" individuals achieve accelerated rank status. The consequences of such a regime for many others subject to the official rules and regulations of the Army was that they could find themselves not only out of favour but also victim to the unchallenged authority and venomous treatment by such individuals. It was often the case that those unfortunate enough to find themselves targeted by these people in such situations generally become estranged from their friends and colleagues who may have feared the risk and consequences of becoming tainted by association.

Progress for enlisted men (and women WRAC) in the army is dependent on annual confidential reports which are written, in theory by their officer commanding, then endorsed and countersigned by the next appointed higher ranking staff officer. These reports then find their way to the annual promotion boards. It should be clear to just about anybody that whilst the reports are written mostly in good faith it would be highly unlikely, particularly in the case of junior ranks for the officer concerned to have sufficient knowledge of each man under his command to be able to produce these crucially important reports with such conviction and any reasonable level of accuracy.

It must be obvious that in most cases the majority of the information in the reports is provided by a third party, usually the junior NCO's immediate supervisor and it should be equally clear that such a process has huge potential for a nepotistic presentation. For those men who preferred to lead their own lives without wanting to spend their entire off duty time drinking or socialising with their work colleagues they would be branded as poor at socialising and for those who were either unable or unwilling to play football or cricket they were to be branded as failing to take part in unit activities. Of course in the case of those soldiers who were fortunate to be working in close proximity to their officer commanding or RSM, whilst performing an important administrative role the officer would be able to report from his own personal observations.

It would probably not be an issue for concern if such third party generated reports were always fair and totally beneficial but sadly this was not the case. Too many were generated not on the basis of professional capability but more on personal or lack of; personal relationships.

I was certainly very naïve in believing that going to work and getting on with the job, quietly without shouting out and mouthing off would ultimately lead to recognition of ability and with this, success and promotion.

Confidential reports provided an opportunity for settling scores and destroying careers and ambitions. The process provided the opportunity for the individual concerned to have sight of and acknowledge the contents of the report but took no account of any disagreement or objections. There was of course a process of redress against any unsatisfactory report but ultimately there was no likelihood or indeed any compelling system in place that would require any officer to change any report. Clearly such a process allowed officers to write virtually anything they wished and the only option available at times of promotion boards in cases of representation from individuals unhappy with their report was for the selection board to consider such unfavourable reports as "rogue" and discount them.

All kinds of vague, fictitious and exaggerated entries might be included without a shred of real evidence or substance. It was also the case that such negative reports would be substantiated by the authors including reference to the subject individual having been provided (fictitious) substantial guidance and support in order to improve any failings or deficiencies. The reality was that support was rarely if ever provided and instead the subject would only discover the depth of his alleged failings and poor performance when reading his annual report. When enlisted soldiers were invited to read and initial their annual reports, they did so as confirmation that they had seen the report and although they may have expressed concern or disagreement with the contents at the time there was actually no provision for any recipient to endorse their unhappiness or disagreement with the report.

It should be noted that I have written this book in relation to events which took place between fifty and thirty years ago. I am of course a good bit older and I would like to think somewhat wiser. In 1964 I was young, naive and totally inexperienced about most everything. Trying to work out now why I acted or responded to situations and people all of those years ago is hardly a mystery but simply because I didn't know any better.

In 1965 I guess that social interaction was not one of my particularly strong personality traits and I was perhaps rather shy. I suspect that my shy and inhibited style may have been interpreted as being aloof and rude when in reality this was not the case.

It may have been this more than anything else that prevented me from making more progress than some of my colleagues. At the time I almost certainly would have considered some of them to be a bit brash and noisy.

Although promotion and success might not have been on my mind on the day that I enlisted, even with my sparse knowledge I k new that enlisted men did not become Generals. In addition and despite the fact that I was keen and enthusiastic from the start I may not have been perceived as particularly ambitious but rather more inclined to just drift along. After a couple of years I realised that it was not sufficient to go to work and do a good job if I wanted to rise to the highest enlisted rank. I am not ashamed to admit that failing to reach where I wanted to be was a very bitter disappointment. Despite the fact that I failed to achieve my ambitions in terms of rank level I know that I did a good job in terms of professional achievement and I know that I made a lot of difference in a lot of places and for the good and benefit of a lot of people.

It would not be possible to produce any such biography without including some reference to my personal life during the same period. Service life is unquestionably bound by some strict rules and regulations that do not apply to the civilian population. Such rules place servicemen (and women) under obligations and liable to consequences that have a far more profound effect on family life than any other occupation. Dependants of servicemen; wives and children are also affected as a result of the unpredictability and the rigours of service life.

The vast majority of what I have written has been dependent on the quality and accuracy of my own memory although I have sought and obtained the views of some of my former colleagues particularly in regard to my early days of life in Osnabruck.

Even though I credit myself with an excellent long term memory I know that I may have got some of the minor details wrong, I certainly would not presume to present a verbatim account of every event.

I certainly wish that I had kept a diary from the day that I enlisted but sadly I didn't. I'm also sorry that I do not have a huge portfolio of photographic or documentary evidence to support everything I have included. Although there were times that I regretted enlisting I later came to appreciate that joining the Army was the best decision that I had made and becoming a member of the Royal Military Police was probably the best job in the world. Nothing since has ever come close to compare in any way. Writing this book has been my way of presenting a picture of life in the Army by sharing my experiences. I also really hope that it will provide some entertainment to other servicemen past, present and future as well as families and friends. In addition I hope this will be of some value to anybody else who has any interest in service life along with those who may have wished to join but were unable to or who may have been persuaded not to.

What's it all about⏐?

DURING MY 23 YEARS MILITARY service I had some really good times and some that were positively dreadful. I may have survived those dreadful times but not without cost and in addition at the time they were painful and traumatic.

The definition of friendship in the Army is questionable and in a Corps like the Military Police there are so many factors that interrupt relationships. I would like to think that I had a number of good friends but changing priorities change people and the consequences of promotion and status change attitudes. The practise of mutual support and protection when military police undertake disciplinary police duties and whilst on operations are borne out of professional excellence and mutual need. It might be the ideal scenario for everybody to be the best of friends at all times but it would quite often be the case that RMP soldiers would find themselves working with people that on a social level they would choose to avoid.

I have no intention whatever to try and hide my contempt and revulsion for some of the individuals with whom I served, some as equal rank, some as subordinates and some of my seniors. This is not about envy or petty disagreement but about the malicious and vindictive agendas of some supervisory ranks and the culture of fear that they promulgated. I was effectively a victim to such regimes on more than one occasion, including one in particular that seriously compromised and came very close to completely destroying my career. It was not however only my career that suffered and one single episode in particular caused trauma and stress within my family and probably came close to causing me a complete mental breakdown. I know only too well that

I was not the only one to have had such an experience and to have suffered such consequences.

The life of an enlisted soldier regardless of which branch of the service he is part of is like no other career or occupation. It really is a case of starting at the bottom of the ladder and progression is at least in theory determined by merit and performance.

Many enlisted soldiers may be destined for a whole variety of reasons to remain at the lowest level during their entire service, some of them are clearly happy to remain in exactly the same place, no responsibilities, no worries and no cares. Regardless of what the civilian population might think in those cases where soldiers do not appear to have been particularly successful or well rewarded the real fact is that the adventure of military service is one of the most positive, rewarding and exciting occupations that any man or woman could choose.

In theory it is possible to train enlisted soldiers from scratch to battlefield readiness in a few months. Special to arm training is of course additional, it would not be logical for every enlisted soldier to aim for a whole service career and a large percentage will only complete three or four years before they leave.

Enlisted soldiers are the real men at the active face of conflict or when it suits their political masters the first and foremost to take part in humanitarian or internal security operations around the world. The British soldier is a special kind of person with an unlimited capacity for moaning and complaining about everything from the nature of his duties, the quality of his food and equipment and his officers.

He learns to put up with being cold, wet, tired and hungry he might be expected to survive for days without meaningful sleep or proper food He survives in whatever terrain or climate he is sent to and willingly eats whatever food he is given hot or cold.

Whatever else; it is certain that the army, specifically the Royal Military Police and in particular the British Army of The Rhine and my service life in the federal Republic of Germany determined my life.

This volume represents my own personal experience and views as a single soldier to begin with and later when I was married.

I have included some reference to my previous life, pre Army days and now that I am able to look back I guess that whilst there were some practical skills that I brought with me to the Army, in terms of social interaction and education I was ill prepared.

I had intended to create a reasonably light hearted but honest account of life in the service of the Royal Military Police but without any deliberate intention of causing any unnecessary embarrassment or offence to the vast majority of RMP personnel.

I do not however have any reservation whatever if I have tweaked the memory of certain individuals without any kind of conscience and who would prefer not to be reminded. These will certainly include those who were complicit in some of my unfortunate episodes and were perhaps unaware or indifferent to the fact that I knew of their involvement or who might have thought that I had forgotten the part they played.

This is not intended or presented as a work of fiction although some of the events about which I have commented might appear at times to be exaggerated so as to stretch the imagination of any reasonable person. It is not intended as a definitive history of the Military Police through the ages as there are already plenty such publications. The changes brought about by my time in the army were not only physical and it really is the case that military life and living overseas completely changed my understanding of life and my attitude towards other people.

Although there were some particularly offensive jokes shared amongst soldiers as the reasons for enlisting there was one particular comment that was particularly meaningful, " The Army Broadens Your Outlook".

One of my earliest realisations after only a short time in the Military was the fact that soldiers normally feel comfortable and tend to talk about aspects of service life and their experiences when in the company of other servicemen. Only servicemen and their immediate families are able to appreciate and understand. Expecting ordinary civilians to appreciate military service life or culture without ever having had any personal experience is a virtual impossibility. This clearly includes politicians who when they come to power seem to identify themselves as military experts and then make strategic and operational decisions on the military without having the slightest idea what they are talking about or the consequences of their actions..

The average civilian is simply unable to comprehend the rigours and demands of service life and in the vast majority of cases; including me the Army provided little or no guidance for life apart from scheduling everyday work. Although enlisted soldiers were drilled and trained to act and respond as part of a team, this process started and ended with duty work hours after which each individual was effectively left to his own devices. It may sound surprising to hear that there was little if any pastoral support after duty in respect of personal development, health, career planning or financial advice. This omission continued throughout an enlisted soldiers service unless he was "adopted or sponsored"; apart from the chosen few it was generally only specific service needs that were ever considered.

Enlisted soldiers including Military Police are probably considered to be more or less expendable; the reality is that nobody really cares about them outside of their essential work.

Enlisted soldiers are in reality, commodities, one of the two categories of available resources, manpower and equipment. The lack of care and support may well be best illustrated by the fact that the army and it's political masters appear to have little or no appreciation of the fact that enlisted soldiers give up the best years of their lives to the Army. Anybody taking the time and trouble to undertake some basic research will soon discover how many former servicemen succumb to the unexpected aspects of civilian life for which they are ill prepared. For so many soldiers their lives in the army created a dependency and reliance to such a level that once released into civilian life they are unable to cope without any support network.

It became clear to me over the years that the motto of the Royal Military Police "leading by example", did not really apply to all supervisory ranks and the way in which they dealt with their junior soldiers. On the contrary it often seemed to me that certain senior ranks were much more concerned with their own well being rather than having any interest in providing positive support or supervision to their juniors.

Although there may be a certain level of humour attached to the relationship between trainee soldiers and their instructors it should be that the language and insults directed at recruits is generic and calculated. Some seniors in the training environment but more worryingly in the operational role clearly delighted in personal, public, offensive and harmful rebuke.

In spite of any internal shortcomings within the ranks of the RMP and regardless of how the role of the Military Police may have changed over recent years I remain totally confident that the overall professional reputation of the Corps will not have been discredited or in any way diminished. There also remains a special kind of camaraderie and loyalty and this becomes clear at service reunions. Although I don't wish to deviate too much from my key objective I must mention that the Royal Military police might not have always been on everybody's Christmas card list. It would be naïve to think that the RMP were universally liked by other branches of the service. I am well aware that some soldiers from other branches of the Army and their families may have had and still do have; some negative memories of the Military Police. British servicemen and their families living overseas, specifically in Germany were not totally law abiding and on occasion would have found them selves on the wrong side of the law. As servicemen or dependants they were not exempt from the unavoidable consequences of criminal behaviour and were subject to both local civilian and military law. It would be understandable in such situations when the Military Police had undertaken investigations which often resulted in some serious, expensive and career changing outcomes for them to be identified as a hate figure. Such situations may have made the Royal Military Police a prime target for some unwelcome criticism and comments. It may also be the case that any real or imagined reasons for dislike of the Military Police has involved not only the junior enlisted soldiers but some seniors and commissioned officers.

Although there may have been some traditional dislike for Military Police it is probable that many of the myths and uncomplimentary remarks as well as the negative attitude towards them from soldiers were probably inherited or institutionally established as part of the normal soldier culture. I also discovered that soldiers are very territorial when off duty and that they would often identify certain establishments, mostly bars as their personal "regimental " territory.

It was not ideal and in fact potentially dangerous for Military Police to visit such places off duty.

Military police are frequently referred to as "monkies", a term commonly used by soldiers in an entirely derogatory sense although if challenged it was most likely that they would not have had the slightest idea why the term was used any more than the Military Police themselves.

Bad mouthing the Military Police may well have simply been part of the culture for targeting a common and universally shared dislike for authority figures in general.

I would doubt if many of the soldiers expressing a dislike or in some cases hatred of the military police would be able to identify the origin of their dislike. I seriously doubt if any intensive vetting of enlisted men took place and during my service it became clear that not all of them were strangers to criminal activities. Those who might have had a real axe to grind would have been those who were arrested or reported by the Military Police. It was often the case that the soldiers would then have been subject to some fairly harsh and what to some might have been seen to be both disproportionate and unfair summary justice; or in more serious cases courts martial or civil court proceedings.

In spite of this and almost certainly in common with other members of the Corps, I had a number of friends serving with infantry battalions and other branches of the service and some of these friendships are still in place after many years.

It may have been good fortune that during my service I never found my-self or my soldier "friends" in any difficult situation where there might have been a conflict of interest and responsibility.

As a consequence of having had the personal experience of working along-side infantry and other soldiers I can appreciate that some may have consid-ered that in comparison to their own military environment, particularly for single soldiers living in barracks the life of the military policeman was far too easy, somewhat protected, elitist and better accommodated. In addition many soldiers may have considered that rank in the Military Police was not so hard to earn as for soldiers from other branches of the service, particularly infantry battalions.

Right or wrong and whatever personal views exist; it is a fact that by necessity the Military Police are something of a separatist and elitist group and form an important part of the establishment with responsibility for and contributing to the enforcement of military discipline.

The off duty social interaction with other soldiers, particularly in public demanded caution. Life for the military police- man has always been very demanding and unlike other servicemen they have the dual responsibility to undertake both a dedicated peacetime and wartime role which would not have been appreciated by the average soldier who generally had only his primary role to manage as it was generally the case that his role in peace and war would be no different.

Although I have always remained totally loyal to the Military Police and proud to be part of the Corps it would be fair to say that my loyalty has been severely tested on more than one occasion. This has been due to some malicious and vindictive treatment at the hands of certain nasty individuals who conspired and successfully managed to directly compromise my career. I'm sure that I was not the only victim and that there will have been others who also suffered a similar fate. There will also have been certain individuals who will have been adopted protégés of the same nasty people and who inevitably managed to achieve considerable success by rising to high rank.

Whilst I might have to accept some responsibility for declining or failing to capitalise on some opportunities including some that were unique, I have no hesitation in expressing my long held view that there was always in place a culture of nepotism and in some cases inappropriate and unfair treatment. By modern standards this would certainly be considered bullying and harassment. Some of the aggressive, vindictive and destructive styles of man management went way beyond the need for reasonable standards of maintaining military discipline. Fairness and equal opportunity rarely featured in the day to day management and although character assassination was probably not unique to the military it was frequently applied with some disastrous consequences. A number of juniors and seniors, me included were certainly targeted by malicious and exaggerated accounts of their previous association or simply the victims of unsubstantiated and fictitious stories. It seemed to me that some particularly nasty individuals had no real purpose in life other than to spread false rumours in order to make themselves look good in front of their own superiors and subordinates whilst, at the same time damage the reputation of their victims.

Regardless of the fact that many stories and rumours were simply mischievous lies started as a result of an individual's own personal agenda the fact remains that when a rumour is circulated often enough even those who should know better; take it as fact and the poor subject victim is convicted and doomed. As my recollection of the years have improved I have been surprised at how, rather than feeling less embittered, I have become even more aggrieved at how my service career was compromised. I think about the individuals who caused me stress and hopelessness and think what might have been the difference had I been able to avoid them. There are several reasons behind my continuing bitterness including the process for promotion, confidential reports and favouritism. I suppose that 2014, the year which marked the 50th anniversary of my enlistment was also of particular significance.

For me there was always a sense of amazement and disbelief as to how certain individuals who would regularly get drunk and behave in a totally inappropriate manner would somehow remain immune to sanctions whilst others who might not have committed such serious misdemeanours seemed destined to suffer more serious, damaging and long lasting consequences.

There was also a sense of despair and disbelief with the annual comedic promotion selection board. It seemed to me that whilst the theory of the process was sound the application certainly seemed to exclude those who undertook and excelled in operational tasks such as garrison police duties and field training. Such activities were supposedly the key RMP function for peacetime and training for war. In reality the process appeared to favour those who were involved in sporting activities or who had found themselves securely entrenched in an administrative post. I know that this was not true in every case but I am also certain that there were those who were elevated into high rank despite their lack of knowledge, of either peacetime duties or operational experience.

I guess that anybody involved in the actual selection board would be very defensive and maintain that the process was above and beyond any criticism.

I suppose that the board were not required or expected to examine the fine details, they had only to consider the total number of points and the level of recommendation.

One of the frequently overlooked and unappreciated skills acquired from military service is the capacity to survive and manage change, to simply soldier on! With every posting exit; often to different countries and sometimes at short notice we could expect our normal, familiar and comfortable lives to be turned upside down and replaced with uncertainty and new challenge.

Contrary to some views about service life, lasting permanent friendships between Corps soldiers such as Royal Military Police are not particularly common. This is not due to reluctance or unwillingness but more as a consequence of the nature of the individual posting system.

It was possible and in fact most probable that RMP soldiers would be posted to different locations to their friends and it was more than probable that they would never share a posting again.

As might be expected; the Army and Military Police have a specific statutory connexion with discipline and this is most often to be seen whilst undertaking garrison police duties. As a consequence of these duties, most unwelcome interventions by the Military Police affect single soldiers during their off duty social time and when excessive consumption of alcohol liquor has been a contributory factor. Alcohol was more than likely to affect the behaviour of off duty soldiers particularly when any group was involved and this would often generate a hostile, aggressive or violent reaction. Internal regimental and inter regimental disputes occasionally took place but these were mostly in private and away from the grasp of the RMP.

It should also be noted that military police are subject to exactly the same rules and regulations with which soldiers have to comply, most soldiers however would probably have held the view that the RMP were somehow exempt. Soldiers and military police are likely to get involved in any number of situations and whilst it is most probable that many RMP have enjoyed miraculous escapes! there are certain offences from which if proven; offer no opportunity for miraculous escape or abdication, regardless of rank, status or connexions.

Apart from desertion, treason or the unsavoury titled "cowardice in the face of the enemy" probably more of a world war 1 legacy than for a more modern era, there are three specific offence categories for which there are guaranteed serious consequences and from which escape is virtually impossible. These are specifically, failure to safeguard arms, losing a weapon or simply not having it under direct control, misuse or theft of public funds and any kind of activity that involves unusual sexual behaviour or indecency with a child or young person. In addition; at least prior to and during the early 1960's and until fairly recently, homosexuality or lesbianism was not tolerated and was in fact an offence against Military Law. Although there may have been cases where it was suspected; once identified; any homosexual would almost certainly face formal sanction and the inevitable discharge from the service. It would be fair to say that during my service, homosexuality was not a frequently debated topic in barrack rooms. Although there may have been occasions when certain individuals appeared to be a bit different! or perhaps somewhat effeminate I can never recall any single occasion when such a topic was discussed openly amongst my network of friends and contemporaries.

Apart from these categories, anything else including loutish, drunken behaviour and what might be described as traditional, normal, sexual philandering was probably seen as acceptable and more of a natural positive social interaction rather than deserving of any sanction. It was always my perception that getting drunk, acting the clown and disrupting the lives of others was a reliable way of establishing a high profile image. As a good old boy or good social member!!!

There were probably three particular activities or service employments that may have contributed at least in my view towards accelerated promotion. These were sport, particularly football, cricket and squash, although squash was not; at least in the early days of my service regarded as an enlisted soldier's game. It was generally the case that enlisted soldiers could only book a squash court after 8 pm when the officers had finished their game and gone home. Also of particular importance was the ability to demonstrate a consistent social involvement in mess life with the necessary stamina to consume considerable quantities of alcoholic liquor. The last of the three most helpful criteria was the good fortune to be in a job that provided a closer relationship with either the senior, warrant officer or even better, the officer commanding. The main advantage of working close to the commissioned officer was the likelihood that the same officer would be the one to write concurrent annual confidential reports. In such situations the same officer would be much more likely to provide the well above average reports, probably graded A or O for outstanding which was a guarantee for rapid promotion. It was always a surprise to me when individuals in such jobs would score either maximum or close to maximum points for every aspect of military police work. This always seemed to me to be rather unfair when they had often been in a relatively secure and cosy little office job protected from the rigours of unsocial hours or invasive shift duty. The fact that such office jobs were of crucial importance to the smooth and efficient operation of any unit should not in my view have provided such incredibly high scoring confidential reports. Each of these was instrumental in raising personal profiles and the key to procuring the necessary fantastic annual reports to ensure accelerated promotion. If anybody was fortunate enough to fit into each of the three categories; the sky was the limit!!

I personally know several of my former colleagues whose only real contribution was to unit sport, football, cricket and rugby.

Unit and regimental sport was at the very least; highly competitive and success in any of the Corps trophy competitions; likely to elevate certain individuals to virtual star status. Officers commanding would almost certainly share the fame and glory. It would be without question one of the topics discussed at very senior level.

Officers also needed good reports and to provide good copy for the Corps if they were to secure the postings of their choice.

The outcome of this would the inevitable walking on water confidential reports, perhaps a nice posting to the training centre and from then on a route to the top.

My only moment of fame and glory was back in 1979 and my success at the Circuite Des Pyrenees (Pau motorcycle rally) some good copy in the Corps Journal and a bit of positive publicity.

I am still however minded of Patton's words "Glory is but Fleeting" So very true but the outcomes can be so different.

Osnabruck and the BAOR

THE FIRST THREE YEARS OF my service, from April 1965 to March 1968 were with the 12th Infantry Brigade Provost Unit which was somewhat unusually co-located with the 2nd Infantry Division Pro Coy based at the Roberts Barracks Annex on Romersesche Strasse Osnabruck.

Osnabruck is one of the largest cities in the area of Lower Saxony with a well documented history. The name itself has generated a number of historical interpretations including, " Bridge to the Gods". There are however some dark periods. Between the years of 1561 to 1639 Osnabruck underwent the most proactive period of witch hunting probably as a consequence of old scores being settled during the period of the protestant reformation. During the reign of Mayor Hammacher 1565 to 1588 there were 163 executions of women recorded, allegedly as witches with most of them being burned to death. During the Reichstag elections of 1930 at least 28% of the population voted for the NAZI party. During the same period the Osnabruck economy also enjoyed a positive change and in the years 1933 to 1938 the unemployment rate went from 10000 unemployed to negative unemployment when job vacancies exceeded the numbers looking for work.

The city sustained considerable damage during the 1939-45 war but was effectively rebuilt and in typical German fashion much of the architecture reflecting the City's medieval influence and historical old buildings were meticulously restored.

At it's height during the 1960's Osnabruck was home to the largest British Military Garrison outside the United Kingdom with over 4000 servicemen based there and over 500 locally employed civilians. When the numbers of dependants, wives and children as well as such people as BFES schoolteachers were taken in to account the size of the British military community may have been closer to 8000.

The garrison was home to the 12th Infantry Brigade; part of the 2nd Infantry Division.

12 Brigade was first formed during the Boer war in 1899 and at the outbreak of the 1939-45 war was deployed with the 4th Infantry Division and part of the British Expeditionary Force to France. The Brigade took part in the Dunkirk evacuation and later saw service in North Africa, the Italian campaign and Greece. The Brigade was disbanded in 1947 but reformed in 1956 and remained so until it became the 12th Mechanised Brigade in 1970.

The Brigade and the Osnabruck Garrison sadly closed down in 2008.

2nd Infantry Division was formed by the Duke of Wellington in 1809 and was integrated into the Anglo Portuguese Army which took part in the Peninsular war.

The Divisional insignia, the crossed keys of St Peter were adopted during the 1914-1918 war.

The divisional battle honours include action at the battles of Waterloo, Porto, Talavera, Bussaco, Vittoria, Pyrenees and Maga.

The Division took part in the Dunkirk evacuation and later saw service in India and Burma as part of the 14th Army.

After the second world war and a series of amalgamations the division took up residence in Tunis Barracks Lubbecke in 1959.

The Division was sadly finally disbanded in 2012.

The Roberts Barracks Annex in which the Military Police were based was a former German wartime Barracks in a rather well appointed and relatively secluded location shared with a number of departments employing local civilian staff. In 1965 there were some remnants of the wartime rail system including a single track immediately behind the single men's accommodation running parallel with the Osnabruck Zwiegcanal. There is also some evidence that the annex was used as a staging post for the unfortunate victims en-route to Bergen Belsen concentration camp.

The Main entrance gate had at some time included one or two stone German imperial eagles as well as Swastica figures which can be seen in photographs taken during the Nazi regime.

I guess that the swasticas would have been destroyed following the end of the second world war, there were several accounts of what happened to the eagles.

A t least one of them survived and was in place at the front of the RMP admin building as recently as 2008.

The RMP single men's accommodation including the ablutions and the kitchen dining room had originally been part of a wartime industrial bakery, some parts of the huge ovens could still be found at the end of the accommodation block. There was no such thing as security and I don't ever recall the subject ever being mentioned. Of course we had our own personal steel locker/wardrobe which we would keep locked. Although it was always the intention to lock away all personal possessions this didn't always happen. Despite this I never had so much as a sock stolen. The corporal's mess would also be locked but the rest of the property was easily accessible at any time day and night. In 1965, at least in comparison with later years we had few valuable possessions other than wristwatch and camera, books, clothes and uniforms. Very few of the single men owned cars and there were no computers or fancy hi fi equipment although we did have some simple basic radios and record players.

Although the majority of the men's accommodation was dormitory style often for up to six and sometimes more men to a room there were a small number of single bunks occupied by senior long service corporals. Perry Edwin John (Jack) Vane was one of the select group, probably fortunate for the others who might not have appreciated his compulsive listening to the Archers. For the very lucky few there was also a small discreet annex section located adjacent to the Special Investigation Branch office away from the main accommodation building, "K Block" this block was occupied by other senior corporals most of whom were in exclusive "employed" jobs.

Single enlisted men were simply allocated a "bed space" Such spaces included a bed, a steel wardrobe and a small bedside locker and a small carpet. This was home!

The accommodation stores which included bedding for the single men's quarters. operational, mobilisation and field training equipment were located in the cellar of the main administration block and the MT lines (motor vehicles) were garaged close by. The barracks included a substantial and pleasant garden which was a regular site for the Sunday curry lunches.

The Sergeants mess was located on the first floor of the headquarters building along with the senior management. This included the Officers commanding, both 2 Div Pro Coy and 12 Brigade Pro Unit, the regimental Sergeant Major and Company sergeant major also had offices on the ground floor within sight and sound of the duty room and close to the main administrative office, the Orderly room.

The corporal's mess was conveniently located in the cellar of the main accommodation block and the kitchen and dining room on the first floor close to the men's living quarters. This meant of course that the juniors would not have to leave the building to take their meal or to get a drink. In theory the single men in barracks would not have to leave the building other than to go on duty, whatever nature that might be, get a haircut, report sick or go on leave.

Privacy and consideration for others in the single men's accommodation was virtually non- existent and this was particularly the case in two regular situations. There was never any thought given on the part of many late night drinkers to men who wanted to sleep without interruption at normal night time. Being kept awake or being woken up by noisy drunks was an institutional hazard for single men. In addition there was scant consideration for the men who wanted and needed to sleep during the day after completing an exhausting night duty. In such circumstances when I had finished night duty I made it a routine that I would have breakfast and then go out for the day and usually ended up having lunch in town.

During weekdays even the men detailed for night duty at 1800 hours, such as the dreaded night desk would be expected to work all day and to be excused only with sufficient time to get changed into duty order although some of the more experienced and "streetwise" would manage to evade such situations.

For those less fortunate this normally meant 0830 to 1500 and then 1800 to 0830, about 20 hours in total.

The daily routine included regular garrison police duties such as orderly sergeant, in charge of the duty shift, desk NCO, standby NCO (duty investigator) standby driver,   who was responsible for taking the investigator to police incidents and the admin driver responsible for a whole host of tasks. These might include collecting married men from their homes, delivering and collecting post from the two main police stations, taking the unit cooks to collect rations and just about every other task that required a driver and land-rover.

From time to time juniors were required to perform security duties to escort female civilian payroll staff around the garrison to deliver the wages to the civilians employed by the military at schools and other installations. It was not a bad task, getting to accompany in most cases a couple of young attractive females and then having lunch at one of the BFES (Army) schools. These school meals for civilian staff were totally different to what we as single soldiers might expect both in terms of quality and quantity. Although we undertook this escort task specifically to protect the two ladies, and the cash; I was never sure how much use I would have been in the event of any attack as there was no means of contacting anybody for help and we were armed only with the standard issue and completely useless short wooden truncheon.

Despite the stupidity of the duty it was a useful break as well as a good lunch and a day out.

In addition to mobile duties, foot patrols of the married quarter areas and the town were a regular task. There were published "beats", routes to which we were assigned but nobody actually took any notice except for one particular sergeant who seemed to derive some pleasure from being downright annoying and would normally instruct us to meet him at a particular location so that he could sign our notebooks.

When the BAOR form 703 (book) was introduced we were expected to increase the numbers of BFG registered cars being stopped and checked particularly around the NAAFI services shop car parks. Although there was a seven day reporting and document presenting requirement I don't recall anybody actually being reported for not producing their documents and I don't think that there was ever a workable infrastructure in place to manage the documentary process.

Foot patrols were a joy in the summer in shirt sleeve order but not so much fun when it was pouring with rain or as I experienced many times during freezing weather and heavy snow.

On one occasion I was on foot patrol with corporal Lenny Want, we were wearing our service issue great coats with collars turned up against the driving snow. We were struggling to walk through the deep snow and I was reflecting on the fact that only the detective sergeant Ray P would have sent us out. Although I don't recall the name, as we passed a local gastatte on the Vehrter Landstrasse a man ran up to us and urged us to come into the bar. My initial reaction was that some soldier was causing a disturbance but when we entered the bar, peace reigned.

The next action from the bar owner was two glasses of coca cola with a healthy shot of grape juice, Reluctantly of course we downed the drinks and spent the rest of the day, eating, drinking and playing cards, effectively strengthening Anglo German relations..

We later returned to barracks and to our eternal satisfaction the intrepid Sergeant Ray P had gone home.

Mobile patrols were normally deployed with the night duties whilst the majority of police tasks requiring any investigation were dealt with by the standby NCO and his driver. Traffic accidents, drunken soldiers, non-payment of taxi and bar bills were the most regular incidents.

In addition to police duties the juniors were required to undertake a whole range of administrative and time occupying tasks (these would appear on the daily detail as "available" a bit of an understatement) Such tasks included cleaning and painting land-rovers and trailers, cleaning stores and equipment and collecting bar stock from the local NAAFI warehouse for the sergeants and corporals messes. There would also be a range of cleaning tasks identified and during the summer in particular plenty of gardening.

In addition there were a number of juniors mostly senior long serving corporals who were employed in essential admin roles. These included probably the most important, the chief clerk and the charges and report office clerk. There were also the corporals and sergeants mess barmen who did not normally attend the morning muster parade.

Normal routine for both duties and admin started with the morning muster parade at 0830. There were two separate parades, the oncoming day duties presented by the off going orderly sergeant and then the general morning muster parade presented by the day orderly sergeant for just about everybody else, including attached cooks and vehicle mechanic. The RSM would normally reserve inspecting the oncoming duties for himself and it was guaranteed that anything less than his exacting standards for both men and vehicles would result in disciplinary action. RSM Roy Standring could however be unpredictable and on one occasion he decided that the turnout of one NCO was so good he should not be on duty and he simply gave him the day off. The general parade was less formal often supervised by the unit WO2 or one of the other seniors and was mostly a case of releasing the employed staff and allocating tasks to the others.

Avoiding work or "skiving" was an essential skill and we all became more effective as our experience of the organisation improved. Learning how to keep out of the way of the seniors and avoiding the most unpleasant tasks.

It was normal for the juniors to take a so called NAAFI break at 1000 until 1030 when we all adjourned to the dining room for tea and mountains of toast prepared by one of the two kitchen helps.. This was always a welcome break and much more so in the winter. Lunch was at 1230 until 1330 and work would normally end at 1700 just in time for the evening meal.

Breakfast was fairly traditional and typical army style, fried egg, fried bread, baked beans, canned tomatoes and bacon. Cereals were not quite the same without fresh milk but we coped!!There was always a substantial cooked meal at lunchtime and another cooked meal in the evening, the menu was a bit inconsistent and determined by a number of factors such as the ration allowances, availability and the creativity of the cook in charge. The ingredients included a mixture of fresh food and composite (compo canned) rations. What might not have been common knowledge to the single men was the fact that the senior cook actually presented the week's menu programme to the regimental sergeant major for approval at least one week in advance.

On the odd occasion we might be surprised by the addition of extra items in the dining room and dinner that included special items presented in much more attractive style than was usual. This was a sure sign that we were "entertaining" visitors.

Although the regular menus and the food were both perfectly acceptable they would probably not have won any prizes and in addition there were some commodities that were simply not available such as fresh milk. Canned evaporated milk was used extensively and although perhaps not quite the same it became an acquired taste all of it's own so much that the use of fresh milk became somewhat alien. Most junior ranks however would make a weekly excursion to the local NAAFI shop to enjoy a carton of fresh Danish!!

I can recall conversations with the unit cooks who had a real struggle to stretch the ration allowance to make decent meals.

Apart from the odd occasion when the sergeants or staff sergeants would take on the duty of orderly sergeant, with the exception of the MT sergeant I always struggled to identify what if anything the seniors actually did. The gulf between juniors and seniors was enormous.

Living and working in Germany provided a wide range of different benefits.

The German social and recreational culture was entirely different and there were, at least as it seemed to me to be far less class divisions than in the UK. I quickly recognised how German workers travelling to and from their place of work would always be smartly dressed making it virtually impossible to tell if they were doctors or labourers. German society is much more disciplined and ordered than the United Kingdom and much cleaner as well as being more socially snobbish.

It may seem extraordinary in light of the cosseted existence and over legislated society of today that in 1965 as a fresh, raw and totally inexperienced Military Police lance corporal there was absolutely no formal induction briefing on arrival in BAOR.

The only mentoring I ever received was on a single occasion when I was detailed for my very first night desk duty and an experienced lance corporal accompanied me from 1800 till 2400 hours, after that it was just a case of getting on with it, sink or swim!

There was never any supervision, guidance or support from the seniors and it seemed to me that the only time they ever got involved was to rebuke or criticise. What a real difference such an induction could have made, getting to know something about Germany, a few useful German phrases, something about the role of the division and the brigade and how the RMP fitted into the operational strategy.

The real reasons might not be obvious but if the general attitude and performance of the seniors was an indicator it was more than probable that the seniors didn't know much themselves.

A couple of weeks of introduction and easing in to the system could have made such a difference even some of the useful tips from senior corporals about preparing for field training and what kit to take along in order to make life more comfortable and improve efficiency.

It seems to me that the whole process was a combination of dereliction and abdication.

In spite of my own experience of some unfavourable treatment I have no regrets about my Royal Military Police service although a fairly typical school report type entry might have been used from time to time, "could do better". I often reflect on what or if I could have done things differently and how I might have made better use of the opportunities that I missed. Perhaps if some of the seniors had taken a bit more of an interest in the personal development of the juniors (including me) I might well have achieved more. During my first Germany posting I was never given the opportunity or ever encouraged to attend any German language course and I don't recall anybody else attending one either. There was never any form of personal development discussion, supervision or mentoring, it was every man for himself, sink or swim. Although I was fortunate to have enjoyed a number of postings in different locations this meant that I also had the misfortune to have either moved on without an annual report or to have seen my officer commanding change and so never had the real continuity I might have wished for and that which provided many others a route to speedy promotion.

What I hope to present now is a picture of my Royal Military Police life; to begin with in the 1960's together with my own personal experiences and some of the most memorable incidents. Unfortunately a number of the events to which I will refer were not those for which I have particularly fond memories. I have however tried to include as many as I can recall.

Whilst those of us in British Army of The Rhine in 1965 were spared the trauma and dangers of active service I was mindful of the fact that there were places where danger was real. Aden was an active posting and was as I recall a dangerous place to be. I also recall that virtually the entire "57" squad of recruits behind mine at Chichester was posted to 24 Brigade in Aden around May of 1965. Despite the lack of immediate danger in BAOR there was always the potential breakdown of détente between NATO and the Warsaw Pact although I can never recall any kind of real urgency or expression of concern.

Even the operational field training "exercises" were treated very lightly they were more of a jolly really, getting away from it all, loads of fresh air and eating and sleeping out. Although it should have been bloody obvious, nobody ever mentioned to me that we were supposed to be training for war. The threat when we were occasionally reminded was real, intelligence briefings indicated that not only was the BAOR and it's NATO allies numerically outmatched in soldiers but also in the numbers of tanks, guns and planes of the Group of soviet forces Germany, the USSR, Poland, Czeckoslovakia, Hungary and East Germany (DDR) as the key players. The regular roll out of field training exercises "war gaming" was part of the overall strategy of being prepared for war but in reality it hardly seemed to generate any realistic preparation. It was always a welcome break from the day to day routine of garrison duties and we certainly managed to enjoy some of the countryside. Another activity was exercise "quick-train", this was a fairly regular operational exercise call out designed to test our ability to deploy in an emergency and our readiness for war. There was normally a period, covertly identified as the quick train season and it was almost certain that any call out would be at night during darkness. The precise call out dates were supposedly secret and the actual deployment intended as a real test. The reality was and although it might now appear rather unprofessional to say but the only thing that it really tested was our patience. To be totally honest we were never in any proper state of readiness, there was never; at least to my knowledge any management oversight of preparation or supervision of the juniors and the whole process was chaos. There was never any briefing on the basic issue of rations or what if the play turned out to be real. There was also some mileage in the view that the Soviet Union and Warsaw Pact forces would have been covertly advised probably via some discrete diplomatic means that the emergency callout would be taking place so as to avoid the suggestion that a NATO attack was being planned and in order to avoid any risky situation or retaliatory response.

Although I always religiously ensured that I refuelled my vehicle after use, there were very few others with a similar sense of responsibility and there was no guarantee that I would be assigned the same vehicle that I had refuelled in the event of any call out.

Although military drivers including military police were aware of the "first parade last halt" process for vehicles there were never to my knowledge any checks and it would have been unlikely that many of the land-rovers used on any urgent deployment would have been fully fuelled even though the rules said that they should be!!. Since Osnabruck and the passage of time and experience I have little doubt that if Osnabruck was in any way typical of how the rest of the Royal Military Police and the Army were managed it was more by luck, poor intelligence (or ignorance) and a lack of determination on the part of the Soviet Union that we were not invaded. I really can't imagine that the Soviet Union knew just how ill prepared we were.

We were really no more than amateurs acting out a professional role.

Apart from an annual (if we were unlucky) gas chamber visit with our respirators I can recall no training whatever in how to function in any Nuclear Chemical or Biological (NBC) environment even though an NBC monitoring and reporting role was one of the key wartime tasks of the Royal Military Police. This was something that was never explained and the only way that we found out was by reading the Provost Training Manual. The Soviets however were in complete contrast; I learned from my own research that they undertook substantial training and deployed whole regiments to operate in any NBC environment without compromising their operational efficiency. I know that RMP NCO s' were occasionally sent on NBC instructors courses but never to my knowledge shared or cascaded anything they had learned. This was clearly very unfortunate as from what I have read the NBC instructor's course was reckoned to be first rate. Anything I learned was a result of my own research and acting on my own initiative.

Off duty time for single enlisted soldiers may well appear at least by contemporary standards to have been very mundane and boring. Television was virtually non existent and there were no equivalents to modern electronic devices. Few soldiers owned motor cars and although some were both smart and sufficiently motivated to learn the German language and meet German girls, they were in the minority. Our daily lives included preparation and maintenance of our uniforms, washing, ironing and making some effort to keep our sparse living accommodation tidy.

I guess that actually going to work on duty was one of the most productive periods.

Most men read a great deal of books and escapist comics and listened to music which in shared dormitory style accommodation was necessarily loud. There was plenty of competition and a wide range of tastes in music. I read the entire catalogue of Dennis Wheatley, Hammond Innes, Alistair McLean as well as Emile Zola and the German satirist author Hans Helmut Kirst

Weekday evenings might also involve a trip to the cinema and Saturday was often the walk into town day. Not really exciting but a welcome diversion.

Unlike married men, as a single soldier in Germany I had no dependants. I often thought however, about how or if; any evacuation plan for families would really work if there were actual hostilities. I'm sure that there was a plan but I don't ever recall anybody sharing with me. Perhaps there was an expectation that we should spend our off duty hours reading the BAOR standing orders. I suspect that there was a whole department at Headquarters BAOR and other places pumping out volumes of standing orders and instructions that were rarely if ever read and would only become familiar as a result of non compliance. Although in 1965 as a junior at the bottom of the pecking order I was effectively out of any decision making fraternity it didn't take me that long to realise that the practise call outs as undertaken (exercise quick train) were really a complete a waste of time. It didn't require any sort of genius to realise that if the Warsaw pact decided to invade Western Europe including the Federal Republic of Germany with the ideal route via the North of the country, they only had to pick any bank holiday with Christmas being the favourite to launch any surprise attack. They could probably have sliced through most of Northern Germany supposedly defended by the BAOR without raising a sweat or firing a shot. Although there were restrictions on the number of personnel being on leave out of station at any one time there was no control on those remaining behind and apart from the very small number on essential duty it would be anybody's guess as to where the rest were or their state of sobriety. I would be the first to admit that I might on occasion have had too much to drink and would not really have been in the best condition. The fact that there was a specific section in the army act that sought to prevent any soldier being unfit for duty due to drinking excessive amounts of alcohol was not so far as I can recall a real deterrent.

In the weeks leading up to Christmas it was more than probable that the vast majority of ranking staff were moving from one party to another and it would have been virtually impossible to assemble anything more than a token command.

It must also be appreciated that in the 1960's there were no mobile phones or email. Very few junior enlisted soldiers or indeed seniors had telephones at home and although there was a British Forces Radio Network (BFN) there was no local British or English language television network. Very few of the enlisted men had privately owned motor cars and there was absolutely no process in place which specifically required married men to be at home when not on duty or for identifying where they might be. If any married soldier was not at home they could be literally any where. The only way for soldiers to be alerted in the case of any peacetime emergency or as part of the quick train call out was for a driver to actually visit their home address and collect them. It requires little imagination to appreciate that this process was slow and very unpredictable. The driver also needed to be able to find his way to each married quarter It inevitably involved waiting time at each address and once the task was completed the unfortunate driver would have to vacate his garrison duty and get changed into operational kit. I can recall occasions when some men were not contacted and simply turned up for their previously scheduled duties totally unaware, or so they claimed whilst others arriving so late that their presence was no longer valid. There was no facility for the married men living off barracks to be able to secure their operational equipment in barracks and I can not recall any occasion when any sort of readiness inspection was carried out. I simply don't have the slightest idea of how we would have managed or survived in the event of a real operational shooting situation. It was never a question of being tough it was straightforward logistics, without food, fuel, ammunition or equipment we would have been totally helpless.

Back in those far off days of the 1960's there was so much happening, that it may have been simple to have missed some of the most important and significant events.

Attitude, perception and responsibility changes with age, I had no responsibility other than getting up in the morning and going to work and when the working day ended it was virtually certain that I would end up in the corporals mess bar until closing time.

Such a routine would now seem totally irresponsible but at the time quite normal.

Newspapers were always twenty four hours old. German television broadcasts were fairly boring and as might be expected were focussed on matters primarily of local German interest.

I don't really think that anybody, including me actually cared that much outside the box or what was going on. It was certainly the case that I was really only interested in anything that directly affected me and the short term immediate future. There was the odd occasion when something stirred the interest such as a case involving the Army making the national UK papers normally as a consequence of a bad news story with most of the facts wrong.

I suppose that looking back on our off duty activities in the 1960's life was rather dull compared to later years and in particular the 1980's. Pay and living conditions had by then improved so much and enlisted soldiers in the military police could easily afford new cars and every modern gadget as well as regular holidays.

Life before

PRIOR TO ENLISTING INTO THE Army I had enjoyed a totally selfish and insular life, work, pub, fishing and girls; nothing else really mattered or was of any particular interest. I had no worries and no responsibilities other than to myself. I probably never considered the future beyond the coming weekend and dependent on the time of year and weather, fishing, pub nights and shopping trips were all that mattered. I had a relatively substantial net income and this enabled me to purchase all of the quality designer clothes I "needed" along with anything else I wanted, mostly fishing tackle and vinyl records. On reflection it seems that this was a very simple lifestyle but of course there was nothing like the diverse range of gadgets available as there is today. I enjoyed regular visits to the local snooker hall, Friday pub night skittles and the Saturday lunchtime poker school when I generally managed to win more than I ever lost.

I had also joined the local Young Conservatives group although not essentially for political reasons, there was a private members only bar, a good snooker room and the members card allowed sign in of two guests (guaranteed female) at the regular Thursday and Sunday dances. I had passed my driving test a few days after my 17th Birthday and had already bought my very first, very cheap and totally unreliable and constantly breaking down banger!! I also managed to run a motorcycle so there was not really anything else of serious concern. So far as I can recall I had no identified ambitions, I was not that interested in anything except fishing going out with friends, cars and girls, although as far as I was concerned any relationship was purely casual and totally mercenary.

The Beatles and Stones along with a host of other British bands were monopolising the music scene around the world and what are now highly collectable and sought after Juke boxes were blasting the music around expresso and coffee bars. Mods and rockers virtually dominated the roadside parking spaces and either war surplus leather flying jackets or sand coloured duffel coats and long flowing scarves were the uniform choices of each of those two groups. The United Kingdom true to form was miles behind the rest of the world and still using an outdated currency system of pounds shillings and pence. The British attitude to food was equally backward and anything other than what was considered traditional was referred to as "foreign rubbish".

Although it might not have been obvious at the time, the sixties was certainly one of the most significant decades of the century particularly in respect of popular music and some classic cars. The Jaguar E type The Austin Healey 3000 and the Triumph Vitesse as my favourites. There were British Motorcycles everywhere and a new style Motorway. Looking back now whilst there were probably many other changes taking place I didn't really take much interest outside of what directly affected me. I was not that interested in British politics and any world events to me were merely news items on the television. I don't ever recall any mention of drugs other than a very generic reference to "Pep Pills"

During the first three years of my military service I don't recall a single incident involving illegal drugs although alcohol featured regularly. Of course it may have been the case that any such incident would have been reported direct to the SIB It was also the case that I never received any advice or training regarding illegal substances aside from the scant reference during basic training.

During this time, there was the Pill, the Mini; car and skirt, a labour government and Carnaby Street. There was a good deal of interest in Lady Chatterly's Lover although anybody reading the book now would struggle to work out what all the fuss was about. There was also James Bond, Doctor Who and Cassius Clay.

I don't know how many prominent presenters have asked, "where were you when Kennedy was shot " ? I remember this clearly, the television newsflash and later that evening when the talk in the conservative club was the big question "could this lead to war" ? Were the Russians responsible? taking revenge for the Cuban missile humiliation. Although it did not mean much to me at the time, the East Germans had built a wall around Berlin and the cold war was getting decidedly colder.

In spite of leading the world's music scene and allegedly creating something of a fashion revolution; England was a tired, drab, old fashioned and class ridden place. Just how drab and out of date I would only come to realise after I had enlisted into the Army and posted to Germany.

I have already made it clear that I have not attempted or intended this record to be either a definitive study of the British army or specifically any of the military units deployed in Germany as part of the BAOR. The BAOR to which I refer in this case is actually the second British Army of The Rhine and that which was deployed in 1945 following the end of the 1939-45 second world war. The first British Army of the Rhine was deployed across the Rheinland Palatinate as part of the stringent sanctions imposed on Germany in accordance with the treaty of Versailles following the end of the first 1914-18 war. The second British army of the Rhine was initially of course an army of occupation which was deployed across the British sector of what was to become the Federal Republic of Germany. Troops deployed to the West Sector of Berlin were not actually included in the operational deployment plans of BAOR. The role and status of the Army gradually evolved into a partnership with Germany and other Countries that developed under the auspices of the USA led NATO.

The NATO countries became united in a protective role to counter the real threat of the USSR and the Warsaw pact. I am well aware that in 1945 the social and economic situation and the way in which the Military Police were deployed would have been very different from that which existed during my service. I have not however set out to create any kind of academic textbook volume on any aspect of Military Police activities. As I have mentioned previously; with the benefit and wisdom of hindsight it would certainly have been incredibly helpful if I had maintained a contemporaneous diary during my service to include the key events and activities in which I was involved or those which took place during the same period.

Sadly I did not retain a complete diary and I have therefore had to rely on a well intentioned, normally accurate but slightly eroded memory. The world has changed so much in the past 50 years and whilst many of the events that took place around the world were not entirely clear to me I did at least have a basic understanding of the key world issues. My world geography although somewhat sketchy was probably better than average so at least I had some idea where things were happening even if I didn't really understand all of them.

As was probably the case for many others I may have learned a good deal about the major political and military issues during my basic recruit training. The practical police training must have worked because there was no follow up training even after posting to Germany. I do however think that much of what was included in our initial professional special to arm training was simply too brief. Without any real practical reference much of it's significance was not understood as well as it might have been.

During the early days of my military service, although I do not ever recall actually asking any of my colleagues why they had joined the Army and the Military Police; I often wondered why they had done so. Nobody ever asked me the same question either before, after I had enlisted, or at any other time. I suppose that several men might have enlisted for no other reason than the fact that in the areas in which they were living there were no jobs. Others I was to learn had enlisted to avoid the only other local employment in the mines. Some men were second or even third generation military police soldiers and it may have been the case that they had been encouraged, coerced or even expected to enlist into the RMP

For others it may have been the search for an exciting and challenging life full of opportunity and adventure.

When I enlisted; my knowledge regarding national geographical areas of the United Kingdom or any cultural differences was virtually non- existent. It was not until I had joined the army that I met men from the countries that made up the United Kingdom. Wales, Scotland, Northern Ireland and some of the regions with Newcastle particularly well represented. These were or at least it seemed to me at the time the majority within the ranks of the Military Police and so far as I can recall they represented a majority in terms of numbers of men who made up the ranks of the Military Police throughout the whole time of my service.

I can offer no sound or logical explanation for choosing a military career and of course as others have probably done, I have often reflected what if I had not enlisted but chosen another career. I can claim no family or historical allegiance to the Army or the Military police. As a young boy my military interests were restricted to playing with toy soldiers. On the culinary side I loved baked beans and this attracted a good deal of comment during my primary school days when my "best friend" disclosed this confidential gem of information to our class teacher, sort of "spilled the beans". Apart from the odd war movie my only source of information was in the form of some probably embellished accounts by my Father of his wartime adventures in Burma as a gunner in the 14th survey regiment Royal Artillery.

Attestation signing on to the unknown

ON A FAIRLY TYPICAL, RATHER dreary and as I recall cold and wet 2nd December 1964 I completed my "attestation" when I enlisted at the Bedford recruiting office. This process involved taking the oath of allegiance to the sovereign, witnessed by an officer and generally agreeing to obey the orders of just about everybody in the Army from lance corporal up. I have to say that at the time I didn't even know what a lance corporal or any other kind of corporal was. Following the attestation I received a days pay and my very own copy of the new testament along with a travel warrant for the train journey to Chichester in Sussex. After a short walk from recruiting office to station I handed over the warrant and boarded the train to London St Pancras, across London by underground and on to Victoria. Despite the passage of fifty years I can still remember thinking what the hell I had done and where the hell I was going. I really had not the slightest appreciation of what signing on meant or the consequences of non compliance. Once I had found the Chichester train I was feeling even more trapped and hopelessly lost.

I can recall having a conversation with another passenger who actually knew Chichester and Roussillon Barracks but I have no memory of what the conversation might have included other than his explanation as to the reason for the strange and peculiar route from London Victoria to Chichester.

I eventually arrived at Chichester and boarded the bus which would take me to the barracks. Of course and to confuse matters even more I debussed at the rear gate and then spent about an hour wandering helplessly around the barracks, which was totally open to the public, before I managed to find the guard room of the Depot and Training Establishment Royal Military Police.

The most astonishing part of this is that as I look back; is the fact that prior to setting off on my journey I had never looked at a map or atlas and had absolutely no geographical idea as to where Chichester was or how far it was from my home. In addition I had absolutely no concept of military life or what to expect when I arrived. I had not asked anybody for advice and nobody had offered any. With hindsight it now seems that this lack of preparation was a serious failing on the recruitment process in general and the recruiting sergeants in particular.

Even the information I had been given about reporting to the guardroom was flawed, when I asked for directions I received a very direct and short lesson on the fact that I should be heading for the duty room and not the guard room.

It was a mixed set of circumstances that would lead me to Chichester, part impulse, part accident, part luck and a touch of desperation. I was hardly from a military family, apart from my fathers national service during the 1939-45 war there was to my knowledge no family military association. Although I am not entirely convinced by any argument for any predetermined destiny some of my experiences have led me to believe that I may have been following a path over which I had little or no control. With my original ambitions abandoned and my then occupation going no place I guess that I simply jumped into the unknown with absolutely no thought of the consequences.

I had grown restless and bored with my agricultural career which had virtually no prospect for advancement. I was not in any way a militant or rebel but I did however resent the class snobbery of farmers and the way that staff were regarded and treated as little more than serfs. Once my boredom and resentment had reached a certain level I just knew that I had to move on although I had no idea to what. Most of my former school friends had chosen a path of apprentice with industry and the farming friends I had made were either looking for a farmer's daughter to marry or had resigned themselves to a permanent and obscure life in farming subordination.

Despite the fact that I had never been on an aircraft and was not particularly fond of heights, when I first ventured into the Army recruiting office it was to the parachute regiment that I initially pledged my interest. Once I had completed the basic recruiting tests, things moved very quickly and the recruiting sergeant processed my application as ASAP with a medical at the now decommissioned local military barracks headquarters of the Bedfordshire and Hertfordshire Regiment.

Due entirely to my complete and absolute ignorance of military and regimental matters and the fact one of the two recruiting sergeants (as I was to later discover) was a member of the Royal Military Police I was persuaded, albeit to my later satisfaction that my future was with the Corps and as a result I found myself at Chichester, the rest; as one might say is history!

Back in the early days of 1964 we managed without colour television, computers, mobile telephones, microwaves, video and DVD. Our cameras used celluloid film and if we wanted to travel to a place that we didn't know; we would have to look at a map or a school atlas, it seems rather strange and totally ridiculous that I failed to do this in preparation for the day that I enlisted. Map reading I would discover was to become one of the most important skills acquired during basic training and one that was to prove crucial not only during field training exercises but also during any overseas travel and peacetime activities in garrison locations.

There was no such thing as equal opportunities, the Army in my early days was entirely male dominated. This was not to say that we did not covet or desire the female species. We most certainly wanted girls but contact was difficult, very few men actually managed to interact with local German girls, I am in awe of those who succeeded. Every opportunity to meet any female was always welcome, the most common occasions were corporals mess functions, taking wives to hospitals and the occasional party and Christmas invitations. To the best of my recollection in my first three years service the WRAC Provost were only deployed to Berlin, Cyprus, Hong Kong and London. Health and safety did not exist but nobody seemed to suffer any ill effects! Racism, and diversity were unheard of and in fact there were very few black soldiers, there were no black or indeed any Military Police from any ethnic minority group.

I have included reference to a number of incidents and events and fully appreciate that there may well be those who find themselves reading this volume and who had direct first- hand experience of the incidents to which I refer. In some cases they may have more intimate or more accurate knowledge of some of these events and therefore might wish to disagree with or challenge my accounts. From the experience gained throughout my entire service career and at reunions I am well aware that different individuals do not always recall identical or exact details of incidents. It is also the case, human nature being what it is that individuals often enhance their own role as this makes for better listening when they retell the story. It always sounds much more interesting when recalling an incident in which the narrator was actually involved rather than having been a third party or spectator. Whilst being able to agree that certain incidents and events actually took place there may be variations on the precise details, the identity of those involved, the level of involvement and the outcomes.

I have set out to present an overview of what it was like to enlist into the Military Police and what life was like as a single, soldier during basic training, in Germany and later in Hong Kong and subsequent postings.

Hopefully I may have succeeded in re-engaging not only with the memories of pleasant times but also of those not so pleasant and at which after so many years it is possible to look back and laugh. I also wanted to share some of my own views about life in Germany and beyond. I am certain that many of my former colleagues will have shared similar experiences.

I am certain that for many members of the Royal Military Police regardless of wherever else they may have served, Germany and the BAOR will have some special memories. I am of course aware that there may be those; a minority who for some reason did not serve in Germany and sadly do not know anything about it. Most members of the Corp will however have completed at least one tour of duty in BAOR and for many there may have been several. Although Osnabruck was my first and most significant Germany posting I consider myself very lucky to have served over fifteen years between BAOR and Berlin.

The German connexion

RELATIONSHIPS BETWEEN BRITISH SOLDIERS AND the German community may have been warm in some towns and cities but unfortunately quite negative in others. I know that a lot has been written about this and I must say that this has been mostly inaccurate rubbish. My overall perception was that the relationship between the British and the Germans was mostly welcoming and I eventually concluded that a majority of the German population was not so much anti British but more anti- military.

Although it never occurred to me as a fairly dumb 18 years old sprog soldier I did at least learn in later years that the German civilian population had not escaped the terror of war and second only to the USSR had suffered over five (5) million dead. A whole generation of German widows had long and painful memories of failed military adventures. I made many German friends over the years mainly during field training exercises and I have maintained these friendships with whole families including children and grandchildren.

There are as many similarities as there are differences between the two countries and I also believe that most misunderstandings and social conflict were primarily the consequence of an inability or in some cases a reluctance or unwillingness to communicate. 1965 was only twenty years after the end of the second war and it is likely that there were some mixed feelings amongst the civilian population.

In many cases, the British soldier of all ranks not only juniors, including some off duty RMP demonstrate the worst example of the Brit abroad, drunk, noisy, argumentative, belligerent and scruffy. It may have seemed to the German civilian population and the authorities, particularly the civil police that the British were a particularly uncultured race and the British soldier seemed determined to provide all of the evidence to support that view. It may have seemed that many soldiers had only one social objective; getting drunk and incapable at every opportunity, acting the clown and getting involved in criminal or anti social activities. Soldiers could expect no mercy from the civil police or the RMP on duty!

The responsibility for such conflict does not rest entirely with British soldiers who often had little experience of the cultural differences and with easy access to cheap alcohol but also with German civilians and officials in particular who generally consider the soldier to be a nuisance, they have little sympathy and even less tolerance when they are involved in any disturbance.

Many conflict situations and difficulties develop in towns and cities during soldier's social outings and often due to the excessive drinking prevalent among young soldiers and unintended, clumsy interaction. The sad thing is that drunken and anti social behaviour by off duty soldiers was often the only image that German civilians had of them and as is the case anywhere, first impressions are the most lasting. Too many soldiers only pluck up the courage to chat up the local girls when they have a skin-full of booze. Eligible young German females do not welcome drunken advances particularly from groups of young soldiers. Laws and regulations in Germany regarding the social activities of young people without parental chaperones are much stricter than in the United Kingdom. In addition many British soldiers simply did not properly understand the social niceties in a country where certain courtesies are expected. In addition to the inability to communicate in German the average soldier lacked understanding of what was expected and this almost certainly contributed to soldiers finding themselves in difficult situations and in direct conflict with the police.

There is also a certain amount of snobbery amongst a large proportion of the German population. There is certainly a part of German ideology and tradition which causes them to believe that they are superior and more cultured than others. The post war progress of the country even though divided had seen a massive improvement in the economy and living standards. In contrast the British economy had shown a marked decline and the British social class system remains as entrenched as ever.

In contrast to any difficulties encountered in the towns and cities and considering the numbers of soldiers involved, the reception generally received in the countryside and the many picturesque villages was surprisingly hospitable and friendly This was the case even when we descended in our hundreds and sometimes thousands complete with whole convoys of heavy vehicles and where we often damaged roads, buildings and crops.

Although it was almost certainly never properly explained to new arrivals, the major annual field training exercises were planned to take place after the completion of the main harvest. These were mainly corn and sugar beet as well as other crops of fruit and vegetables that were not sufficiently robust to withstand any peacetime or wartime military incursion.

The Germans are by nature a generous and hospitable people as well as incredibly hard working. I could provide many examples but one in particular best illustrates this generosity. As a platoon commander later in my career whilst on a major field training exercise a particular farmer on whose land we were encamped made a complete brick built barn available to accommodate the entire platoon where we could assemble our camp beds as well as moving his tractors from the Dutch barn to save us the trouble of camouflage. He had also built a small shower and toilet facility for our exclusive use, for a totally unexpected encore his wife proceeded to cook food for the whole platoon whilst he provided an inexhaustible supply of beer and schnapps. In addition he point blankly refused to accept any of the barn money on offer. On one occasion after leaving this location earlier than had been expected and having missed the food being prepared by his wife, the same farmer accompanied by his daughters and son in law managed to track me down via exercise control in order to deliver a food parcel, much to the amusement of the directing staff and I suspect a little envy.

I know that a substantial number of corps members and other soldiers married German girls and later made their homes in Germany. In what I consider to have been one of the biggest mistakes of my life compounded by the fact that I had already decided in my early days in Osnabruck that Germany was to be my chosen country I eventually returned to live in England. Without reservation this has to be one of the decisions that I most bitterly regret. It was also clear how important the teaching of English was in German schools, this was something that was obvious when even the youngest child we met on exercise could speak English. I often reflected on the stubborn and outdated British attitude and wondered how many English primary school children would have been able to communicate in German with any visiting German soldiers.

I have no hesitation in expressing envy of those that have made their homes in Germany. It's a strange irony that I should have served in BAOR for fifteen years and spent all of that time never wanting to leave as well as encouraging others to make their homes in Germany that I should be the one to exit. Unlike Great Britain, Germany values it's own heritage and traditions whilst developing new and modern ideas.

Although I have no current or accurate data regarding the number of British soldiers and particularly Military Police married to German Girls it is an interesting fact that the British Governments ban on British soldiers marrying German girls, following the end of the second world war was lifted on 1st August 1946 barely one year after hostilities concluded. Despite this legal amendment it was not until the 1960's that such marriages were actually permitted by the military authorities. As part of this process it was necessary for servicemen to apply for permission to marry, this was not automatically granted and in many cases, to prevent such marriages the applicant was likely to find himself posted rapidly to a far- away destination. I have no data or any information to suggest that soldiers might have used this process as a ruse to get away from Germany, or indeed how many were shanghaied against their will to prevent such marriages.

In the first year following the end of the 1st world war there were 700 marriages recorded between British soldiers and German girls and in the years following world war two until; 1965 there were over 2500 recorded.

I have mentioned; albeit briefly the first world war and it is right that I should include some reference to the first British Army of the Rhine from 1919 to 1929 which was primarily based in the demilitarised Rhineland. Strangely enough this deployment was in partnership with the French military as a consequence of the aftermath of WW1 and the Versailles Treaty. This was a substantial force of nine divisions so the Military Police, Military Foot and Military Mounted would probably have been kept fairly busy.

Having personally made a number of excursions to the Rhineland Palatinate I would guess that in those early and less frenetic times life for the army would have been reasonably enjoyable although it is more than likely that local community relations would not have been particularly good in view of the fact that the Versailles treaty imposed very harsh financial penalties and these would have affected virtually the entire population. My research however indicates that the relationship between British soldiers and the German civilian population would have been considerably better than the relationship between the French Military and the Germans.

As a member of the Royal Military police, particularly in Germany my colleagues and I almost certainly considered ourselves somewhat elitist and right or wrong superior to the average soldier. It would be fair to say that working to a motto which extolled the virtue of setting the very best example was entirely compatible with an elitist and egotistical attitude. It may also have been the case that the Military Police were perceived by the local community as something akin to a gang of military enforcers. Many of the German civilians and Military would probably have associated us with the ruthless reputation of the German wartime "Feldjager" or Head-hunters. This might not have always encouraged positive interaction only twenty years after the war as it has been well evidenced that literally thousands of innocent soldiers and civilians were summarily executed by the head hunters particularly in the final days of the war.

The majority of married British servicemen lived in service quarters which formed part of some very substantial estates. There was a clear demarcation between officers and other ranks (enlisted men) not only in terms of location but also as regards size and standards. Although some enlisted juniors were provided with houses, (usually because they had a number of children) the majority of junior enlisted ranks were accommodated in flats most of which were very modern, purpose built and others in multi- story or converted buildings.

Warrant officers and Commissioned officers were usually accommodated in houses with gardens, well away from enlisted men and of a size and standard according to rank. The higher the rank the (bigger) better the house!

Two particularly advantageous aspects of service quarters in Germany was that virtually all were fitted with double glazed windows and efficient shared central heating systems. The vast majority of service flats were well appointed and of a high standard. Another advantage was that most enlisted men's service quarters were relatively close to Barracks with easy access to the primary facilities such as NAAFI service shops, service schools and medical facilities. Although such easy access was advantageous to the soldiers, make no mistake it was of even greater advantage to commanders who were there-fore able to call in their soldiers more quickly in the event of any emergency.

In strong contrast to German civilian housing areas which would accommo-date a wide age range of families, as in any civilian community, the military were generally all the same age under 40 years. A natural consequence of this was that there were always large numbers of young children concentrated in military estates at a level not found in the German community. It sounds very judgemental and snobbish to make any negative comments about service-men and their families but it is a well documented fact that many of the service married quarter estates occupied by enlisted soldiers did not present a par-ticularly good image. During 1965 and 1966 the very large service quarter estates at Belm and Powe outside Osnabruck became the focus of a National German newspaper story when it was reported that organised coach trips were being made to view the British Army Ghettos. The story also made the British National press. As part of the clean up and damage limitation exercise military police foot patrols were deployed every day into the offending estates with orders to report back.

Each military unit would send out clean up troops and in addition the married men living in the quarters would be hauled out in the evenings to clean up. Make no mistake, the press reports were not untrue or in the least exaggerated because the place was a real mess.

Roussillon The first step

JOINING THE BRITISH ARMY AS an enlisted soldier in 1964 was a unique experience and one that could not possibly be replicated anywhere else or indeed with any other organisation. I don't think that the real implications of signing away personal freedom and accepting military rules were always immediately understood. It still seems surprising after so many years that I should wonder why after enlisting and agreeing to serve the queen and obey orders that there was actually no clear explanation provided regarding the consequences for not obeying orders and in particular what might happen if I simply did not report to the training centre.

Having abandoned a totally class dominated culture to enlist I should probably have realised that I had swapped such a regime for another which was much more sophisticated and with a draconian enforcement potential. I think also that I retained some resentment for a number of years and never immediately came to terms with the class dominated and effectively segregated organisation. I may have given some indication of how I felt even though I meticulously obeyed the rules and observed the protocols of rank.

Looking back and reflecting on my times, both good and bad; I can say with absolute conviction and apart from anything else, service life was never boring or routine. Unlike Regimental whole unit moves, in the case of Military Police; postings were on an individual basis and whilst friendships were made, many were lost and it was often the case that friends and colleagues would never meet again

As instructed at my Attestation I found my way to the Training Centre at Roussillon Barracks Chichester and on arrival foolishly asked for directions to the Guardroom, it was probably only a consequence of my obvious and naive ignorance that spared me a bawling out. Following a short briefing on the difference between a duty room and guard room I was consigned to the temporary safe keeping of a (two weeks service) recruit who was to deliver me safely to the stores for issue of the immediate essentials, then to the dining room and finally to my living accommodation.

My initial reaction when watching my escort was amazement, I had never seen anybody either walk as the recruit did or swing their arms with such abandon and I was certain that it was far from natural or normal. I also thought that it must be very painful as well as potentially damaging. As was the case for all new recruits such arm swinging, shoulder high was the mark of the untrained soldier together with a small red band worn on the shoulder epaulette to denote, "Not yet trained to salute"

Arriving at a training centre store and being issued on your first day with the basic domestic needs, a mattress, 4 blankets, 2 pillows, 2 pillow cases, 2 sheets, an ashtray, a bedside rug and the most important accessories for any soldier, a pint mug and a knife fork and spoon was bewildering. I barely understood the stores language used but managed to complete the operation after which I made my way to the accommodation. Having deposited my newly acquired possessions I was escorted to the dining room where I arrived right at the end of mealtime and as cleaning was in operation. This was not the optimum time to dine and I recall that whatever meals I had taken in my life to date I had seen nothing that looked as unappetising as that now on offer.

This was no gourmet supper, there was a large bowl of a white runny substance masquerading as mashed potato and which I was to later discover to be POM (a reconstituted potato substance) a bowl of cabbage and some pale raw looking sausages of dubious origin floating in water. There was a small pile of dried up bread slices, a dish of margarine and the remains of a pot of jam. The real prize however was an aluminium urn containing luke warm tea. I was never so glad of the fact that I had packed a few packets of jaffa cakes and some cheese sandwiches.

After the dreadful meal my next unpleasant surprise was my living quarters. This was a large room on the first floor containing nothing but six metal bed frames. I really was wondering what I had let myself in for and asked what am I doing here?

My first night in the army was not pleasant, I felt lost and trapped. The bed was tiny and uncomfortable, the windows rattled non stop, every sound in the building appeared to be magnified and the room was freezing. I was glad that I had brought along an ample supply of cigarettes, this was not the ideal time to quit smoking. Thank god for Senior Service!

The following morning I managed to find my way to the canteen and I was at least able to find something fit to eat, beans and toast as well as hot but not very nice tasting tea. This was to be effectively my constant cookhouse diet for the next four months mainly due to the fact that little else was recognisable or eatable.

Once my mind had grown accustomed to the reality of enlistment and my stomach had reached a compromise I was able to enjoy breakfast and for the next fourteen weeks I survived on the real basic and very simple diet apart from the morning cheese roll in the NAAFI junior ranks club.

The issue of uniform took place during the following days together with the identity card, in those days the AFB 2603 and the plastic case AFB 2604.

We were also issued with and instructed to memorise our 8 digit regimental number Our uniform issue included Boots DMS, shoes, plimsolls, shorts, towels, socks, pt shorts and vests and the housewife, sadly not the usual human model but a small cloth bag containing such precious commodities as buttons, cotton, wool and needles.

Cleaning utensils consisted of two shoe brushes and a button stick; this in 1964 was in reality an obsolete item more useful when enlisted soldiers buttons were made from brass and not stay-brite. To the novice soldier it seemed that descriptions of clothing were somewhat amusing but time and service would make it all much clearer such as shirts, khaki cotton and shirts khaki kf and shirts cotton no 1 dress and one wondered why there was any confusion in the first place.

Probably the most welcome event during the next few days was the arrival of several other newly enlisted recruits with whom I would later share rooms as members of my squad (56). We were all in this together and it somehow made life much easier. Outwardly, everybody else appeared calm and reasonably happy, I may of course have been mistaken and I wonder what impression I gave.?

In total disregard of all the rules I recall one of the newly arrived men getting himself dressed up and heading for the town on his very first night. Those of us who witnessed his covert departure and the fact that he had to sneak back in after lights out without permission was considered very daring and reckless About one week later following some disturbance he mysteriously vanished from our lives along with all of his possessions and was never to be seen again. An unsubstantiated account suggested that in a drunken and violent rage he had smashed a number of glass windows and sustained some serious injuries.

However hard I try; I struggle to recall the actual routine of the first few days.

I was almost a zombie, left on my own for the first two or three days having no idea what to do or where I should be. I recall being rescued by my squad instructor, Sergeant Bob Sacco, I was beginning to think that I had somehow been overlooked or missed and I must have been sorely tempted to jump ship. Certain later activities are fairly clear in my mind, particularly my very first pay parade. This involved a long winding queue along the top corridor of Sandhurst, block marching to the table where the pay officer was sitting, taking the pay book taking the money and confirming that the pay and pay book was correct accompanied by the smartest possible salute, once we had been trained sufficiently well to do so.

I really thought that the amount I received £5.00 must be a mistake. Prior to enlisting I was clearing at least twice and often four times that much every week. It was of course no mistake, the simple fact was that it was what 6 year enlisted soldiers received and about as much as was needed to pay for the daily cheese roll, the haircuts and cleaning kit, kiwi polish, blanco and brasso.

For virtually every enlisted soldier except perhaps for those who had been to Boarding school there was another unfamiliar experience, dormitory life! Sharing a room with a number of other men who were unknown to each other and made worse by the fact that some of them did not appear to take personal hygiene seriously. This was not an easy matter to deal with although things did improve over time. In addition to personal cleanliness there was also the issue of cleaning and polishing the barrack room. The corporate responsibility simply evolved over time and the regular morning inspections served as a motivator to maintain the standard. I can recall one incident in another squad where a trainee recruit had failed to maintain the basic standards and had apparently wilfully ignored the approaches of his colleagues. He was unceremoniously carried to the bathroom and given a thorough scrubbing with a large sweeping brush with the promise of further treatments if he did not do as he was instructed.

Every day was filled with activity and the routine rarely changed. There was never any spare time or dull moments. The constant instructions regarding every aspect of our daily lives as well as the urgency and sheer physical effort of marching from one place to another became more manageable with each day. Our development also included the ease with which we could change clothes in moments, from drill to PE from PE to classroom all of which we developed to a fine art. At the end of the working/training day and the evening meal there was little time to relax. Although there was a television set in a communal room it was rarely used, any time spent watching television would have been time lost on the two primary occupations after evening meal, study and cleaning.

Most of the young soldiers were totally unprepared for such a culture which included the early start to each day. Reveille was at 0600, there was no tea in bed but plenty of noise from crashing dustbin lids. As the days passed and we became accustomed to army routine we became almost robotic in our response to the myriad of essential daily tasks. Making our beds, complete morning ablutions, shower and shave, breakfast, get dressed, tidy personal locker, leave no dust or dirt, polish the floor and leave no marks or smudges. Under normal circumstances these tasks were simple except for the most challenging time when returning from night guard duty as it would include having to iron service dress uniform and clean the boots worn during guard duty ready for morning parade. The worst guard duty to pull was the 24 hours on a Sunday and if as it was for me; raining, utterly soul destroying. Running from the duty room to the barrack room and then Ironing what had become virtual cardboard trousers and transforming our boots from virtual destruction to parade standard in the short interval from 0630 to 0730. Along with having to share the task of preparing our barrack room for morning inspection, completing the whole package was nothing short of miraculous.

On days like this breakfast was the usual casualty.

Arriving at any military establishment as an enlisted soldier at evening meal time is not an experience to either encourage or recommend. This was a lesson to be taken around the world and in particular the need to avoid arriving at weekends.

It might be fair to say that this phenomenon is not restricted to the British army and my experience of other, particularly European and especially the French army is no different. Trying to identify what it was you were being invited to eat required imagination, courage, a strong stomach and a desperate appetite.

My first few weeks generated a whole mixture of emotions and challenges, learning how to stand up straight and marching in a group and in step was a real effort for virtually every new soldier and the daily routine in the gymnasium really demanding. The combination of intensive classroom lessons and the demanding physical routine generated a new experience, this included the total body ache every evening, during the first few weeks it was almost permanent debilitating pain. There were other lessons to learn, ironing uniform, polishing boots and the mystery of green Blanco applied to our field webbing and the intricate application of white Blanco to our waist belts along with the need to produce highly polished and smudge free brass accessories..

Although as recruits we were instructed to Blanco our kit and polish our boots by our squad instructor it was effectively left to those recruits with previous service to demonstrate the actual skills of applying spit and polish as well as the other intricacies of sorting out our kit. My room was fortunate in that we had an ex RAF regiment national serviceman "Daniel" Boon who was a real boot bulling expert and an accidental mentor.

The legal military obligation to recognise authority and rank was a new experience and one which I believe I resented and with which I was never fully compliant or indeed comfortable. Over the years it seemed to be the case that some seniors would give orders or instructions with which I could readily and willingly comply whilst others would serve only to challenge or intimidate. On more than one occasion I thought to question in my mind how on earth certain individuals came to be in positions of authority. Such experiences provided for me a profound lesson in mis-management and one that I would keep in mind for the future. I determined that I would be far more considerate than some of the seniors I had met in those early days. Sadly this transition would not take place overnight and during the following years I would experience more than my fair share of institutionalised and legalised unsavoury behaviour.

In addition to the maintenance of our uniform, particularly our boots which had to be highly polished as well as ironing the awful green denim overalls there were other tasks. Each day these became easier and included the routine of bed making which in the early days of training required blocks constructed from blankets and sheets. There was also the huge task of cleaning our room which included bumper polishing the wooden floor to inspection standard and any place where dust could hide we had to find it first.. Not every soldier was able to cope with this catalogue of tasks and during the first few weeks there were a number of recruit casualties who were to find themselves departing from the training centre. There were some who could simply not apply themselves to the level of self discipline demanded, this included finding the time to study, housekeep the shared barrack room, clean our own kit and get smartly dressed in time for every morning muster parade. From my experience and although the tasks became less challenging with every passing day, there was little free time except for the eagerly awaited weekend. On Saturday mornings except for those detailed for guard duty every recruit had to parade for litter- picking around the barracks and other general tidying up tasks. Perhaps well ahead of its time this routine was described as "interior economy". This was not a particularly onerous task and it had the effect of making the remainder of the day seem even more enjoyable and valuable.

The Training Programme

The Army and the Nation induction

The initial introductory programme, the first two weeks, in 1964 was as I recall referred to as "The army and the nation". This included instruction regarding the Army rank structure and the deployment of the army in the UK and overseas in both peacetime and wartime roles. The programme also included details of the international treaties with which the United Kingdom was involved such as NATO and how the forces were actually involved. Having sworn an oath of allegiance to the Crown it came as no surprise that the training included an explanation of the relationship between the monarchy, the government and the armed forces.

Although we were barely into our training in early 1965 after just a few weeks we could at least march reasonably well and in step as a squad. On 30th January 1965 the entire training centre, recruits and staff assembled on the barrack square and marched to the corps chapel for a service to mark the funeral of Sir Winston Churchill. As befitting the occasion it was a cold, overcast and very wet day. The actual march was made very difficult (as many may recall) due to the fact that all training centre staff were required to wear the issued rubber proofed (RP) coats. This particular item of uniform was very effective in helping to keep the rain at bay but the noise of the rustle from the coats seemed to affect the hearing and caused all of the recruits in training to lose the marching step. The result of this was that the training centre sergeant major lost his cool and summoned one of the squad instructors a former guardsman to march ahead of the column beating the time on a drum to help us to keep in step. This changed what had been a chaotic situation into relative order but did not make the day any more enjoyable. In later years I identified the same coat to be not only a fine waterproof but also a very useful emergency blanket.

Weapon Training

Following completion of the introductory induction phase the real training programme actually began, as for all enlisted soldiers and what was to prove to be the first real demanding topic was the weapon training phase. This training forms the basic introduction for all enlisted soldiers and reinforces the objective of developing a reasonable level of proficiency in the primary skill of how to fight and kill with weapons. There was no inference or suggestion of political correctness in 1964 and why should there have been? Soldiers are trained to use weapons and weapons are for the express purpose of killing. As we were frequently reminded throughout our initial training and later; we were soldiers first and foremost and policemen second. Although we were to hear this very same statement many times over the years, it proved to be something of a con-tradictory claim when priorities were prone to change to suit the management. As potential military police non -commissioned officers our initial training in-volved learning to handle and fire what were then the standard military police weapons, the .38 Smith and Wesson revolver and the standard 9mm sterling sub machine gun. Although I had occasionally used smooth bore shotguns and air rifles this was my first experience of real killing weapons.

Although I can't be certain why, it was as I recall that during the initial stages of this training I became very disenchanted after my very short tenure of military life. I remember discussing this with my squad sergeant "in con-fidence" or so I thought and for my trouble I was ridiculed by the weapon training sergeant (Ramshaw)for being a "quitter "at every subsequent session. This approach must have had the desired effect as I managed to "soldier on" for another twenty three years.

I was not however let off the hook and I reckon that I had more than my fair share of doubling around the parade square with sand filled boots and carrying boxes of empty cartridge cases. The in barracks weapon training programme involved a lot of pointless and demoralising activities such as the bizarre and persistent stand up sit down stand- up routine!!! It may have been this phase along with the dreadful food and the aggressive bullying attitude of the senior physical training instructor. In addition to the more exciting live firing on the ranges we continued with our practise of loading magazines timed against the clock, stripping and assembling weapons, TOTS (tests of trained soldiers) making range declarations, collecting spent cartridges and probably the most unpleasant experience, an introduction to the gas chamber whilst wearing respirators and later practising drills of eating, drinking and decontaminating with fullers earth when removing our respirators. Exposure to CS in a closed environment is not a pleasant experience and standing in the gas chamber having to recite number rank and name without respirator before being allowed to leave reinforces that view.

During these early days of drill, PE, parades and room inspections we were also introduced to the world of green and white webbing, shiny brass buckles and shiny boots. Once again such matters which at first seemed impossible to manage became ever easier with each passing day and the results so much better..

Daily PE and marching drill became very painful when our muscles ached at the end of each day, this probably lasted for about two weeks after which both activities became easier day by day.

During the weapons training phase we were introduced for the first time to outdoor field training supposedly designed to acclimatise us to active service conditions. There was not to the best of my recollection even the most basic advice on what to expect and there was no help or support with the preparation. These failings resulted in some very unpleasant experiences along with some hard learned and never to be forgotten lessons. In my squad this training phase took place in early January, the weather was cold and wet with some night time and early morning frost. The ground quickly became a muddy mess and a real challenge, having to work, live, sleep and eat in such conditions was anything but enjoyable. Digging trenches, mounting defences against imaginary enemy attacks, learning to cope with thunder flashes thrown into tents and trenches, lack of food and sleep all took their toll and we were never so pleased as to return to barracks on the Friday afternoon. I don't ever recall being told although with hindsight it should have been obvious; that we were training for what we might expect during war. It was a sad fact that we received no guidance or instruction on how to actually look after ourselves and it was very much a question of personal survival. At the time it was a matter of doing what we were told to do and with little consideration of what the aims might be or what we were supposed to be learning. We were not provided with sleeping bags and had to make do with the same blankets that we used in our barrack rooms. The main priority at the time, at least for the training staff seemed to be making life as difficult and as unpleasant as possible for us. The officers and training staff may well have thought that the process was designed to create something akin to the realism of the battle field and character building but the only thing it proved to me was the same old story of making life unpleasant.

Meagre and indifferent as it may have been, at least the food, mainly "COMPO" rations of canned food that we received during this training was no worse than that in barracks.

The unpleasant and mostly pointless experiences from the field training would stay with me throughout my service and although there may have been occasions when my own methods may have seemed harsh and not appreciated by everybody I always made certain that any soldiers under my command were properly trained, well prepared and suitably equipped.

Social hours
In between work and sleep there was, when time and opportunity became available after our first four weeks the chance to visit the local town centre, this involved the process of booking out at the duty room. The first step involved knocking on the door, waiting for permission to enter, marching in, halting and requesting permission to book out. Once inside the duty room the NCO's on duty would subject us to the ordeal of being inspected to ensure

that we were properly dressed in a style that was acceptable. This provided no guarantee of success, on some occasions we were refused and then had to return later to start again at the end of the booking out queue. There were also times when the queue was so long that it became a pointless exercise trying to book out because by the time we might have succeeded it would have been time to return. During our forays into town we learned that there were certain hostelries where as short haired young soldiers we were really welcome although not every place was the same. During a rare visit to the nearby town of Arundel we learned that in certain places there was an open policy of discriminatory snobbery and we were not in the least welcome. This was clearly demonstrated by the bar staff who deliberately yet silently ignored us whilst serving other customers who arrived after us. We might have been mindful of our corps motto even at this stage of our careers but we were really pissed off with the snobbish attitude of the bar staff, we made sure that we told everybody and chose never to go Arundel ever again.

When we were out of barracks we couldn't help but notice how the very easy to spot recruits in training seemed unable to walk normally even though they were wearing civilian clothes. Vigorous swinging of the arms had become quite normal along with walking in step and in pairs. There was never to my knowledge any demonstration of dislike of the RMP recruits on the part of the local Chichester community and although we could not disguise who we were, we were treated at least in my experience no different to any others. During an exploration of the Chichester Cathedral one Saturday afternoon I was treated to tea with the vicar and his wife although I was never sure if this was a consequence of him and his wife identifying me as a good Christian, a potential conversion or just plain hospitality.

During these very early days in our barrack room we discussed the cost of the frequent haircuts and one of the four men sharing my room, a former RAF Regiment national serviceman suggested that we all contribute towards the purchase of the equipment needed to cut hair. We shared the cost and he did the cutting, although we never made a fortune we were able to reduce our own personal expenditure "save a few lives" and spend the small amount of income. This continued until a well meaning informant spilled the beans and we had to close down the enterprise because the camp barber did not like the competition.

We also discussed the option of purchasing our own steam iron as an alternative to the hiring process that was in place, to the best of my memory this idea was shelved because we couldn't locate a suitable model in the town.

POLICE DUTIES

Having successfully, at least for most of our squad completed the weapon training programme we moved on to the next Police Duties phase. Prior to this transition one of our colleagues who had attempted, much to our annoyance to portray himself as an experienced and skilled territorial warrant officer was suddenly removed from training. The official line was that he had failed to make the mandatory minimum height of 5'8" but I think it was because he was simply too mouthy and could not live up to his arrogant claims. This police duties part of the training represented the actual start of our specialist introduction to the military police role and despite the fact that this phase coincided with the spectre of having to perform the dreaded guard duties was a great time. The horrible guard duty started with a small parade outside the duty room and then being inspected by either the duty officer or sergeant. We then took our places inside the duty room and started the patrol duties which involved two beats, the most dreadful was the six minute armoury patrol which involved walking from the duty room to the armoury and return to knock on the duty room door literally every six minutes. The second beat involved a roving patrol around the barracks, this was not nearly so bad as the six minute beat and it was least possible to find a dark place to hide for a crafty smoke. The length of duty was two hours patrol and then four hours off. Undertaking this duty on a weekday night was bad enough but the worst of all was the Sunday duty which degenerated into a total nightmare if it was raining.

The police duties phase included the benefit of being instructed by long serving sergeants and corporals with years of actual experience and endless tales of engagement with soldiers around the world. This was both motivating and highly entertaining. How could we fail to be in awe of the accounts of the immaculate military police man holding back riot and disorder by his mere presence, immaculate uniform and boots along with his unflappable composure both in peace and war-time. This was also the first time that we were permitted to wear our service dress (training) uniforms and forage caps. This change was a welcome development particularly for those of us who had been obliged to wear the 1950's style impossible to look smart in overalls.

I think that at this stage we actually began to look as well as feel the part. Our service (no 2 dress) shirts were a legacy of the past as they were fitted with detachable collars that required fixing with studs, I can recall that one of our roommates who had never, so he told us, ever worn a shirt with any kind of collar and was completely baffled by the process for fitting the collar and then using the tie. Sadly and although he received a great deal of help with the preparation of his kit, uniform and boots he was simply unable to manage the tasks and it really came as no surprise that the detachable collar proved to be his final downfall. David; left the training centre for transfer to another branch of the army, the newly created Royal Corps of Transport having been formally identified as no longer suitable to continue training as a military policeman. He was not the only casualty and a number of others made their exit before the end of the fourteen weeks.

We were now becoming seasoned recruits; morning parades held no fear, the drill sessions were no longer the challenge of those very first days. Strangely, marching in unison as part of a trained squad became a real pleasure and a source of team pride. We learned to listen to the sound of our "in time" feet striking the ground and the ease with which we performed the wide range of drill movements, right turn, left turn about turn and saluting, marking time as well as quick and slow marching. Our training and confidence was rewarded later when we completed our drill test under the instruction of our squad sergeant and observed by the company sergeant major. The whole training centre routine became second nature and any fears or inhibitions banished. We walked with a new pride and self- confidence and developed a sense of competition always wanting to be the best and hear the Sergeant's praise. How things had changed? we were no longer at the lowest level, we watched in disgust as the new recruits following us made their pathetic start to marching and wondered if we were ever that bad.

MILITARY LAW

The Police duties phase was followed by Military law and an introduction to the legal definitions according to both civil and military law as well as the statutory powers granted to military police. We were expected to learn the definitions by heart and this was tested at the time of the end of phase written tests. This knowledge was crucial to identifying the nature of the offences committed by soldiers, over the years there were a number of changes in criminal legislation and this resulted in changes in criminal offences to be replaced by others which were naturally accompanied by new definitions. Despite the many changes in civil criminal legislation the bulk of military law remained unaffected. What was not included in our basic Military law training were the differences in criminal legislation in other countries around the world and how severe some laws were compared to that of the United Kingdom.

This phase was crucial to understanding the rules under which criminal investigations were governed and undertaken. In 1965 the so called "New Judges Rules" were introduced which governed the whole process for interviewing those suspected of criminal offences. These rules would stay in place for twenty years until the Introduction of the Police and Criminal Evidence Act (Pace) in 1984.

Although this phase included the procedures for interviewing suspects, cautions and taking statements, it seems to me that more could have been done during training. There was never, at least in my time so much as a role play or demonstration and it was not until we were deployed on our very first posting that we would have the opportunity to actually put the theoretical skills learned, into practise.

Study and retention of information became much easier and the classroom routine more comfortable, we were at ease with our training and eager to learn. We were now also now free of the dreaded Guard duty rota and selfishly grateful that those recruits in the squads following us had taken on this task. This phase demanded a good deal of personal study in order to master all that was required in order to ensure that we passed the necessary course test. At this stage neither I or anybody else wanted to be kicked out!! Throughout the whole of our training and particularly during this phase our main source of reference was the Corps "Bible" the magnificent red coloured Provost Training manual.

PHASE 5 TRAFFIC CONTROL

Traffic duties was the next specialist phase and this included such tasks as mobile and static speed checks, military police escorts and what was probably the most frequent undertaking; car parking. Many of the skills learned here would prove to be essential in both our peacetime and operational roles and car parking in particular would feature at practically every major or minor event at which we were deployed..

Traffic duties would certainly feature one way or another in just about every theatre of deployment, in every unit and in every country. Some of the most basic activities such as car parking at major events could become masterpieces of control or total disasters. The main piece of equipment was the rather vintage Lamp Traffic Control with it's option of green or red lens covers and a bit of a headache. This piece of equipment was paraffin fuelled which would burn for about 4 hours and which required about the same amount of time to clean after use. Naturally the real merit and disadvantages of these lamps would only be realised later on in my service in Germany.o far as I can recall it was at this stage that we had earned a weekend pass, the first time we were allowed to stay out and go home. This was after work on Friday until return on Sunday, not a particularly long but nonetheless a welcome break.

Of course there is always a cost and in this case during the Friday morning Commandants inspection a number of our squad recruits were judged to have "dirty" webbing on top of their lockers and were placed on OC's Orders.

This process involves soldiers being charged with an offence and then being marched in front of their officer and mark time (tapping the boards) in front of the officer's desk to answer the charge. In this case the cost to them was forfeit of their weekend pass. It was really a load of rubbish and in reality simply a question of emphasising the concept of military discipline. In just about every similar case the unfortunate soldier would have been charged under the catch all section 69 of the Army Act 1955 specifying that the soldier either did something or omitted to do something which was "Contrary to good order and military discipline".

DRIVER TRAINING

Due to the fact that all military police NCO's need to be able to drive or ride, the next phase of training was referred to as MT, the mechanical Transport period. This training of two weeks was designed to train the recruit sufficiently to be able to pass the standard Driving Test. The Royal Military Police training centre was in the ideal position of being it's own licensing authority and therefore able to provide the training, the testing and the test pass certificates.

The general practise was to teach any non -driver using land-rovers or Austin 1 ton trucks and to teach some others or those who already had a vehicle licence to ride a motorcycle.

It was my understanding that failure to pass the standard car test on two occasions prevented any further training and in such cases it was an early exit from the Royal Military Police.

For those recruits who took part in the MT phase those days were relatively easy with no guard duties and a fairly relaxed atmosphere with the civilian instructors. The driving instruction was focussed on the total novice learner and was in reality no different, other than the type of vehicle in which any civilian would be trained. The level of training was basic and there was nothing additional or specialist provided. This clearly did not take account of either the need for military police to be able to demonstrate above average skill during peacetime duties or, possibly more importantly during any operational field deployment when there was a need to negotiate rough cross country terrain.

I was fortunate in that prior to my enlistment I had already accrued several years of driving a whole range of motor vehicles on cross country terrain and was highly skilled with land- rovers, lorries, tractors and towing a variety of trailers single and double axle. I was already the holder of a full vehicle and motorcycle licence and after undergoing a first day one hour review of my driving ability along with a small number of other recruits I was removed from the MT phase and transferred to a different squad. As a result of this move I joined the new squad who had started the final and what was rumoured to be the hardest training phase, Provost Ops. This move also reduced my overall basic training by two weeks.

Provost Operations

The final phase and that which was rumoured to be the stumbling ground of many recruits was Pro Ops (provost operations) which focussed on the war time operational role of the military police. This phase introduced some really new military police tasks, which included NBC (nuclear biological and chemical) monitoring, prisoners of war, anti- vice, looting, refugees and stragglers. It also included the introduction of the army deployment process and how the military police undertook route signing both to and from the front of any combat zone and the use of route signing along lateral routes. Route signing was one particular task that featured significantly throughout my entire service during both operational (field training exercises) and peacetime activities. Even though the signed objectives would be entirely different the general process and requirements, route planning and map reading were the same. The anti-vice topic was never discussed in any detail and there was a general assumption that this was related to prostitution. Drug misuse and addiction hardly featured. Pro ops also included an introduction to internal security duties; much of which was based on the style of dealing with public disorder and violent protests around the world in British colonies. I recall the riot control film involving a squad of soldiers marching into action and then displaying the disperse or we open fire banner. This was how riots were dealt with under British Colonial rule although it was not made clear as to exactly what was the specific role of the RMP.

Pro Ops also presented the historical role of the military police who took part in military executions by firing squad. This particular task, as my research has shown and as anybody might expect did not enhance the image of the Military Police.

In the event that a condemned man was not killed by the firing squad the men would be marched away and it was then the sombre responsibility of the Deputy assistant Provost Marshal in any division for delivering the coup de grace with his service pistol. Provost operations was certainly the most interesting phase and of course its successful completion marked the end of the initial training programme.

Looking back

BASIC TRAINING PROVIDED THE MINIMUM level of the essential skills that every enlisted military policeman needed as a soldier and in addition the basic special to arm skills necessary for the soldier to undertake his duties as a military policeman. Many of the routine lifesaving and additional basic skills such as shining boots and brasses as well as blancoing web belts and equipment were not part of the training curriculum but essential to successful completion of basic training. These essential but undocumented skills were effectively overseen and delivered by the older soldiers with previous military service and without whom the process for the novice recruit to learn would have failed. The squad instructor was clear about what was expected from us but it was in reality up to us to find out for ourselves

In addition to the technical and academic phases, marching foot drill on the parade square and physical education took place every day. I can recall only one planned swimming lesson which involved a trip to the Naval base at Portsmouth, unfortunately the trip ended in disaster due to the fact that when we arrived it was discovered that the facility was double booked and we returned to Chichester having not even got our feet wet. In addition to being marched in a squad to and from every training session there were also regular morning parades and inspections. Some of the parades involved our lone squad, some involving the recruit training group and on other occasions the whole training centre, on some occasions the junior commissioned Squad officers took part, essentially this was training for them. It was on such occasions that we had sight of the Depot Regimental Sergeant Major who also put in an appearance, it was a bit scary to hear him actually shout at the junior officers if he thought that they were not making the effort. I have to admit that in the early days of my training I felt a bit overawed and intimidated by the parade experience. It was strange and unfamiliar but as was the case for every part of our training our confidence grew with experience and practise.

During our training we also received a very basic introduction to first aid which was entirely classroom based theory. There was no practical training, demonstration or role play. We also received some rudimentary self- defence and restraint techniques colloquially referred to as "police holds " during the gymnasium sessions but once again barely sufficient to be able to develop more than a modicum of proficiency. As our training progressed even the gym work became easier and the aches and pains that we had experienced in the first few weeks had all but disappeared. Although we could hardly have considered ourselves expert, some of the restraint techniques we were taught were fairly helpful although it would take a number of real life practical applications before we would really master the techniques.

I have always failed to understand why, even after so many years there was never any practical instruction during basic training in the use of handcuffs or the standard wooden truncheon. Neither of these items were routinely carried by military police patrols and so far as I can recall required the permission of an RMP officer before they could be issued. Both items were secured in locked cabinets in every RMP duty room and in fact each truncheon had it's own personal page in the official truncheon book which recorded every minute imperfection. In the event of any issue each truncheon had to be examined before it was signed out and again on it's return with details of any new imperfections and details of how these were acquired.

There were other not specifically practical military matters which received no input, these included personal hygiene, cleaning, ironing, independence and survival, ironically none of these topics featured on the training agenda but were simply learned or shared by other soldiers. The army may be all about team work but every soldier has to learn to take care of himself and to be prepared for the times when he is alone out on his own with no colleagues and no support. Most of these "social and domestic" skills simply developed as part of the group association and in particular from those recruits with previous military service, including the rather well trained Junior Leaders. It was really clear to me even at this early stage of my service career that some of my colleagues would never learn all that was required no matter how any times they were shown or told.

Being an enlisted soldier creates some opposing concepts, the first of which is following orders without question or debate and the second although not obvious at the initial stages of basic training was the expectation on every soldier when separated or estranged from his superiors to be able to think and act independently.

Self- survival and taking care of yourself becomes a really important issue because in reality and although it might appear an unpalatable statement the fact is that nobody else really cares about anybody but themselves. Everybody has to learn to take care of themselves. Staying fit, staying healthy, taking care of your weapon and equipment, all of these demand commitment, determination and self-discipline. It always seemed to me that the supervisors had little interest in the care and welfare of the juniors but could always be relied on to apply sanctions if it meant saving their own skin i developed my own personal philosophy for prioritising when on operations. Safeguard my weapon at all times and in my case I always attached a pistol lanyard particularly at night in the sleeping bag, look after my vehicle, take care of my body and in particular the feet by staying clean and dry at all times. I also made a particular point of eating at every opportunity even when not hungry or having just eaten and when everything else has been completed sleep.

In summary, when not in battle, work tasks, clean, eat, sleep.

The end of the initial basic training was marked by a formal parade in no 1 dress ceremonial (blues) uniform with the whole squad formed up in three ranks, open order outside the commandants office. I guess that there was an air of excitement, having successfully completed our training and getting ready for the final parade. Our parade positions were pre-planned and marked out so that we could assume our place without any unnecessary drill movements.

I can recall a number of rehearsals which mainly focussed on how we should walk the several hundred yards from our barrack room to the form up position without ruining our highly polished boots or getting our uniforms covered in dust. This was also as I recall the first and only occasion when we were allowed to walk unaided and not marched in a group.

On the occasion of our squad pass out the weather was fine and despite our anxiety, the walk from the barrack room to the parade site did not totally destroy the fine polish on our boots. It was fortunate that the grass had been well cut. The passing out parade was a celebratory event to which the families and friends of the recruits were invited to watch and then to take tea in the junior ranks club. We were all handed our little congratulatory certificates and that was it. I recall that together with many of my colleagues I made a pretty rapid exit to catch the next train and this was the only time I would ever travel by choice in uniform. Friday afternoon travel into London Victoria was never the best option but there was never any other suitable route to take.

A few days before the pass out day our squad instructor had announced the postings for each man on completion of training. In 1965 Great Britain still retained a number of overseas colonies and there were several possible destinations. Although Germany BAOR took the lions share with as I recall only two of our squad being posted by choice to the UK. Although the other options included Cyprus, Hong Kong, Singapore, Malaya, Borneo, Brunei, Aden, Bahrain, Malta, Gibraltar and Kenya none of our squad were destined for any of these. There were postings available within the United Kingdom and what was later described as a gardening posting to Northern Ireland. Together with three of my squad colleagues I was posted to Osnabruck Germany me and John Hodgson to 12 Infantry Brigade Provost Unit and Gordon Price and Terry Whitfield to 2 Div Pro Coy.

Following completion of our training and prior to leaving the centre after pass out parade we had been granted a period of well -earned and eagerly anticipated privilege leave.

In most cases the end of training was the last ever time the squad members would meet. Apart from John, Gordon and Terry I can't recall ever meeting any of the training squad again with the exception of Harry good when we both found ourselves on the long service list at HQ BAOR in September 1986, 21 years after completing training.

Germany here we come

THE TRAINING WAS NOW COMPLETED, we had our first stripe and we were officially, "Trained Soldiers and "qualified" military police "non -commissioned Officers". We were now permitted to re-adopt a normal walking/marching posture and no more windmill, shoulder high arm swinging. I think that we were all justifiably excited as well as relieved that the training was successfully completed and that we had survived. So far as I can recall there was not a sign of apprehension or nervousness and everybody appeared to be happy with their postings. I don't actually recall how much leave I had at the end of the training or what I actually did during this time. On our return to the training centre after leave we had our very first experience of the MFO box, although our limited possessions would hardly justify a whole box we managed to find enough. I recall travelling with two suitcases, one traditional service issue that contained enough of my uniform to accommodate whatever tasks I was assigned, the second suitcase contained enough of my civilian gear to get me through the coming weeks. Although I had considered myself reasonably independent I was probably somewhat relieved that I would not be making the journey to Osnabruck Germany via rail to Gatwick and then on by British United Airways alone. I made the journey with John, Terry and Gordon who had previous military service in the Royal Engineers and had actually requested his posting to Osnabruck where he had served. Prior to his inter regimental transfer to the RMP.

The journey included two major firsts for me, the first time I had ever travelled beyond the English border and the first time I had ever flown in an aircraft.

I can vividly recall the day of travel, boarding the BAC 111 jet at Gatwick airport for the 45 minute flight to RAF Gutersloh, the take-off particularly and the whole flight was for me a bit of a scary first time experience. It's hard for the first time flyer to imagine what the flight will be like but once I was able to light up the senior service and down a few brandies accompanied by the in-flight lunch I actually began to enjoy the trip. Apart from the occasional bit of turbulence the flight was smooth and uneventful. It was actually amazing how soon we had arrived at RAF Gutersloh in Germany, less than an hour. I was to learn to appreciate the speed and comfort of the jet when I made many more flights including some in vintage piston driven aircraft.

Following a coach trip from Gutersloh through some picturesque but very flat German countryside we arrived in Osnabruck in the early afternoon of 21st March 1965, a mere 109 days after I had enlisted.

I was on foreign soil for the very first time in my life.

I was not sure what kind of reception I had expected or what our living quarters would be like. I had not actually given any thought to either. What I do remember is that it's never really nice being a new boy and this was no exception, we were not made particularly welcome by everyone. I can recall that I felt more like a new laboratory specimen than a person. I can also recall one particular sergeant who rather than welcome, encourage or motivate seemed to have no other objective other than to make us feel uncomfortable and this personal perception of mine was to be strengthened by his overbearing and unhelpful attitude during my service in Osnabruck and until he was posted out. It was also unfortunate that he held the responsibility for the issue of bedding and other equipment, he was a total pain.

I was to meet him during a later posting, I was not in the least surprised that he had not been promoted beyond sergeant, he had probably exceeded his ceiling with his first stripe. His general attitude had not changed either and he was simply a perennial fool and a boring pretentious know it all as well as a pathological panic manic!

As was to be the usual case for enlisted juniors, on our arrival in Osnabruck we had to collect and carry our bedding from the store to our new barracks home. Although the room was more basic than that I had occupied during my first night in Chichester it was at least very close to the dining room and little more than a very deep breath away from the corporals mess. Once settled and unpacked we (all four) set off to explore and meet the resident members of the army catering corps who we would get to know in the coming months and years when they would provide all of our meals.

We were very lucky that one of our colleagues, Gordon who had travelled with us from the training centre had actually completed previous service with the Royal Engineers in Osnabruck prior to his transfer to RMP. As a consequence later in the evening I can recall that under his guidance we made our first excursion to a local Gastatte where we were able to sample the local beer and schnapps and to receive a quick briefing on the local language so that we could at least order a beer. By a somewhat bizarre coincidence we arrived at the bar on the Natruper Strasse at the same time as a local German gentleman was celebrating his birthday. Having easily identified us as British soldiers he insisted that he buy us all a drink and then proceeded to share his rather dog eared wartime photograph collection. He produced the most amazing pictures of himself and other German soldiers taken during their incarceration as prisoners of war in England including some group shots of the prisoners and prison guard football teams. He certainly did not appear bitter at his experience and if anything he may have considered his capture and subsequent incarceration in England fortunate and less risky than fighting on the Eastern front..

Even more bizarre was when I discovered that the camp in which he had been held captive at Bolnhurst was literally no more than five miles from my own home in the UK and that, even more bizarre was the fact that along with other German prisoners he had been assigned to work at a number of farms including the one at which I had myself worked prior to enlisting into the Army. He could even remember the American Allis Chalmers lend lease tractor which had still been on site after more than 20 years in 1964.

I was able to explain to him that after the war the site of the camp where he had been held had been returned to farming. The camp buildings had been converted into a modern facility using the original accommodation huts which had housed the prisoners to actually accommodate a herd of Danish landrace pigs. He clearly found this highly amusing and after making a long speech to everyone in the bar, he asked that I should take some photographs for him the next time I was in England, he even gave me his address so that I could visit his home and family.

Sadly this was the only occasion I was to meet the gentleman and in addition I never remembered to take any pictures and I must have lost his name and address.

After a few beers in the Gastatte we made our way to the corporal's mess which was to be the focal point of our social lives, in my case for the next three years.

On arrival at the corporal's mess and as was the case for all new arrivals we were invited as part of our indoctrination to drink the "boot". The boot is literally a boot shaped glass drinking vessel with a capacity of about 1.5 litres. This object was filled with a mixture of beer and a selection of other drinks and as part of the welcoming initiation every new boy was required to drink it. It took a lot of effort and immediate access to an empty fire bucket. All but the most hardened drinkers experience the need to evacuate what they drink and in most cases no real or lasting adverse effects are experienced. I had no real issue with this initiation although not everybody was happy to take part. The most painful part was that we had to pay for the privilege of filling the boot and then seeing the entire contents wasted.

Although the reception in the corporal's mess on our first night was welcoming and friendly, once we joined the ranks of the duty rota things were not quite so pleasant. Some of the more senior corporals from whom we might reasonably have expected encouragement and guidance appeared to be more intent on maintaining their own image rather than sharing advice on how to carry out duties. In addition and rather than offer any mentoring I recall how one particular single, senior corporal made adverse remarks about our "untailored" and baggy KF shirts when we went into summer dress, shirt sleeve order and also criticised the fact that our SD cap red covers were not as smart as they should be. When I managed to ask him about these and other issues, particularly report writing he responded by complaining that it wasn't his job to teach new lance corporals and that when he had done so in the past he had never received the credit due to him whilst the recipients of his advice had been applauded. All new enlisted arrivals received a formal welcome interview with their officer commanding followed by a very brief pep talk from the sergeant major. With hindsight I think that I may not have made the best impression on my OC. I was not particularly experienced at such meetings and it may have also been the case that I didn't tick the sports boxes or talk myself up. I hadn't learned the importance of creating the right image and it had never occurred to me to embellish my previous history. As a very naïve 18 year old I'm sure that I must have appeared to be quite dumb. After this interview it was a case of learning to be in the right place and at the right time. I was never quite sure about what was expected of the new boys and there was never any assessment as to the level of our knowledge and skills. Even during the formal interview, as I recall the only question I was asked was about what, if any sport I played. I guessed that snooker, darts and poker might not have fitted into the company sports category so I left them out. In those early days it was really a question of watching and listening. The key to always being in the right place and at the right time was the "Daily detail" this document which listed the nature of each NCOs' duties was posted on the unit notice board every evening and it was the individuals overriding personal responsibility to read and comply. Failing to read and comply with this all important document could have the most serious consequences and I was witness on many occasions to those who got it wrong. Neither the RSM or CSM would take kindly to any junior who failed to turn up on time properly dressed in the style of uniform that the nature of the duty demanded.

After 50 years I have again read my first annual report, this describes me as shy and retiring with a lot to learn about the job. I suppose that this was an honest appraisal and not entirely demoralising or negative.

Living in Germany was a totally new experience, apart from the language, driving on the right and the tax free concessions such as cheaper drink and cigarettes the whole country was different. Although 1965 was only twenty years after the 39/45 war and despite the fact that Osnabruck had been severely damaged there was no outward sign of any war time damage. A testimony to German hard work was the fact that the town centre had been completely rebuilt and formed part of a thriving economy. Later exploration and research revealed just how much damage had been caused; although the centre of the town had been rebuilt, a great deal of time and effort had been applied to restoring and retaining as many of the old buildings as possible.

Getting to know and understand the German culture and diet involved a lot of enjoyable eating out and becoming familiar with some of the traditional specialities. Although Germany is renowned for a diverse range of Sausages, bread and beer my early experience was focussed on the local, regional Bratwurst. This really delicious pork sausage is traditionally roasted, fried or grilled and is available in a variety of sizes and shapes. My later travels and exploration of Germany would reveal how tastes varied according to regional preference and tradition. Without any doubt the best bratwurst were to be found in the small Schnell Imbiss located around the town, on market stalls and often in roadside caravans. Normally served with a small bread roll and mustard. In the Osnabruck area the same sausage was also served as a Currywurst normally sliced into small pieces and served with a hot curry sauce. Other delicacies included the shaslick which was a Turkish import and comprised a combination of meat and other food stuff, onions and peppers prepared on a wooden skewer and also served with a hot curry sauce. There was also the frikadelle, small (pork) meatballs very spicy and served with either mustard or curry sauce. German pommes-frittes (fried-chips) were available everywhere and in most cases served with a delicate mayonnaise or occasionally a spicy tomato ketchup.

kartoffel Salat (potato salad) was also served everywhere and frequently as an accompaniment to another local pork sausage, the bockwurst; also served with mustard. These sausages were cooked in heated water or occasionally steamed.

Sauer Kraut (Kraut salat) pickled cabbage was also available although not to everybody's taste and not a firm favourite of the British soldier Away from the street vendors there were plenty of affordable food outlets and a much wider menu. Although the German diet may have been described by some as bland, I never considered this to be the case. Apart from regional variations there are two additional food items of particular interest and universally popular throughout the whole country. The popular roast chicken normally dressed with a hot red paprika (pepper) and normally served as half chicken portions. This firm favourite can be seen in virtually every German fast food outlet or restaurant. The second real favourite is the schnitzel this may be made from pork or veal and served with a range of sauces generating different description. Jager (hunter) and Ziegoiner(gypsy) schnitzel.

The German bakeries (Backerei) offered a huge range of bread, cakes and biscuits, later I was to discover that although there were some universal and national favourites such as the Doughnut (berliner) and the Danish pastry (plunde) the regional variations were extensive. Chocolate, fresh cream and ginger all featured, the list is so huge that it would take up so much space here that I will have to leave any list to your own imagination and memory!!!.

Sweets and chocolate confectionary were available everywhere and I was to discover to my great delight the pleasures of the huge selection of chocolate covered Marzipan.

The one German commodity that I could not enjoy were the cigarettes. I can recall a few brands that I tried, Lux, HB, Ernte 23 and Stuyvesant. They were all totally different to English brands both in taste and smell, pretty much an acquired taste and only to be used in cases of real emergency.

Our social activities which primarily involved excessive drinking were not entirely restricted to the corporal's mess and on Wednesday pay day there was the occasional outing, into town when we would visit one of the local night clubs; usually after a spell in the corporals mess and a meal in town. There were so far as I can recall, three regular destinations, the La Parisienne, the Krystal Palast and the Zanzibar. The Parisienne was probably the favourite and unlike some establishments did not offer any visible objection to British soldiers visiting.

Although there was not usually any entry cover charge there was a requirement to purchase a schnapps on arrival. We became adept at making this drink last the duration of our stay although on occasion by some sleight of hand somebody would produce a bottle of brandy from their coat pocket. On a number of occasions we abandoned restraint and collectively bought a bottle of cheap German Sekt (champagne) at a grossly inflated and insulting price. The nightclub which normally closed around 4am produced a varied show, a fairly modest stripper, a singer and on occasion a magician. I suppose it was fairly tame but it was at least entertaining and for me a totally new experience.

re were a number of "popular" places to eat out in Osnabruck town centre which were easily affordable although not specifically up market. A couple of these became effectively our eating out locals. The well established "Kochloffel" wooden spoon served a variety of dishes but the most popular was the simple Bratwurst and pommes frittes. The second new venue which had its opening during my tenure, the Romer grill which had as it's speciality the giant "riesen" bockwurst served with Kartoffel salat. Just outside the main Roberts Barracks there was a small schnell imbiss which served two main types of Bratwurst and frittes along with a variety of other dishes. This place was extremely popular both with local soldiers and military police and always incredibly busy every night until the early hours. There were also plenty of small kiosks around the town where it was possible to purchase Bratwurst and enjoy an Osnabrucker bier at the same time.

One of my favourite haunts was the Gastatte," Muhlen Ecke" on the corner of Natruper and Sand Strasse, This place had two real specialities, the universal and inevitable half chicken and my personal favourite the Jager Schnitzel. The schnitzel was enormous and took up the whole of the plate so that the frittes were always served separately, German frittes are really best served with maionaise and it seemed to me that without this addition they were never quite the same.

Away from the town centre there were also plenty of small traditional gastatte catering for the more refined and cultured customer. These establishments offered a much more diverse and less common menu. Occasionally the doors would display a small brass notice "Out Of Bounds" These discrete signs were fitted by the owners of the establishments and had nothing whatever to do with any official military authority.

I simply ignored these and I am pleased to say was never challenged when entering. I simply interpreted the notice as a bit of snobbish quality control process on the part of the owner designed to deter any drunken, rowdy or scruffy British soldier. I liked to think that I was a sharp dresser. I still had my Hardy Amies suits, Russel &Bromley shoes and my Jaeger shirts. Along with a regular drinking partner the late Steve Blundell I took to carrying a brolley! Most military police off duty NCO's chose to wear a smart suit, collar and tie rather than the generally scruffy casual clothes worn by other soldiers. I had also managed to improve my spoken German. As a result of my personal experience of just how off duty soldiers often behave I can't say that I would blame the bar owners in the slightest for trying to deter the unruly.

There were in Osnabruck a number of official, out of bounds establishments which were regularly subject to mainly drive by visits. As usual it was never made clear exactly why these places should have been posted as off limits although in the case of one particular establishment, "The Golden Anchor" I was informed by a German police patrol that any call to that location was treated as risky and potentially dangerous. The bar was owned by two sisters who apparently held a total disregard for any authority including the police and was known to be a favourite haunt of Osnabruck's most unsavoury criminal elements. British soldiers would have been not only most unwelcome but also particularly vulnerable. Although I had driven past the place on many occasions I never actually went inside and I can never recall being asked to go there. I would guess that any incidents or disputes would have been quickly resolved with some vigilante style action. The German police were as usual the barometer for such places and they would only enter when it was absolutely necessary and mob handed. I understand that this bar was also favoured by the local Gast Arbeiter Turkish population who were known to carry knives and who were not reluctant to use them.

In 1965 there was no such process as formal mentoring or tutoring for new joiners to the unit and it was a question of parachuting in and hitting the ground running.

I have never been certain if this was a consequence of a failing in the basic training programme at Chichester together with an assumption that every recruit had been adequately trained or an abdication on the part of the senior management at the receiving unit. It was a case of learning on the job. There were huge differences in the attitude of the experienced NCO's both junior and senior towards us novices, some were really helpful and there were those who presented the attitude of we all had to manage so get on with it. I guess that the majority of juniors who were involved in the normal police duties rota may have been pleased to see new boys arrive on the scene as this reduced the number of duties they were assigned, particularly as desk NCO duties were predominantly allocated to the new arrivals.. Whatever the intentions and official objectives we generally managed to struggle along and overcome most challenges and get to grips with the duties allocated without too much drama.

It was not simply a question of learning and completing whatever tasks we were assigned but to apply in practise the theory of what we were supposed to have learned in training. We also had to master a new portfolio of tasks and jargon unique to Military Police duties in Germany, such a topic had inexplicably never formed part of our basic training programme. In addition to the whole re-learning work process we also had to do our best to make sense of the German language.

My first official duty was as night Desk NCO and surprisingly I had the benefit of an experienced and very helpful mentor, lance corporal Gill Waddell until 2400 hours, after that it was having to manage on my own. Although this duty from 1800 until 0830 hrs was really tiring it was not particularly busy and at least there was no micro managed interference or intimidation from the seniors who had all gone home by 1800 hours. It was difficult to stay alert and awake and I learned just how difficult it was to try and record everything accurately and clearly into the official diary, the dreaded daily occurrence book (The DOB)

I did however manage to get through the night and although there would be many more similar duties they would never get any easier.

Recording entries into the DOB demanded a specified and uncompromising format and entries would be rigorously scrutinised by the duty sergeant during the course of the duty and more rigorously by the RSM the following morning. It was usually closer to 0930 hrs before the totally exhausted night desk NCO could be allowed to stand down from duty and even later if the RSM had spotted any errors, spelling mistakes or unanswered questions in the DOB entries or if there had been any serious overnight incidents.

Having survived my first duty as desk NCO I found myself only a few days later detailed as duty investigator in the company of an experienced corporal, George Mcdermid as my driver. I am not sure if this was part of the testing process or an attempt at professional mentoring. In any event I was as I recall somewhat apprehensive particularly as my experienced driver disappeared on some private mission and left me on my own. My fears were considerably enhanced when I was ordered by the duty sergeant (Ray P) to attend and investigate a road traffic accident on Romeresche Strasse about a hundred metres from the gates of the barracks.(It might come as no surprise that this was the very same sergeant responsible for accommodation stores and who appeared to think that his main purpose in life was causing havoc for new lance corporals) He made it clear that I should be able to walk to the scene and added that I should manage this task without the aid of an interpreter. The details of such incidents remain indelibly ingrained into my memory and I can vividly recall arriving at the scene to find that a trailer had become detached from a military police land-rover carrying a number of NCO's and the trailer had then collided with the front of a civilian Volkswagen beetle carrying a group of Nuns. Fortunately there were no injuries and the damage only minor. I was fortunate that I was helped at the scene by the RMP driver involved in the collision who was able to speak German. He persuaded the German police who attended the scene to accompany me back to the military police office where the RMP interpreter provided me with the details that I would otherwise have struggled to obtain. Although new to military police vehicles I was no stranger to land-rovers or trailers and it did not take me long to determine that the cause of the accident was a consequence of the driver having failed to ensure that the locking pin was in place in the tow-bar. The military police driver had the privilege of becoming my very first interviewee under caution.

The driver as might be expected was subject to disciplinary action and this incident served to remind me throughout my service how what might be considered a trivial issue, if not dealt with properly could lead to serious consequences. .

Duties were neither excessive or particularly demanding, the general exception was without question the dreaded night desk NCO. This duty lasted from 6pm until 0830 the following day and there was, at least officially no opportunity to sleep although there may have been the occasional nodding off if only for a few moments. Not only was it difficult to stay awake all night and remain alert but it was also necessary to be able to remain coherent when answering the telephone and to be able to make proper sense of calls and record details. The documentary and evidential part of this dreadful duty was not only the task of completing the daily occurrence book but also a collection of other books such as vacant married quarters, key books and several others. The DOB demanded virtually verbatim, details of every incident that was reported no matter how trivial and in accordance with a definitive template. There was no excuse or mitigation for inaccurate information, bad handwriting or poor spelling.

There was a generic and incontestable template for every reported occurrence

Place Date Time Involving Quite simple really

The accommodation for single junior ranks was part of what had been a wartime bakery. Rooms were shared by several men, privacy was virtually non existent and there was little or no guarantee of peace and quiet even at the time between midnight and dawn when most men wished to sleep. Not every man wanted to go out drinking and get totally pissed every night. Some men did however get totally smashed and many of these seasoned drinkers had little or no respect for those who wished to retire at a reasonable hour and sleep. It would be accurate to say that at one time or another we were all disturbed by groups of noisy drunken and totally inconsiderate idiots. Incredibly many of these individuals were supposedly experienced so called role models, not only single men but married as well and who should have known better. Many of the younger juniors may well have felt intimidated by the experience which was nothing more than bullying and abdication of professional responsibility I guess that such behaviour was considered to be acceptable A certain amount of bullying and intimidation were the normal routine and probably considered as not only an acceptable part of army life but also entertaining, just good old boys having fun.

The barrack rooms were structurally very poor and austere, there was never any redecoration during my three years in Osnabruck although there was one small rebuild to accommodate the increase in the number of single men.

Apart from the barrack rooms the remainder of the accommodation was hardly any better. There was a single communal shower and as for toilets so far as I recall no more than three cubicles shared between something like forty men. The kitchen was permanently infested with the small brown cockroaches indigenous to Europe and the enormity of this problem only became clear when visiting the kitchen in the hours of darkness and to hear the sound of crunching bodies underfoot.

The task of the military police patrols attending incidents was certainly made easier when assisted by the German civilian interpreters. During the period 1965 and for a number of years the key personalities were Herbie Nigg, Willie Westphal and the senior Heinz Korte. As was the case with so many civilians in similar occupations Heinz had served with the German armed forces during the 1939- 45 war and had been a senior lieutenant in naval intelligence. Heinz certainly had a liking for his beer and schnapps and he had a particular favourite watering hole very close to the Roberts Barracks. Heinz was I think very pro -British and on the many occasions that he accompanied me to incidents whilst always remaining polite and respectful he presented an air of superiority when dealing with German civil police.

In addition to the regular formal police duties, desk NCO, mobile patrol, duty driver, orderly sergeant and foot patrols there were a number of routine admin tasks which included vehicle cleaning, gardening and collecting bar stock for both the corporals and sergeants messes. There was very little or anything ever provided to assist the cleaning process for the only vehicles we had, land-rovers except for water and rags. It was no wonder then that fresh paint was a favourite resource along with the inevitable oily rag. Collecting bar stock was a regular weekly activity and normally led to an impromptu lunchtime drinking session and with any luck we could avoid any additional work in the afternoon.

I can also recall being sent out to the married quarter of the officer commanding to undertake some gardening although I did not receive any clear or specific instructions. I guess that I could not have done a particularly good job and received a severe bawling out the following day from the RSM who lectured me on the fact that the Officer commanding was entitled to a batman. At least I was not sent gardening again.

With hindsight I really could have made the effort to do a better job than I did and it might well have done me some good at annual reporting time.

Soldiers serving overseas along with their dependants, wives and children are not immune to the kind of activity or incident that might involve the civilian police in the United Kingdom.

The most common offending activity apart from road traffic accidents involved drunken behaviour by young enlisted soldiers, fighting and disputes over bar and restaurant bills. Of course there were other more serious incidents most of which were dealt with by the Special Investigation Branch although any initial action would normally be taken by uniformed NCO's. Certainly during my service in Osnabruck I never had to deal with any incident of shop theft. I can however recall several occasions when the SIB declined to take on certain investigations which they may have considered too trivial.

It may seem strange now but in 1965 and until the introduction of the RSA 67 in 1968 the Special Investigation Branch also investigated drink driving. I can recall a number of occasions when I had to collect the Duty SIB investigator from their home, unsurprisingly they were rarely in a hurry to get dressed in the middle of the night. I'm sure that there would have been occasions when the long delays would have affected the outcome of any drink driving investigation.

Apart from scheduled duties and admin commonly referred to as fatigues and the deployment on military field training there was virtually no incursion into either our free time or any positive planned activities by way of training, either professional or personal development. It seemed that most juniors were only sent on courses when quotas had to be filled.

The only real exceptions were for junior lance corporals the opportunity to progress to full corporal which involved, in the first place studying and hopefully being successful with the 4 part upgrading examinations (grade1&2), not only was this the precursor to attending a junior promotion course but also attracted a welcome pay increase. I remember my first attempt to pass the upgrading and the horrible failure, it transpired that I had failed only one of the four topics, Provost Ops but by such a margin that I could not make up the surplus pass marks on the other three papers.

I can remember the two questions that I cocked up totally. One of these was to illustrate by diagram the organisation of provost in a theatre of war, I must have missed that one completely during study and secondly explain the rules regarding the use of force for which I quoted practically verbatim the wrong page. I did however manage to pass soon afterwards with a very good grade one but of course and through no fault other than mine, my promotion to full corporal was delayed.

Sporting competitions played an important part in the RMP BAOR calendar, specifically football for the Stanley cup and cricket the Swindon cup. Competition for these cups was fierce and for the players they provided the occasional exemption from normal garrison duties. Although not obvious to new starters it later became clear to me that being part of any unit sports team was a real starter for ten towards a good annual report and an accelerated route to promotion.

For the more experienced NCO's there were other opportunities referred to as employed jobs. These included chief clerk, postal clerk and charges and reports. These were mainly Monday to Friday appointments, prestigious, envied and much coveted positions. Although I would not have known it at the time, employed roles and sports teams generally attracted more positive reporting from unit officers than the everyday police duties roles. In my early days I might not have even suspected that working normal daily hours without nights or weekends, and playing football would be an advantageous sure fire route to success. Although this would certainly become more obvious to me in later years when it became a particular source of irritation and anger. I was amazed when I eventually realised how regular sporty types could race along the promotion ladder as a consequence of receiving brilliant annual confidential reports. Although these reports were supposed to focus on every aspect of military police work these chosen individuals would avoid most duties in favour of their sporting commitments.

Of course there were those who were not only good at their primary job and who took part in team sports and who deservedly did very well but these were a minority.

The primary element in the social life of most single men was the corporal's mess and although not every junior was a regular drinker, most were and probably to excess. The bar was open every day from early evening and usually till early morning. Although the official opening times were published in unit orders the reality was that the bar was usually open well into the early hours. Conflict or arguments were very rare and generally everybody managed to get on very well with each other. Credit in such forms as bar tabs in military establishments such as corporals messes were prohibited by Queens regulations for the army and repeated in both BAOR and unit standing orders. Despite these rules, but unofficially and discreetly, bar tabs were accepted as a normal part of mess routine. Back in the days prior to 1970 and the changes in soldiers pay system and the military salary concept, enlisted soldiers, including Military Police were paid weekly, each Wednesday in cash and in the local currency. Although it might not appear in any written instruction it was clearly understood that the first priority for every NCO, immediately after being paid was to head to the corporals mess and to settle any bar bill, any defaulters were assured of a fairly robust response from the RSM.

This routine was of particular importance due to the fact that the corporals mess was subject to the weekly stock check every Thursday when the barman had to pay in for the weeks sales. Any case of noncompliance, not settling a bar tab would be likely to affect the barman's cash float and any defaulter could expect to be dealt with harshly.

Whilst there may have been a deal of emphasis on teamwork and collaboration during duty time and whilst there were obviously different levels of skills, knowledge and experience, every junior was supposed to conform to exacting military standards and protocols. Fortunately there was a good deal of discretion applied particularly when dealing with young soldiers as there was clearly no moral or practical justification for arresting every soldier that had had too much to drink..

Osnabruck Military Police had its share of unique individuals including Jinx who was able to sleep in virtually any location, including where I always considered to be the impossible! Squashed and cramped bumped and jostled in the rear of a moving land-rover. Ricky the only man I ever knew who somehow managed to sleep without a break or interruption from early on a Friday morning after finishing night duty until tea time on Sunday afternoon.

Gambling was forbidden under the provisions of the Queens regulations for the Army but this still took place although mostly on a fairly modest scale. Unfortunately there was the occasional exception and in addition the odd man who managed to lose all self control and succeeded in getting far too involved. I can recall that on a number of occasions a certain married man managed to get drunk and then lose his entire weekly pay in an extended afternoon card session trying to recover his losses. This was a real recipe for disaster as he then had to face the music at home when he had to tell his wife that he had lost his weeks wages. I have no idea how he would have managed in such situations, nobody had local bank accounts and most juniors lived from pay day to pay day. I really struggled to defend a regime that was already aware of this mans domestic problems and his unfortunate habit of getting drunk and gambling. It was also the same idiot, the very same who always ended up causing a disturbance in the single men's accommodation because he couldn't pluck up the courage to go home and face his wife.

I actually got to know this particular man very well, when sober and away from drink he was very capable but once he had sunk a few beers he seemed unable to resist the temptation of the cards. His common sense seemed to desert him and on one particular occasion when he had been gambling all afternoon and evening he got drunk and lost his weeks pay. He later arrived at the duty room and after making a nuisance of himself for about a half hour, the orderly sergeant instructed the duty RMP patrol to take him home. Because he resisted every attempt to put him in the back of the land-rover and take him home whilst continuing to insult the duties he was not exactly treated gently and in simple terms he got a bit of a hiding. Incredible as it seems he arrived the next morning without any signs of his experience and as though nothing had happened.

As part of the mess management regime the senior warrant officer held the position of Mess president and in addition every corporals mess was required to elect a committee in order to plan and organise a range of functions and catering requirements. This generally comprised the president of the mess committee, president of the entertainments committees and a number of members with a range of responsibilities. A monthly evening mess meeting took place normally chaired by the RSM/CSM (mess president) at which time the mess finances would be presented and future plans and expenditure discussed. All junior ranks including attached soldiers from other arms such as REME vehicle fitters and ACC cooks were included as members. Attendance was mandatory except for those on leave or duty and there was no casual dress permitted. Although the process involved a democratic system of voting for social events and the money needed to pay for them, it was generally accepted that any function of particular interest and involving substantial sums of money were effectively presented to the meeting as already done deals and would not receive the nod of assent without the president's approval or recommendation

The corporal's mess hosted a range of regular social activities. There was always a monthly function which was either a Saturday evening dance or a Sunday curry luncheon The menu was fairly consistent, Curry, pork cutlets and a selection of meat rolls. As was usually the case the single men only managed to get to the food after any guests and the wives of the married men had been to the buffet and in most cases carried off more than they were likely to eat for themselves in order to provide for their husbands. The unfortunate outcome from this practise was that by the time the single men got to the food there was very little left and the evening usually ended with a trip to the local schnell imbis.

The Sunday curry lunches usually took place during the warmer months or on special occasions such as Remembrance Sunday after the church parade or on the regimental Corps day which also included a church parade. Special events also took place at Christmas usually a joint sergeants and corporals

event and normally at a neutral venue that could accommodate a larger attendance including invited guests. Preparation for such events involved the
juniors doing virtually all of the work such as moving tables and chairs, carrying the drinks and transporting the food to the venue. As a reward the same
juniors would be invited to clear up after the event.

These bigger events of course meant that not only was a great deal of
money spent on food but the menu was also much more grand and ambitious.
The same old call of ladies and guests to the buffet before anybody else was in
place and once again there was not a great deal left by the time the single men
reached the food tables.

In addition to the fact that the food was not fairly distributed at these
functions the juniors could also feel aggrieved at the fact that the corporal's
mess would almost certainly have made a significant financial contribution to
the end cost.

Apart from the corporal's mess and visits to other local drinking establishments there were few other social activities, this was a world with limited
television. German programmes were virtually limited to opera, news broadcasts and reruns of wartime newsreel. There were occasional British television
series such as the Saint dubbed over in German and from time to time a pop
music programme.

There were a number of local German cinemas however the choice of
films was little better than the television programmes and were not particularly inspiring. In Osnabruck there were also two local SKC (Service Kinematic
Corporation) Cinemas, one of these was located in Sedan Strasse next to the
NAAFI services shop complex and the other in one of the largest service married quarter estates near to Imphal barracks at Dodesheide. The films on offer
were generally compatible with what was available in the UK and were rotated
regularly. The cinemas themselves were subject to the National German regulations which included a no smoking rule. The NAAFI services shop included
a range of gifts and durables, clothing, household goods, vinyl records and
a food hall which stocked a wide selection of groceries, alcoholic drinks and
tobacco goods. The nearby church army facility comprised a bookshop and
cafeteria. Newspapers were of course at least twenty four hours old (always

yesterdays) unless in the case of transportation problems or inclement weather several days old. The church army was however a very popular venue for soldiers and RMP, it was also the Local collection and dropping off point for the RAF Gutersloh air trooping flight bus service.

The corporals' mess barman was an important part of the junior NCOs social world. He was entirely responsible for ensuring that there was always a healthy stock of every drink that customers wanted as well as a supply of snacks and miscellaneous cleaning materials. The barman also needed to keep a close eye on the accounting side which involved paying in the weekly takings in cash and carrying out the weekly stock check.

For some NCO's; taking on the job of corporals mess barman was a hazardous and time consuming occupation. There was an expectation that the bar would always open on time and stay open well into the night. Drink was cheap and the constant temptation for drinking to excess led to some serious health and professional difficulties. I can recall one NCO who arrived in the unit with a real drink problem and was given the job of corporal's mess barman whilst he was living in barracks and waiting for a service married quarter. He was usually so drunk that he would regularly be carried into and out of the bar and had virtually no control of the sale of drinks or the receipt of money. I got to know this man very well, he was intelligent and very knowledgeable, he had a beautiful German wife, two children and also spoke fluent German. Sadly he was an alcoholic yet to my knowledge never received any help, support or counselling. After what would not have been a very successful time as Barman he was reassigned to general police duties. Sadly he was always struggling to cope with the basics of Military Police life, unable to sort out his uniform, always in trouble and although it pains me to recall, the final failing was the day on which he was detailed to accompany me on motorcycle patrol. He had not checked the daily detail and had not turned up properly dressed for such a duty. Even worse was the fact that his uniform was not ironed and was dirty, his boots were also dirty and he had not shaved properly. As I stood next to him on parade I could smell his alcoholic breath and I shuffled a few steps away from him closer to my gleaming motorcycle.

This was the only time in my service that I felt afraid on parade, my heart was pounding and I was shaking even though I had absolutely nothing to fear. As we were called to attention by the off going night orderly sergeant I saw the RSM approach the duties and watched his face as he saw the poor man standing next to me. He literally screamed at him, he was so angry and shouted for one of the sergeants to " get this man off my parade". The poor man was literally shaking and his face was ashen, probably due to a combination of being drunk and afraid and then as I glanced to my left to watch him I saw the wetness spreading over the front of his trousers as he lost control and freely urinated as he stood. He was then manhandled into the back of a land rover and taken to the nearest guardroom. I don't' recall ever seeing him again.

I can clearly recall how one morning during our NAAFI tea break the then PMC and Chief clerk Bob Lodge came into the dining room and announced that the corporal's mess would be closed until further notice. This was a shocking and unexpected event and for reasons completely unknown. The corporal's mess was more than a bar it was the heart of all social and off duty interaction. We might not have been actual addicts to alcohol but that evening we all adjourned to one of the local Gastatte, affectionately known as the Oxo Cube. There was absolutely no way of knowing how long the closure of the corporals mess would last however the following evening the mess was back to normal but with a new barman.

A few days later it emerged that during the weekly stock check which on this occasion had been more thorough than those preceding, had revealed some serious problems. It eventually emerged that the barman had successfully concealed the fact that he had sold a great deal of bar stock and did not have the funds to cover what had been sold. He had managed on several previous stock checks to mislead whoever had carried out the check by disguising empty boxes of spirits as being full. It also emerged that he had purchased a substantial share in one of the local nightclubs, the La Parisienne and had probably; been living and spending well beyond his means. He had or so it would seem to have used the corporals mess takings to fund his late night drinking although probably with the intention of making up the shortfall once his finances were sorted out. He was subsequently arrested, charged and later sentenced at a court martial which was the end of his military police career. Although he received a fairly modest yet significant sentence, when it came to the confirmation of sentence by the Brigade commander his previous unblemished career, his age and the fact that he had been effectively suspended since his initial arrest were taken into consideration and as a result he served a bare minimum and was discharged from the service.

It would be fair to say that compared to other military units, Royal Military Police enlisted juniors generally enjoyed a better standard of accommodation and more exclusive facilities such as the corporal's mess and private dining facilities" than soldiers in other branches of the army.

Under the sponsorship of the RSM and ably led by one of the senior corporals (later to rise to the highest commissioned rank possible for a former enlisted soldier Tex Pemberton) the corporal's mess underwent a major transformation. Most of the juniors undertook some of the unskilled work during the rebuild and when it was completed a high ranking visitor later described it as the best junior NCO's club that he had ever seen. This must have been a view shared by the Sergeants mess as they chose to borrow the club for their own Christmas functions rather than try to squeeze their members and guests into their own tiny bar. It was also rumoured that some of the seniors had suggested that the corporals mess should be handed over to the sergeants for their own use. I suspect that this move was only vetoed by the RSM because the sergeants mess would have been too small for the corporals. The corporal's mess was always busy and a place where it was a pleasure to go, it was effectively a refuge and the closest thing that single men had to home.

The catering in barracks which included the day to day meals, special occasions and field training exercises was undertaken by a trio of ACC cooks whilst most of the hard work cutting and chopping preparation, as well as all of the post catering cleaning in barracks was undertaken by two German civilian ladies, the kitchen help. These two ladies one of whom Maria was well into her sixties and subject to some extreme mood swings. I regret that I did not really try to find out about her previous life or her status. I may have tried to engage with her on a couple of occasions but my poor German and her sometimes bizarre behaviour made it very difficult. My enquiries revealed that she was widowed and had most probably lost her husband along with many thousands of other German soldiers whilst fighting on the eastern front. I also understood that she lived alone but I never managed to establish whether or not she had any children. I do know that she was an exceptionally hard worker. I also know that on the occasions when there were television newsreels of the second world war she became visibly distressed. I was informed that Maria had died shortly after I had left Osnabruck in 1968. The second lady was Irma some years younger and who lived close to the Barracks she was also a real hard worker.

I think back at the times that I saw these two ladies struggling under the weight of a kitchen full of dirty dishes and cooking pans, all to be washed by hand, there were no dish washers.

It was a great shame that these two ladies were really taken for granted by just about everyone, me included and particularly badly by the unit cooks. I can also recall the odd occasion when the cooks failed to turn in for work and the kitchen ladies managed to save the day by sorting out either breakfast or lunch.

Whilst the general standard of catering might not have been in any way comparable to home cooking and involved a combination of fresh and composite (canned) rations, most of the time the cooks did a reasonable job and on important occasions such as Christmas functions they produced some incredible stuff. Despite any shortcomings the meals were regular, dependable and pretty much well presented and on time. There was no fear of starving due to lack of money and for those wishing or happy to live a frugal life there was no requirement to purchase extra food or in fact ever dine out. Considering the constraints of the budget, the level of rations supplied and the sheer numbers involved our cooks managed very well. I personally think that the real skills and talents of the regimental (ACC) cooks were always best demonstrated during challenging field exercise conditions during harsh and inclement weather when they were totally out on their own with no other support or assistance.

In addition to the civilian interpreters and kitchen staff there were a number of lady cleaners (putz Frauen) and a gentleman with the job as unit sign writer. During my entire service in Osnabruck I can't recall ever seeing this gentleman undertake any sign writing task. I guess that he was simply maintaining a low profile because painted signs often materialised for special duties which he must have produced. I did spot him on a number of occasions having had a bit too much to drink although strangely enough never in the corporal's mess.

The cleaners attended each weekday and were normally well advanced into their work by 5 am. Unlike their British counter-parts German workers always travelled to work smartly dressed and it was virtually impossible to tell what kind of work they were into from the clothes they wore en- route to work where they would change into their working clothes

There may be a combination of reasons for such a process which includes a dedication to their work, being suitably dressed and in regard to travelling a certain pride in their appearance as well as an element of social snobbery.

Everyday life for juniors involved a mixture of garrison police duties, general admin which included vehicle cleaning, field training exercises and getting our uniform kit ready for whatever the published routine demanded. Away from regular daily routine there were other events which made life more interesting even though they often interfered with our personal plans and days off. One of these spectacular events was the massed bands display at the town sports stadium. Any such event involving Military bands would be immensely popular with the German community and their love for the military spectacular. Seats for the stadium were quickly sold out and the stadium filled to capacity for every performance. Sadly as was the case with many other similar events most junior NCO's were only able to hear some of the music but not able to watch the display as they were almost certainly deployed on the essential duties of either car parking or security. Even with these tasks there was virtually no supervisory or management support. It was a case of park the cars here or there and then try to control them when the show is all over. There was never any consideration for any comfort break or any indication as to where any bathroom facility might be and there was not the slightest hint of any kind of refreshment break. I have however no doubt in the slightest that the seniors would have been able to enjoy the show, take a break whenever they wanted one and to be certain that they enjoyed whatever hospitality was on offer as well as being able to enjoy a smoke.

I can not recall any single occasion when we were deployed on such "special duties" that any attempt had been made to reorganise our meal times so that we could eat before we started or any provision after the event. The only really positive aspect was the fact that on most occasions, once we had returned to barracks the corporals mess would be kept open where we could enjoy a welcome and much needed drink as well as organise a "Bratty Run"

The RSM at this time, Roy Standring was very creative and keen on local initiatives, one of these was his blitz-weeks on military traffic. This coincided with the National German police winter lighting checks, virtually every military or BFG sponsored vehicle was stopped and checked. On a number of occasions I was assigned the task of chase bike specifically with the objective of pursuing fail to stop vehicles. I don't recall actually having to chase anybody and unless I had kept the engine permanently running I may have had some difficulty catching anybody who had a head start as the service motorcycles were notoriously hard to start in urgent situations.

On a number of occasions these were joint, RMP and German civil police initiatives and in such situations I would find myself parked with my motorcycle alongside the German BMW.

Away from our insular and cosseted existence in Germany there were other events shaping the status of Great Britain and the armed forces. The new labour government in Whitehall had initiated a series of economic measures and drastic cuts to the armed services, in some ways we were largely immune to these but when the government started to close down overseas military installations and reduce the overall number of servicemen we started to take notice. When the pound sterling was devalued this meant of course that our pounds would but fewer deutschemarks and if we went to any other country, normally Holland, fewer guilde.

As part of their spending cuts programme the government decided to cancel the highly advanced TSR2 aircraft project, the blue streak missile and then decommission our aircraft carriers, this was unquestionably the signal for the demise of the British imperial military status and a serious reduction in our capacity as a world power. In addition to the dismantling of much of the British defence capability the devaluation of the pound sterling bit deep into the value of the pound against the deutsche mark and made everything in Germany and the rest of Europe that much more expensive.

One of the most interesting although totally biased sources of propaganda and one that really enjoyed efforts to emphasise great Britain's demise as a world power was Radio Tehrana. This station broadcast on the medium wave band close to radio luxemberg and would have been heard by many soldiers who may have found this when searching for other more suitable stations. Radio Tehrana was the voice of the Albanian communist (puppet) satellite of the peoples republic of China. During this period the Chinese Communist Leader Mao Tse Tung launched his great leap forward, the cultural revolution and unleashed his Red Guards throughout China with the aim of re-educating the intellectuals and professionals. I have some memories of the confrontations in London between the Chinese embassy staff and the British Police who had no proper equipment and used dustbin lids as shields. There were some significant consequences of the Chinese revolution (1966/67) the Government of the Portuguese Colony of Macau effectively surrendered control to China and this prompted the disturbances in Hong Kong which then generated the emergency reinforcement of the Provost units with NCOs from Germany and the UK.

During the early part of summer 65, along with a number of other junior lance corporals and under the careful guidance of sergeant Ray Pleasance I had to complete the BFG matrix (Tick) test. This test was the essential precursor to being allowed to drive motor vehicles in Germany and was considered to be a bit of an obstacle. For some reason the test could not be taken until we had completed six months local service.

The process was simple and involved a multiple choice card with questions regarding German traffic laws, road signs and priorities. It was simply a case of "ticking" the appropriate answer and the papers were checked by placing an answer template relevant to the question sheet. Naturally I was pleased to overcome this minor hurdle and a few weeks later I was summoned to the office of the regimental Sergeant Major, Roy Standring. Roy was in my view a real gentleman and a good RSM. He was always impeccably dressed and very articulate. He was a strict disciplinarian who expected everybody else to conform to his required standards but he was also a fair man. With Roy Standring you were left in no doubt and you knew exactly where you stood and what was required.

I had no idea why I had been summoned and after knocking the door and being told to enter, I stood in front of his desk, expecting the worst and hoping for something a little better. Roy told me that I was being assigned for MT duties under the management of sergeant Joe Harding who was the unit Mechanical Transport sergeant. I was ordered to report to Sergeant Harding immediately and that I should expect to be on duty as duty driver the following day.

I left the office and went direct to sergeant Joe Harding, he promptly "issued" me with the keys to what was to be my personal responsibility land-rover and instructed me to prepare this for my first duty. The vehicle I was issued was certainly the oldest in the fleet, it was a right hand drive ¾ general service land-rover registration number 18 DM 09. Not only was this some kind of dinosaur but it was also fitted with what were effectively obsolete desert tyres and filthy dirty inside and out.

I had no time to lose as I knew the RSM liked to inspect every vehicle at morning duties parade and did not accept any excuse for anything that did not measure up to his standards.

I rapidly got stuck in with hose pipe and water starting underneath the body work and the wheel arches. I used a mixture of kerosene (paraffin) and some waste oil to clean and then rinse off the engine compartment, I used a mixture of kerosene and waste oil to wipe under and behind the seats and inside the cab and rear compartment. I used a brush to clean off the top of the battery and made sure that the battery and oil levels were correct and that the tyre pressures were exactly as they should be. I used an oily rag to clean the spare wheel and all of the vehicle tools which were laid out carefully behind the front seats. I checked that the lights, windscreen wipers and vehicle horn were all working properly.

I used newspaper to clean the windscreen and when that was completed first wiped the whole of the body work with a fresh oily rag and then dried it off to leave a smart clean shine. I repainted any of the scratched paintwork and finally applied a fresh union flag transfer to complete the job.

The following morning I took my place on parade standing next to my virtually reborn land-rover. As expected the RSM took several minutes to inspect the vehicle and I was rewarded with a very positive "immaculate" duty vehicle.

Being assigned to the MT section was a very positive and constructive move for me, it generated a new level of independence and sense of responsibility as well as a sense of pride in what I was doing. It was entirely up to me to ensure that my vehicle was properly maintained and serviced as well as being presented in immaculate condition for each start of duty.

In 1965 her majesty queen Elizabeth made her first state visit to the federal republic of Germany which naturally included a visit to the British army of the Rhine. Part of this visit involved meeting the Army at the Sennelager Training Centre. There were two separate parades, the dismounted exhibition of military vehicles and the most visually effective the afternoon display of marching troops and bands. This display took part at the windmill site in the vast NATO training area. I was privileged to be involved in the duties deployed in support of this event and was assigned the rather prestigious role of VVIP car park NCO. Her majesty was due to arrive at 3pm and as I had been in position since early morning I had the time and opportunity to watch the parade forming up. The display site was in fact a huge flat field and around lunchtime I could see and hear the massed troops and bands advancing towards the reviewing base and spectator seating. Although it was a grassed area it was possible to hear the sound of the marching feet keeping in time to the bands and I guess that there were several thousand troops actually on parade.

I can recall that in this very exclusive enclave to which I had been assigned, entry was restricted to a total of thirty two cars carrying Members of Royal families, heads of state or other high ranking guests.

My task was actually very simple, all I had to do was to note the parking space reference number at the front of the car and then march smartly to the same numbered space on the ground and indicate this to the driver. The VIP guest would have already disembarked and the process was made easier due to the fact that the cars were arriving in numerical order. At the end of the parade I simply had to stand in front of each car and then allow the driver to proceed as the numbers were held aloft for me to see.

At the time of this deployment I had spent only a few weeks in Germany and was with hindsight totally unprepared. I can recall being on night mobile patrol duty the day before, from Saturday 1800 until 0800 Sunday morning and had actually arrested and handed over three soldiers into close arrest at the guardroom for being found on out of bounds premises. Typically I was left to complete the necessary paperwork whilst the senior member of the patrol went to his bed. I was summarily ordered into the back of a land rover at 2pm en route to Sennelager having had no sleep and no food. I don't recall having ever received any kind of preparatory briefing regarding departure time or anything else but this was fairly typical of the style in which such events took place. It also demonstrated the total lack of consideration and care regarding the fact that I had been the only NCO to have been assigned night duty on the very night preceding the deployment and had not finished until 0830.

I can recall thinking about and comparing the accommodation and the food provided in Sennelager with that to which I had become accustomed in a relatively short time in Osnabruck. I remember the filthy, noisy and austere rooms, inadequate showers and toilet facilities and above all the massive queues for the terrible and literally uneatable food. The accommodation in Sennelager was in fact a German wartime barrack block and had almost certainly had little money or time spent on it since 1945. it was probably in a worse condition than after the war. Despite this the experience of taking part in such a momentous historical event may have been well worth the temporary pain and discomfort even if it meant standing around for hours and hours and not even getting a decent meal. I remember having spent two whole days rehersal on a traffic point only for me to be moved to my rather exclusive VVIP car park.

In 1965 I also took part in another challenging adventure when I was assigned on loan to 1st Divison Provost Company from Verden Alle. This was for a period of six weeks at the Bundeswehr (German Army) Barracks located at Putlos on the North German Baltic Coast. The event was the 1st British Corps annual support platoon weapons concentration. The purpose of this was to allow British soldiers undertaking their annual regimental training to take part in live firing their Mortars and anti tank guns at the German military firing ranges on the coast and into the sea. Our accommodation was as assigned to German conscripts although there was a supplementary catering facility in a tent provided by the Army Catering Corps. The menu was chicken every day as it appeared that was the only meat provided, it was certainly the worst cooking I had yet experienced, the chicken was more raw than cooked and invariably ended up in the bin. Although I had not had the foresight to pack six weeks of rations, I had at least received some advance notice about this deployment and I had been able to ensure that I had sufficient clothing and equipment as well as cash and cigarettes. The barracks was a short distance from what at that time was a desolate and deserted beach area. The sea was very cold even in the height of summer, I was however to discover many years later that this particular coast line was virtually perfect for wind surfing. Due to the desolate surroundings the beach was particularly popular with naturists and the sight of many beautiful naked females provided a welcome distraction and we needed little motivation to return on every occasion we were on duty. During the entire six weeks attachment I was assigned with five other juniors and one sergeant to provide Military police support to soldiers and deal with any incident or crime, we were tasked to only one incident which was a case of alleged theft and I can also recall that following a brief investigation, jurisdiction was handed back to the soldiers unit for an internal disposal.

During this time I also met for the first time a number of staff from the MSO Mixed services organisation. The MSO was formed under the sponsorship of the post war Federal German Government and was staffed primarily by displaced servicemen from those countries which had subsequently been absorbed into the control of the post war USSR and who would have been at serious risk of harm if they attempted to return or who had effectively been declared stateless.

In particular I can recall a senior supervisor who had been the equivalent of a brigade commander in Poland prior to World war two. When the country was occupied by the German authorities he escaped to England and remained there as part of the free polish army.

Following the end of the war and the political changes in Poland he had been unable to return home and had remained in Germany. Over the next few weeks whilst he was supervising the movement of military vehicles in and out of Putlos he was quite happy to talk about his life before and during the war and how he had fled Poland when the army was destroyed and when the Germans and the USSR had occupied his country. He had spent time in England with the free Polish army. He had left a wife and family behind but had never seen or heard from them since he escaped the country with the remnants of his Brigade. This man was clearly a real intellectual and very smart, apart from his native Polish he spoke fluent English without the slightest trace of any accent, fluent German and as he told me Russian and French.

I was later to meet a number of MSO during my time in Osnabruck many of them undertaking menial roles as cleaners in support of military staff in Barracks and on field exercise. I also met some of them socially and found them to be charming, polite and appreciative of what they had, even though it was clear that they had all experienced considerable loss and trauma.

Putlos I was assigned another detachment, on this occasion to another provost company providing the administration for Exercise Watchtower. The Watchtower is the title of the regimental march of the royal military police and this aptly named exercise was an annual competition involving all BAOR military police units as well as guest teams from the USA and other NATO countries.

On this occasion the exercise was located in the Rheinland Palatinate around the Eiffel mountains. This is one of the most beautiful scenic areas of Germany and shares borders with France Belgium and Luxemberg.

During the exercise I was assigned the duty of sergeants mess barman and waiter, not essentially a task which I would have chosen but it didn't take me all that long to appreciate the benefits. I not only had a bed provided in a very large tent with plenty of space but I also took all of my meals in the mess annex, much better than those provided to my junior colleagues mainly due to the extra messing contributions paid by the sergeants. I was also frequently included in the rounds of drinks purchased by the sergeants. I think that this generosity was mainly due to the fact that there were no cash transactions and that a bar tab was raised for all mess members to be paid equally after the exercise. I suspect that such a process rather than encouraging moderate drinking tends to encourage the opposite and most of the individuals involved wanted to ensure that they received their fair share rather than abstaining and ending up paying for those that did not.

Although I was not included in any direct conversation regarding the competition activities I may have occasionally overheard some of the planning and preparation talk and may have shared some of what I heard with my unit team colleagues.

On one such occasion I heard that a foot inspection was to take place the following day. Naturally I dropped few hints about feet when I met my Osnabruck colleagues.

My team ensured that they were all wearing perfect condition socks, with no holes, they had also trimmed their toenails and applied a good measure of the regulation army foot and body powder, result top marks. I also recall that one NCO from one of the two teams from 7th Armoured Brigade under the leadership of Staff sergeant later Major Richard (Dickie) Poole had a hole in one of his socks and subsequently blew the entire teams points score for the inspection. The whole of the exercise was a thoroughly enjoyable time and during the mid weekend an outing was organised which included a boat trip along the Moselle river. This trip on a splendid boat was complete with traditional German brass band, free flowing wine and ample food. The boat trip was followed by a stopover in the town of Cochem located at the intersection of the Moselle and the Rhine. I know that I drank far too much and probably needed some help in getting back to the coach for the return trip.

Following the end of the exercise, I managed to escape the admin clearing up and tent dismantling as I was instructed to return to Osnabruck with my own unit team.

On my return life progressed and the summer came and went. There were some small training exercises mainly TEWT (training exercise without troops) that the military police took part in along with elements of the local brigade headquarters and on the social side we discovered the pleasures of the closest equivalent of, but vastly superior to a British fun fair; the "Shutzenfest" (Shooting Festival) These traditional events take place throughout Germany and include, the best of German Bands, dancing, drinking and eating on a scale beyond anything any thing that I had ever experienced. During this period I also celebrated my first birthday since joining the army and since living in Germany.

I can remember that I celebrated the occasion accompanied by my good friend John Hodgson by visiting a small and exclusive Gasthaus which Heinz Korte used as his hideaway. For the first time I was able to enjoy a real traditional Jager schnitzel served in what was effectively the front room of the owners home.

Along with another NCO Perry Edwin John (Jack)Vane in September 1965 I was assigned the task of signing a number of road routes from Osnabruck to the Royal Air Force Station at Gutersloh and to various locations within the station. This route signing was in preparation for the deployment of the 12th Infantry Brigade for the Exercise Bar Frost to Bardufoss in Norway. Bardufoss airfield is located on the north west coast of Norway, several hundred miles inside the arctic circle.

A few weeks after the signing task in company with most of the 12 brigade Pro Unit I flew to Bardufoss. Although we received a short pep talk regarding the deployment process and the dangers of mosquitoes, the talk really concentrated on the transport arrangements and the flight from RAF Gutersloh. What was never explained, at least as far as I can recall was what we were supposed to be doing in Norway and what was the military objective of the exercise. I suspect that the majority of the seniors had any better idea and would probably not have been capable of explaining in any event Prior to deployment all of the juniors had to present themselves for "weighing" along with large pack and kit bag clearly stencilled with last four name and flight chalk number. These items had to be packed in accordance with a list provided and then surrendered until the day before departure. There was no space for any extras as this equipment was to accompany us on our flight to Norway. It was only after we had arrived in Norway that I discovered to my annoyance that the seniors and some of the juniors who had accompanied our vehicles by sea had secured extra items in the vehicles without allowing us the same opportunity. A few extra items of clothing might have made a considerable difference to our comfort. Apart from the strict planning and control over what we were allowed to pack for the trip there was never any briefing about the RMP aims and objectives for the exercise. An advance party with our vehicles left several days ahead by Ferry. Those of us in the main party, making the journey by air reported to the RAF base at Gutersloh and after sitting around for several hours boarded a Caledonian Airlines Bristol Britannia Flight to Bardufoss in North West Norway. This airport is in a very exposed location and was used extensively by the Luftwaffe during the German occupation of Norway during the second world war.

So far as I can recall this flight took about six hours. It was a pleasant and comfortable journey made easier by the fact that we were provided breakfast on board. Arriving at the windswept Bardufoss in late afternoon it was very cold and following a short road trip we arrived at our base camp. Facilities were sparse and despite the fact that we were literally surrounded by water we were told that water rationing was in place.

It seemed to me then even as a young 18 years old lance corporal that some of the logistics planning was poor.

The accommodation provided for the juniors comprised a small two man bivouac tent which I shared with another junior, once again my old friend John Hodgson, these tents barely provided enough room for one yet alone two men. Any dressing or undressing had to take place outside, there was only head room when seated not standing. Meals were not provided and we had to cook our own compo food rations using the portable hexamine block cooker. Our water ration was a single aluminium bowl which had to sustain our drinking and washing needs. Prior to deployment to Norway the only briefing we had received was that it would probably be very cold and that we would have to deal with mosquitoes.

I recall not being surprised about the weather warning but it seemed strange about the danger from mosquitoes. I guess that mosquitoes were normally associated with warmer climes. Whatever warnings we had received it had not included the rain. It started raining the day after our arrival and never stopped until a couple of days before we left. In spite of our best and with hindsight our amateur and untrained efforts to keep dry, within a couple of days our clothing and kit were thoroughly soaked through. There is nothing more depressing than the prospect of remaining in the field soaked through and without any hope of changing into dry clothes. Although we were not troubled by snowfall which always remained a constant threat; the mountains which surrounded us were snow covered and we witnessed regular snowfalls not really that far away. We heard of a number of infantry soldiers from a Scottish battalion undertaking patrols in the mountains whos' leaders had clearly underestimated the ferocity of the weather, thinking that they could overcome the cold and as a consequence several of their men had succumbed to frostbite and hypothermia.

In addition to the small portable cooker with which we were provided we were also issued with mosquito repellent and emergency rations. These rations consisted of a small metal container holding a single block of hard dark chocolate. Our instructions were to secure these tins, guard them with our lives and in the event of being marooned or caught without rations we could eat them but only in an emergency. The chocolate bars were divided into small cubes and each cube we were instructed would provide sufficient nutrition for up to twenty four hours. I think that this instruction was generally ignored and the chocolate sampled without any emergency situation in place. I also heard that when some soldiers had given the chocolate to local children they had thrown it back at the soldiers because it was simply too hard to bite through and eat.

Exercise Bar-frost was the first military exercise to take place in Norway since the end of the 39/45 war, this was mainly a consequence of the Norwegian government not permitting foreign troops to be based on Norwegian soil. Bardufoss is located in what was then a totally rural and very remote area. Bardufoss airfield was established in the 1930's and was partially developed by the occupying German Luftwaffe during the 1939/45 war. There was however no modern road infrastructure designed for anything other than really light farm traffic and the mainly dirt or gravel roads soon began to crumble as a consequence of the constant rain and heavy military vehicles. I recall many occasions when even the recovery vehicles became stuck and the entire exercise programme was in real danger of becoming a serious catastrophe because of the continuing damage to the roads. The local road infrastructure was also being compromised and there was a real danger to the soldiers and their vehicles, I would not have been surprised to have seen or heard of soldiers being swallowed in a se of mud. In between the rain and traffic nightmare the war games and the discomfort continued. I still struggle to recall any actual war game scenario. Trying to stay dry became the main priority, there were no support facilities and no opportunity to change into anything dry as whatever dry clothing we had with us was soaked.

I can recall moving to a farm where there was a substantial wooden barn filled with loose straw. The cold, wet and desperate military policemen had burrowed into and were totally submerged in the straw. The only clues to their location were the ascending tell tale curling whisps of steam. Despite the problems the "war play" apparently continued although there were some confusing episodes, in one case I allowed traffic to pass my point when I should have stopped it whilst a one way system was in place. This earned me the biggest and most sustained bollocking I had ever received even though I protested my innocence and ignorance of the plan that had never been properly explained to me. I guess that with hindsight common sense should have told me that I had made a cock up and worked things out for myself. I was later to discover that the NCO who should have told me what my task was and to escort the end vehicle had failed to stop at my traffic point and brief me but had simply ridden away on his motorcycle, perhaps assuming that I already knew the details of the plan.

Suffice to say it had not really been his responsibility but that of one of the seniors who may have not properly understood the differences between, responsibility, delegation and abdication.

I have to admit that the misunderstanding caused some serious inconvenience and traffic problems for a while but this was eventually sorted out without any injuries or damage although it hardly enhanced my reputation. I think that thick as two short planks was the best accolade I earned that day.

The exercise war play eventually came to a halt and we all returned to our base camp in preparation for the return to Germany. The water shortage had now ended and in its place we were instead presented with a serious lack of food rations. Yet another classic example of the poor planning and logistics failure.

Every man was ordered to surrender any compo rations in his possession in order to assess the level of the shortage and to ensure that any rations were shared equally. Imagine the surprise of everybody when during the search of every vehicle and trailers, as well as the odd few ration cans in every vehicle; one trailer was discovered to have been packed to capacity with whole un-opened ten man ration boxes more than sufficient to sustain the whole unit for the next few days.

The individual responsible had as it later emerged allegedly secured the rations for his own personal use during his own time camping holidays. I guess his personal account might have been more akin to claiming that he had simply secured the rations for safe keeping. Suffice to say that not only did he lose the rations but it was no secret that he also had some serious explaining to make when he returned to base camp and later found himself tapping the boards back in Osnabruck. For the final few days the rain thankfully stopped and we were at least able to hang out our clothes to dry. We were also permit-ted to visit the nearest Norwegian military base for a welcome shower. This was not a simple exercise and we were to discover just how paranoid and secu-rity sensitive the Norwegian forces were. On arrival at the barracks we had to temporarily surrender out identity cards and our personal weapons and whilst we were in the sports hall shower facility a guard was placed on the entrance to ensure that we didn't wander around. We were not allowed to make use of any other facilities which was a real shame as we could all have managed some hot food and a decent coffee

At the time of the Bar frost Exercise and ever since I have struggled to ap-preciate what on earth we were supposed to have achieved. It must have been obvious to anybody that the roads could never cope and that if the weather had deteriorated into snow conditions or if the rain had continued, the whole British contingent would have become incapacitated in much the same way as Napoleans Grande Armee in Moscow and Hitlers 6th Army at Stalingrad and we were not even at war.

The fact is that we were not trained, dressed or equipped for the Norwegian conditions. So far as the military police was concerned virtually all of our time was taken up with controlling traffic in some challenging real police situations as a consequence of the deployment of a large number of heavy vehicles on roads that were entirely unsuited. Lessons were however learned on a personal if not strategic military basis. Our uniforms were totally unsuitable and incapable of providing the basic protection against the prevailing weather conditions. Although land rovers might be one of the best all terrain vehicles the other types of vehicle used by the army were totally unsuitable and unable to operate on the dirt and gravel roads.

Although the main logistics strategy may have been a success ; for example transporting the vehicles by sea and transporting troops by air, at operational unit level and particularly RMP the management was simply not good enough. Base camp did not provide sufficient quality facilities and having to live in mini bivouacs was hardly the right way to start a training deployment. Rations almost ran out and whilst there is always an acceptance of the need to apply realistic training in preparation for actual battlefield conditions this can only be really effective with quality equipment and good food. I always wonder how we would have coped in such conditions if this had been a real war. Another month and we might have been knee deep in snow and ice.

A number of soldiers had succeeded in interacting with the local farmers and discovered that access to and the availability of alcohol was virtually non- existent. Hard liquor could not be obtained in Norway except in certain shops in cities and towns and then subject to the most stringent regulations. Some bartering may well have taken place although I had no personal experience and although I heard a few rather colourful rumours I have no evidence or examples. I would add that when our advance party was dispatched by sea, one of the trailers had been loaded with corporals mess bar stock, this was subject to some strict allocation and intended to last for the duration of the exercise. There was absolutely no local source of any alcoholic drink and until the last week of the exercise I can not recall actually seeing a single retail shop premises.

I imagine that the indigenous population would be rather better prepared than the visiting British Army and would need to lay in plentiful stocks of food and supplies to see them through any winter. It would have been a great idea if prior to our deployment to Norway we had been able to meet some real Norwegians with personal knowledge of the Bardufoss area and who could have told us what to expect.

Apart from the one rather chaotic traffic point duty that I had been assigned to and had somehow managed to get wrong it seemed to me that we had no other real tasks other than standing around in the rain and getting soaking wet.

Everywhere we went we saw British military vehicles abandoned in some very precarious positions where they had fallen victim to the collapsing roads and where recovery was almost impossible. Many of the recovery vehicles also became stuck in the mud which had at one time been a road.

Just before the end of our deployment a number of us attended something of a social function hosted by the Norwegian Military Police. This organisation wore the exact style of uniform duty order that had been previously worn by the RMP including blancoed white webbing and cross straps during the 1950's. Although as I recall our small group of juniors remained sitting in our land rovers the seniors appeared to have been able to enjoy the hospitality including food and drink. During the evening some beer was smuggled out to us and I can recall that one of the Norwegian officers who saw us drinking became absolutely incensed that we were in his words, " drinking on duty". Matters could have become even worse due to the fact that on the way back to our base camp our driver somehow managed to crash the land rover into the steel gate of the Norwegian camp. There was some tough negotiating but not at my level and I remember just sitting and keeping quiet.

Eventually the exercise ended, thankfully our departure day arrived and we made our way back to Bardufoss airport. This location must be permanently cold and windswept and our departure day was no different.

Once again we embarked on a Caledonian flight ready for our return journey to RAF Gutersloh. Although I gave it little thought at the time and although most of us had managed to get a shower a few days before we left we must have presented as rather shabby and unsavoury as we were still wearing what were really dirty, damp and probably very smelly clothes

I particularly remember that on the return trip we were totally mortified to be told that we were not to be provided with the eagerly anticipated and much hoped for in-flight meal. It was never explained why this was the case and just who had made this decision. Was it just our flight? Or all of them, was it just for flights carrying enlisted men and what about the officers? I remember that the cabin staff were only able to tell us that they had been told to fly to Norway and that in-flight meals were not on the loading manifest, no explanation had been given

I suspect that it was simply the MOD just saving money. For whatever reason, this omission made the flight something of an anti climax and not the pleasant conclusion expected as we had all been looking forward to an in flight meal. As if to confirm my suspicions about the MOD and saving money the cabin crew were able to sell alcoholic drinks and they were kept busy for the entire trip back to Gutersloh

It was something of a relief to return to Osnabruck and our safe and familiar surroundings. After living in virtual swamp conditions in Norway we had at least a dry bed, central heating and a well stocked bar. I think that everybody made the excursion to the local schnell imbiss after a session in the corporals mess.

After Norway and return to Osnabruck, life quickly returned to normal although it probably took several weeks to get the vehicles, stores and equipment clean. The single biggest task was getting our own clothes and uniform clean when there was only a standard domestic twin tub washing machine shared between forty men.

There was no plan to dry clean our sleeping bags or combat uniforms and as I recall we were straight back onto the duty rota.

Although the weather in Norway had been decidedly unpleasant it had not been exceptionally cold except for the infantry soldiers who had played at imitating mountain troops and who had suffered as a consequence of inadequate training, unsatisfactory equipment and most importantly poor leadership. The main problem was the fact that we were soaking wet for the duration. Back in Osnabruck we resumed our normal military police duties. We were however in for a bit of a shock and surprise when the German winter decided to arrive shortly afterwards and the reality of undertaking police duties in long-wheel base often right hand drive land-rovers with no cab heaters.

These vehicles were great for coping with the icy road conditions but useless when trying to see where to drive. Osnabruck that winter received a good supply of snow, plenty of freezing rain and a good amount of fog and ice. Most of the roads around the town were manageable except for the rather ancient cobbled surfaces which were a real challenge in anything but warm summer weather.

I had never had any real enthusiasm for Christmas however my first experience of this Christmas 1965 in Germany and in a military environment was to change my attitude completely. The whole lead up to service life Christmas in Germany was great fun, there were regular visits to married pads homes and outings to other military units. There was a spirit of excitement that I had not experienced since my early childhood and although I took a couple of weeks annual leave in mid November to visit my parents, I was desperate to get back to Osnabruck in time for Christmas week.

Just a few days before Christmas I was introduced to carol singing military police style, in the company of a small group of single men carrying crates of beer and bottles of whisky knocking on the doors of the married men's quarters.

The Germans have managed to retain tradition close to the Christian ideology and the real spirit of Christmas and to have retained true family values. As soldiers in Germany we were able to enjoy the best of both worlds of German and military tradition. In every Garrison town including Osnabruck any real or imagined conflicts were either forgotten or postponed in favour of some real festive good will.

It seemed that every German home was displaying a Christmas tree in their front window mostly just dressed with a set of lights and not the pile of rubbish that the English would decorate their trees with. In contrast to the British tradition, the Germans celebrate Christmas in a completely different way. This starts on the afternoon of the 24th of December when virtually every German arrives at the location where their Christmas is to be celebrated. A traditional dinner takes place that same evening after which the gifts which have been placed around the Christmas tree are handed out and opened. This allows Christmas day to be a day of rest and without hours of slaving over cooking.

It would not be right if I failed to mention one of the army's Christmas traditions. Although the exact origin is not clear "Gunfire" takes place when officers and seniors pay an early morning Christmas day visit to the single soldiers barracks sleeping accommodation and serve tea laced with rum. As a morning person I personally found the experience quite pleasant but I can recall that a number of my colleagues who had perhaps had far too much to drink the previous evening did not appreciate either the noisy early call or the powerful rum laced tea or coffee.

Apart from normal mess functions there were also the traditional children's parties. There were two such events hosted and mostly paid for by the corporal's mess. The first was the party for the children of our own married personnel and the second was for local orphans. Both events took place in the corporal's mess and although the unit party was supported by single men it was largely managed by married men and their wives. The orphan's party however was almost entirely managed by the single men and not just because they felt a sense of moral and righteous obligation. The orphans were always escorted by a group of young, attractive female nurses and teachers and the opportunity and experience to meet them was worth every effort.

I guess that some of the men may have made considerable efforts to get to know the ladies much better and this would have started at the bar with a few drinks.

Of course the confident German speakers would have been more assured of a positive outcome.

There was a general policy that NCO's could expect to be on duty either during Christmas or new year. In my case as I recall the Christmas stand down commenced around the 20th of December so I was free from duty for almost two weeks.

The major social events during this period included the corporals mess and the whole unit party but aside from that it was business as usual in the corporal's mess bar.

On my first new years eve in Osnabruck I was on local mobile patrol and parked outside the Cathedral. Immediately following the clock striking midnight the door was flung open and both my colleague and I were besieged by a group of new year revellers. The fact that this group comprised a party of young ladies who felt it necessary to hug and kiss us and offer glasses of champagne made it a very memorable evening. This was certainly the best new years eve that I had ever experienced and I was already looking forward to next year!!!.

1966 my first year completed

I HAD NOW MOVED INTO my second year of service and I was by now reasonably competent but by no means expert. A number of new lance corporals had been posted in and this somehow made those of us with twelve months service feel pretty superior. I had enjoyed 1965 and had on reflection done quite a lot, I had gained a lot of police duties experience, travelled to new places and enjoyed my first Military police and German Christmas. Nearly a year of overseas service and experienced in all of the peacetime garrison duties. Desk NCO day and night, duty driver, standby patrol driver, duty investigator and foot patrol. Each of these duties presented its own unique challenge and difficulties. The duty driver, particularly during the week was virtually guaranteed a non stop routine of admin tasks and was lucky to be able to manage a decent meal break. The standby driver had the main task of responding to call outs to incidents accompanied by the duty investigator. The duty of day desk NCO was always hectic and always under the scrutiny of the seniors. The night desk duty was far less hectic but staying awake and alert for 15 hours was no fun!

Like many of the more experienced NCO's I had learned not to respond to direct calls from bar owners but managed to redirect any such calls back to the military exchange operator who managed to filter out a number of mischievous and bogus calls.

There were occasional rumours regarding the vulnerability of RMP lance corporals serving in BAOR and in particular the 1st British Corps Provost company at Bielefeld seemed to be the most risky posting where a large number found themselves reduced to the ranks (busted) and discharged. I don't recall that there was any specific or common explanation as to the reasons why and it may have simply been foolish rumour. I don't ever recall that in Osnabruck there was any sense of anxiety although there was one former lance corporal who had been reduced and was awaiting transfer. This soldier " Bugsy" had by all accounts been a highly competent military policeman but had fallen prey to an unusual set of circumstances.

Soxmis (Soviet Military Mission) cars were seen around military establishments from time to time and there was a specific protocol in place regarding any reporting or sighting which required to be passed to the RMP duty room. These reported sightings had to be recorded in accordance with a strict template. It would have been fairly obvious that a number of sighting would be reported and although this could be a fairly onerous task for the duty NCO each one had to be fully recorded

It would appear that whilst Bugsy was on duty as desk NCO several sightings were reported at different times and from a range of locations. Although Bugsy logged a number of these reports he was alleged to have failed to record one reported sighting. In most cases such an omission, regardless of whether it was deliberate of otherwise

Would not have attracted any undue attention.

Unfortunately one of the reported sightings was from an officer who later mentioned this to the RMP officer commanding. When the OC checked the Daily Occurrence book there was no such report from the officer recorded. As a result "Bugsy" was charged and somewhat harshly reduced to the ranks. This was of course the end of his RMP career and as I recall he spent around nine months as a private soldier living in the RMP accommodation due to some difficulty securing a transfer to another branch of the Army.

Soxmis was the Soviet military mission to the commander in chief BAOR. The British version, Brixmis. These organisations provided for teams from each country, SOXMIS to travel around West Germany FRG and for BRIXMIS to travel around East Germany DDR. This was an authorised intelligence and information gathering process. The USA France and Australia also had missions.

There were of course some permanent and some temporary restrictions on travel areas and every SOXMIS sighting in the BAOR area was to be reported to RMP.

Of course this was a form of legalised, approved spying. Although I was never personally involved I had a number of friends who were and it seemed that the whole game was both demanding and exciting.

The British mission commenced on 16th September 1946 and remained in place until the two Germanies were reunified in 1990.

Soxmis were provided with their own base (compound) at Bunde near Herford West Germany and Brixmis had a similar reciprocal arrangement at Potsdam north of Berlin in the DDR.

The arrival of a new officer commanding 12 Bde Pro Unit presented an unusual opportunity in the form of an attachment to an infantry Battalion. In my case with the 1st Battalion the Duke of Wellingtons regiment (West Riding) based at the Brigade Headquarters in Quebec Barracks. In 1966 the normal headdress worn by RMP on non static police duties (Exercise) was the Khaki SD cap this would not have been suitable whilst working with infantry soldiers and so for the duration of the attachment along with several other lance corporals we wore a navy blue beret but with our own Regimental cap badge.

On arrival at the regiment I was assigned to Corunna company 10 platoon and later introduced to the platoon sergeant and men.

This attachment was to be a challenging and hard lesson in basic soldiering.

I discovered that many of the men in the platoon had served for a number of years and had not progressed above private soldier. I spent several days sharing the soldier's accommodation and food, well below the standards to which I and other military police were accustomed and also joined the soldiers during their social outings to local bars. During the time in barracks I received a rudimentary introduction to the 432 AFV tracked personnel carrier and the Ferret scout car. We also received some instruction in the use of the vehicle combat radios and the general issue weapons including, SLR, mortar, Carl Gustav and the vigilant ground to ground missile.

I guess that some of the infantry soldiers may have thought that as a lance corporal I should have had a bit more experience in supervising other soldiers but I did not.

After a few days in barracks we made our way to the Osnabruck freight Bahnhof and about 0200 hours we boarded the military train for the journey to the Soltau training area. Not only was the train exceptionally slow but because British military trains in Germany were given very low priority ours was diverted from the main line to allow virtually every other civilian train to pass. There was clearly some efficient intelligence gathering in operation as at every stop which lasted at least an hour a mobile snack van operated by either the church army or Toc H appeared selling food and drinks. This was just as well as there were no meals provided on the train, the haversack rations we had been given had long since been consigned to the bin and we had no idea when we would get our next meal.

On arrival at Soltau we had to detrain our AFV 432 and then make our way on foot to the tented area where we would be living for the next two weeks. Over the next few days I learned how to debus and evacuate my section from the 432, as well as some basic infantry tactics. This included ambush drills and preparing defensive positions. I had the opportunity to drive and command an AFV 432 armoured personnel carrier. Although this was a tracked vehicle I soon discovered its limitations when loaded and confronted with very deep mud and water, such difficult conditions required the driver to have a great deal of experience and skill without which there was a strong likelihood of getting bogged down. As for all junior NCO's I had to undertake other tasks, guard and picket commander and the supervision of the morning "hot water" for washing detail. This was a fairly tough assignment and my first real experience of supervising soldiers most of whom had considerably more military service and army knowledge than me, I was probably a bit of an easy touch and too soft for some who were determined to take as much advantage as they could get away with. This water duty was potentially a real challenge with the most difficult part ensuring that soldiers taking hot water actually topped up the boiler with cold.

I was helped in this task by a tough lance corporal also from Corunna company named Clinton Mcgee. Clinton was a mixed race veteran of many fights, not only did he have the scars of battle but also a fearsome reputation for enforcing discipline amongst the soldiers and took no nonsense. Although Clinton was part of a different platoon so I did not actually work with him, he became a willing and supportive ally for me when I was struggling for advice and support.

During the attachment along with my whole platoon I made a visit to the NATO artillery ranges where we took up position at a comfortable observation point. What had not been explained, at least to me was that the firing points were some miles behind us and the targets in front. As we listened to the commentary we could also hear the whistling of the shells passing over our heads. The grand finale to this demonstration was the firing of an Honest John missile. We listened to the countdown and expected to witness something akin to a gentle lift off and majestic flight. What we actually saw was a flash followed by a distant dot in the sky as the missile disappeared over the horizon on it's way to the target some ten miles away

There were other lessons learned from the infantry soldier, in terms of rations they organised what was issued into what each of them could easily carry, they were not reliant on motor transport and were always prepared to slog it out on foot. What they didn't want or couldn't carry was simply dumped. I learned how to dig emergency slit trenches and how to make best use of local camouflage. I practised running around in respirator and steel helmet. During the field training exercise phase I learned how to engage an entrenched enemy and then to move into a fortified defensive position.

During the exercise along with my section and the entire platoon we were flown by helicopter to attack the enemy (The Queens Own Highlanders) behind their lines. This was my first terrifying experience of operational tree top, low level combat flying and although I did my best to hide my angst, I probably failed by the mere fact that I was the only passenger to use the seat belt. Most of the men I was supposed to be leading were leaning out of the open door taking in the view. I suppose that they could have been inclined to take the piss but they didn't and considering the fact that I actually knew nothing about proper soldiering I was treated with a good deal of respect and tolerance. I would like to think that they were simply being decent but of course some of the soldiers may have been looking ahead to ant potential peacetime contact.

At the end of our flight when we were supposed to be launching an attack on our enemy the Queens Own Highlanders were waiting for us and we were surrounded as we disembarked from the helicopter in the middle of a cornfield.

As "prisoners of war" we were effectively written off by the Exercise umpires and simply abandoned. Without our vehicles which we had left elsewhere prior to our ill-fated attack we simply had to tab it on foot to our pre arranged rendevous.

It was not much fun having to carry the vigilant missile which was secured in a heavy metal box or the very awkward to carry the carl gustav anti tank weapon.

I think that after about an hour we arrived at the RV and pleasantly surprised that this was a gatstatte where we were able to buy some breakfast and also enjoy a beer whilst waiting for the end of the exercise and the platoon vehicles that recovered us a couple of hours later.

The end of the exercise also marked the end of the regimental training and at this stage it was a case of packing our kit and making our way to the railway siding and loading our vehicles onto the rail flats. Once we had completed this we boarded the train again for the return journey to Osnabruck. I recall that this journey was much the same as the outward trip, very slow and constant shunting into the sidings to allow every other train to pass. We were however better prepared and had kept plenty of compo rations as there were no meals provided. We eventually arrived back in Osnabruck about 1600hrs and moved in convoy back to Quebec Barracks. I had hoped to remain in Barracks at least for a few days which would have allowed me some time to say my farewells to my platoon soldiers however I was recalled to my own unit and had to return without even taking part in the post training clean up programme.

Although my involvement with the regiment had come to an end I was able to maintain my friendship with Clinton until the regiment moved to Stanley Fort Hong Kong in early 1968.

In 1966 English football clubs strange as it may seem now were full of English footballers and this year was marked with the only ever world cup win by England. Live international Television coverage was not as sophisticated as it is now and it may be because of this that the early stages of the cup competition did not attract a great deal of interest except perhaps for the dedicated supporters. Media coverage in 1966 was technology limited and the real excitement only developed when the competition drew towards it's climax and the final match between England and in some quarters the arch football foe, Germany.

The 1966 English national football team was full of talent and led by Captain Bobby Moore.

The competition may have been about football but the final match was something much more. It might have been a football match in name and on the surface but in reality it was far from a question of sport. This final event was a battle between two arch enemies and fight to the bitter end. Although by contemporary politically correct standard it might have seemed inappropriate there were many British soldiers as well as some RMP who delighted in counting the "Final" as one of the three great victories over Germany, 1914-18 1939-45 and then 1966.

The German press and by all accounts the German team were supremely confident despite the home ground advantage for England where any German support would likely be dwarfed by the English spectators.

There were a number of RMP NCO's who were married to German girls and who would probably have had access to local television. I suspect that watching the final at home may have created a conflict of support and for this reason virtually all married men joined the single men in the single men's accommodation to watch the match on the rather antiquated and by modern standards very basic black and white television. English audio commentary was via a radio tuned to BFN British Forces Network.

I can recall that the corporal's mess remained open throughout the entire match and there was a constant stream of men adjourning to the bar to top up the drinks and loads of loud cheering every time that England looked like scoring and even louder for every goal.

Following England's victory I can also recall that the mess stayed open without a break until the following morning. We never really needed an excuse for an extended drinking session but this was a Bonus.

In Osnabruck in 1966 a "British week" took place primarily sponsored by the British board of trade with the aim of promoting British trade in Germany. I always struggled to identify anything other than Scotch Whisky that the Germans would want to buy from Great Britain. For the duration of the programme two of the senior military police corporals were selected to take part in the official activities and celebrations in the company of officials from the Town authorities. There were several accounts fed back to us about how the two RMP had been able to enjoy the corporate hospitality and over indulgence of the town council and business-men. In addition to the shops in the town centre displaying a range of British goods there was a major attraction at the weekend in the form of a Garrison at home open day in Roberts Barracks. Each military unit from the garrison had displays of their regimental silver and historical uniforms. There was a display of British military vehicles and equipment. All of the local military bands were providing music in addition to a massed bands and marching display..

For some reason which I could never fathom, the German visitors had an amazing appetite for English sausages and all of the other food items on sale. There were of course several bars selling English beers and spirits and these were also very popular. Although I had no personal knowledge or involvement and have never seen a single scrap of evidence, I certainly heard the "rumour" that one enterprising soldier had offered a piece of the equipment display, a very expensive engineering vehicle for sale. Whether or not any money ever changed hands I can't say or even if the alleged deal was serious or a prank. I was however informed by a fairly reliable source that the proposed deal only came to light when the purchaser arrived with a low loader trailer to collect the vehicle some days after the exhibition.

Any reasonably observant soldier would be able to confirm just how much the German population enjoy any military parade and in particular the world's finest traditional musical displays produced by the British army. The Germans also have considerable affection for and a fascination with the British royal family. Tickets for any military display or bands concert would always be sold out quickly. This might seem a bit strange to some but it confirms to me just how much the Germans love the tradition and pageantry of the military even though the consequences of disastrous wars sometimes leave them with a degree of anti Military sentiment.

During this year I was also able to undertake some useful training which included what was then known as the ACE 2 (army certificate of education) this was a great time, during four weeks at the local army education centre I learned a great deal about German history and the national and local economy.

The course also included a number of field trips to local industries. One of the trips was to the local Volkswagen Karman Ghia (VW sports cars) auto factory. What a shame I did not have the foresight (or the funds) to purchase a dozen of those incredibly beautiful sports cars which now sell for a considerable sum.

The factory was in part built as a joint enterprise between the federal Government and Turkey in order to provide jobs for the Turkish population who were at the time defined as Guest Workers. It was during the course that I also learned the economic importance of the Turkish workers in Germany and that their income was the largest single source of revenue to the Turkish government.

This year I also successfully completed my upgrading, my understanding was that apart from one WRAC NCO who did not take the same final paper on Pro Ops, I scored the highest marks world wide. Shame I could not have done this the first time. The most immediate benefit as I recall distinctly was that my net pay increased from dm 75 to dm 90 per week. Hardly a fortune but I managed reasonably well, no dependant responsibilities, no worries and literally not a care in the world.

Also this year we had a long serving corporal (Lenny Want) posted in who was a lot older than most of the juniors and who claimed to be a bit deaf, I suspect that this was a selective condition to filter out what he did not want to hear. Also I recall that he wore two rows of medal ribbons and had little tolerance or indeed respect for most of our seniors who I think did their best to keep out of his way. I got to know him quite well and in time discovered his incredible military history of how to came to be awarded the medals. The same man I also discovered to be a bit of a wheeler and dealer with a keen interest in photography and cameras. Within a very short period of time he had established some kind of business arrangement with the local Photo Porst shop and had assisted just about every single man in the barracks, me included to purchase a camera. Amazingly he claimed to be unable to speak any German!!

Lenny also managed to secure some rooms in the accommodation block along with a selection of sports equipment with which he set up a mini gym and boxing ring. Along with his many other talents, Lenny was an accomplished boxer and undertook to teach the rudiments of the skill to other juniors.

There was only one occasion to which I was witness when his good nature and best intentions were abused. One particular NCO who considered himself a real exponent of the noble art ignored Lenny's instruction when sparring to punch soft and threw a flurry of deliberately hard, vicious and potentially harmful punches.

After another ignored warning from Lenny he decided that a lesson was needed, he stepped up a gear, went into fighting mode, threw a package of serious punches and his partner was suddenly lying immobilised and flat on his back.

This year, two of the most senior corporals, Tex Pemberton and Wally Holloway attended the London Metropolitan police advanced driving course and on their return they provided some training to other juniors. In my case accompanied by Lenny Want and Gordon Price I took part in the training under the guidance of Tex Pemberton.

I think that translating the training that Tex would have received using standard saloon cars on British roads into equivalent training on German roads using army land rovers was a bit of a risk. It was clear that Gordon was a bit of a daredevil driver and Lenny appeared to have no fear whatever and both seemed quite happy to drive as fast as possible and hurl the vehicle into some very risky and hazardous hazards.

Although I had considered myself a fairly competent and confident driver I was also cautious by nature and being a passenger when either of them was driving literally scared the pants off me. I had to admire Tex for saying that he was not nervous, he didn't look so but I probably made up enough scared for the both of us.

For reasons which were not entirely clear, this year I was assigned to some motorcycle training under the guidance of Sergeant Ray Pleasance. Ray was not the easiest man to get on with and always attempted to portray himself as an expert on every topic. I was perplexed by this training assignment because I already had a full licence for motor car and motor cycle, I had passed the matrix tick test and had been assigned to the mechanical Transport section some months earlier and was a regular driver..

The aims of the training were a bit of a mystery as we did nothing except ride around the town ring road making stops and starts. I was surprised that we did not receive any instruction in off road riding as that would have been really worthwhile and of benefit if we were ever deployed to ride motorcycles whilst on field exercise training.

In the autumn of this year along with other members of both 12 Brigade pro unit and 2 Div Pro coy I took part in the annual 1 British Corp annual FTX. At least by this time of my service I had gained enough experience to be able to make sure that I was well prepared and self sufficient. I had packed plenty of extra food and some medicinal brandy and my planning proved to be well worth the effort.

The same old routine prevailed and on more than one occasion I was simply dumped on a remote traffic point in the middle of nowhere to direct non existent traffic and left there for the best part of 24 hours with no support, no food and no idea what was happening. If I had not made my own support plans I may well have starved. On other occasions I was similarly dumped in the middle of a town which in some ways was even more difficult because it was virtually impossible to answer any call of nature in full view of the mystified local population.

As I mentioned earlier although life for single men in the Military Police in Osnabruck was good, virtually no additional responsibilities outside getting to work on time and keeping on the right side of the RSM this mainly involved smart uniform, shiny boots, clean vehicle when on driving duty and tidy entries in the daily occurrence book when on desk duty.

There were however occasions when events outside of one's own control generated some unfavourable reaction. On one particular occasion I had been on duty for 24 hours as duty driver and early in the morning just prior to completing that duty I was collecting married men from their homes in order to bring them to work. During this time the officer commanding had occasion to call the duty room to request transport for himself as his own car had broken down.

It was probably only a few days earlier that the incumbent RSM 2 Div Pro Coy had left Osnabruck having been commissioned into the Corps. As an interim measure and having been promoted to WO1 (RSM) the incumbent CSM 12 Bde Pro Unit WO2 Terry Clift took over the role of RSM for reasons not entirely clear on this particular day, all of the remaining junior NCO's on duty were absent from the duty room and had apparently adjourned to the kitchen in a separate building for an early breakfast. This should never have happened however and as a result the duty room telephone was unmanned and unanswered. A short while after we had been stood down from duty the OC informed the newly promoted RSM who then recalled the entire night shift to his office for a sound bollocking.

Despite the fact that I was the only NCO who had an "alibi" for not being present in the duty room at the time the OC called I was rebuked by the RSM for wearing what he described as a dirty white belt.

He then warned me that I was to be placed on OC's orders, he then confiscated my belt presumably as evidence and I was charged (section 69 Conduct prejudice to good order and military discipline) for wearing a dirty belt on duty. This was a classic case of military bullying by a warrant officer wanting to prove how tough he was in front of the officer commanding. Having lived in the shadow of RSM Roy Standring for nearly three years this was his first big occasion. It didn't require much of a brain to work out that after 24 hours anybody's white belt would not be as clean as it was when the duty started. He simply wanted a scapegoat and I was to be the victim. I still can't fathom why the other NCO's on duty were not charged. In particular the one who was detailed as duty sergeant and who should by any measure have ensured that the duty telephone was manned and as he failed it was he who should have been charged, not me.

In any event a few days later after I had finished night duty and what was part of the process of humiliation and lessening of mental and physical resistance I was marched in front of the OC on "OC's orders.

What then took place was another example of the medieval and grossly unfair system of summary "justice". I was marched in front of the officer who had complained to the RSM by the RSM who had decided to charge me, as usual the outcome of the process would have already been decided. Somebody needed to be punished and I was the selected victim when it should have been the night orderly sergeant and the night desk NCO who were not even reprimanded. I was duly marched in and listened to the charge, I provided an explanation for what had taken place and in another example of the malicious attitude of the RSM and OC the matter of the unmanned telephone was ignored and it was quite clear that they just wanted to punish me for allegedly wearing a dirty belt. Even my explanation for this was totally rejected by the RSM and the Officer commanding and when the inevitable question was asked, " are you willing to accept my punishment or do you wish to elect for trial by court martial"? I responded by saying that I would not accept any punishment and elected for trial by court martial.

The question of being asked whether to accept punishment indicates a finding of guilt as charged and the intention of the officer to impose a financial punishment by means of a stoppage of pay.

I had already submitted a redress of grievance as I felt that I had been unfairly treated and should not have been charged. I was also aggrieved that the other NCO's on duty and who had neglected to man the telephone were not punished. After being marched in several times as was the usual process for wearing down resistance and after continuing to elect for trial by court martial, and being told that if I was to be tried by Court Martial I faced a possible two year prison sentence I was reprimanded and dismissed so that I could return to what was left of my day off. The issue of a reprimand removed the question of accepting or refusing punishment.

The whole process of summary justice is intended to humiliate and nearly always takes place when the individual charged has just finished night duty and supposed to be on a day off. Such an arrangement helps to compromise any resistance and being tired make the brain less effective. This process started at 0900 hours and continued all day, with the intention of breaking my resolve and actually finished at 1600hours.

I was actually feeling fairly contented with the outcome and believed that I had secured a small victory, I had not given in and the officer commanding and the RSM would have been well aware that the court martial outcome they had predicted was an empty threat.

I returned to my barrack room and waited for the evening meal at 1700 hrs. My day and the attempts to punish me were not however completed. About thirty minutes after I had been dismissed from "orders" I was summoned to the RSM's office. Incredibly he greeted me in an exceptionally friendly manner and following a long winded explanation that another RMP unit was short of men he instructed me to collect a land-rover from the MT sergeant and report to the Military Police Unit (6 Infantry Brigade Provost Unit) at Munster to help out with duties for a few days. I was not that stupid and it was clear that they wanted me out of the way for a while as I was a temporary embarrassment. I did not for one moment believe that my detachment would only be for a few days and I therefore gathered all of my possessions to take with me.

When I arrived in Munster the CSM WO2"blinky" Moyles told me that he knew all about me refusing punishment however there were no implied threats or warnings as I might have expected. In confirmation of my view I was employed for three months as the admin driver for the unit ration storeman (Lenny Want) and had a thoroughly enjoyable time.

Lenny somehow managed to acquire rations for the single men that were much better and well in excess of what most Sergeants and Officers messes would have been provided. I never asked any questions and the single men were all very happy.

In Munster Westphalen where the British Army and the RMP were located there was a large concert hall the Munster Halle. This place was the venue for many British Bands concerts including as well as many others, The Rolling Stones and the Who.

Although I have no idea who might have organised it, a number of these groups made their way to the RMP corporals mess and I suspect it was an opportunity to really relax and enjoy a "quiet" drink.

Following my instant removal from Osnabruck I was never given any indication of how long I was to remain in Munster. I was simply called in to see the CSM one day and told to return to my own unit in Osnabruck. Punishment completed

By the time I returned to Osnabruck both the RSM and the Officer commanding responsible for my "punishment" had been posted elsewhere, this was in my view a positive change and rather than make waves decided that it would be best if I just put the entire matter down to experience and by my own judgement felt that I had achieved a small victory. Despite the passage of time and the fact that the final outcome was more or less satisfactory, to this day I have not forgotten or forgiven the individuals who caused the problem in the first place. It was due to their negligence, effectively being absent from their place of duty that created the situation and still managed to escape any form of sanction. Similarly I have not forgotten or forgiven the grossly unfair and bullying attitude of the RSM or the Officer Commanding and I am certain that this would not have happened under the watch of the RSM's predecessor Roy Standring.

1967 Two down

AWAY FROM MY FAIRLY TRIVIAL personal challenges there were some far more serious events taking place around the world in 1967 these included, the Chinese cultural revolution and the rampage of the red guards in China. I must say that I did not pay any particular attention to the events in China although I had watched the events in London with more amusement than anything else. I was however quite fascinated by the events in the Middle East and the Arab Israeli 6 day war. This conventional conflict in terms of how it compared to the British Army will always be a classic reminder and an example of how strong government and a determined military can defeat a numerically superior, well equipped and resourced enemy.

The war in Vietnam was too distant to make any real impression on me and in fact was probably not all that newsworthy. I had at least remembered the history of Vietnam and it's Imperial record as French In do China, I recall that this attitude remained in place until I was posted to Hong Kong and listened to the AFN radio which included daily body counts of the Vietnamese killed by the US forces. Later I was to discover how many serious US forces casualties were treated at the British Military Hospital. Whilst recognising the importance of each of these world changing events there was however something else happening much closer to Germany and which really captured considerable local German and European interest..

The Eurovision Song Contest.

Although this competition had been around since 1956, in 1967 this particular event staged in Vienna (Austria), so close to Germany created a great deal of interest. I have to admit that I had a massive "crush" on one of the artistes (Sandie Shaw) and I can claim the dubious privilege of being the very first member of her official fan club launched by her mother. The British entry "Puppet on a String" was already a huge success in Germany prior to the event and my constant playing of this and her other songs was probably a source of annoyance to my room mates.

Sandie Shaw and the writer of many of her songs were both very popular in Germany. There was some rumour that the British entry was at risk of being disqualified because of it's alleged unfair airplay exposure and the potential influence on the "voters". This negative campaign never succeeded, I think it was a plot by one or more of the other entries and the result was that the song by Sandie Shaw won the event outright and actually received more than twice the number of votes awarded to the second placed Irish entry.

I had been a fanatical supporter and admirer of the barefooted Sandie Shaw since her very first hit record (Always something there to remind me) and so I was particularly glad to be able to watch the event on Television. I made no secret of the fact that I was overjoyed by the result and I certainly managed to celebrate her victory well into the night and the early hours.

Music was a significant part of our domestic social life in barracks and it was no secret that there were some serious differences in taste. It was not easy sharing a room with four or five other men each with their own record player and stock of different artistes records including Sandie Shaw, Dusty Springfield, Beach boys and Hank Williams. Astonishing as it might seem, each room member had to connect their own record playing device via a rather untidy series of plugs and cables via single wall power socket. This would have presented a challenging and almost certainly a very dangerous environment, fortunately, as it was we had never heard of health and safety regulations and nobody ever had ether the time or trouble to look at what we were doing.

1967 Berlin The divided city.

In 1967 the military police unit in Berlin (247 Berlin Provost Company) made calls on other military police units throughout BAOR for manpower support in order to maintain their important deployment tasks. Although I did not appreciate this at the time I was later to discover that the main reason for the call on other BAOR Military police units to provide men to support Berlin was for no other reason than to allow their sports teams to concentrate on training and competitions.

In May of this year I was detached to Berlin and discovered that the main task to allocated to visiting NCO's was the "Autobahn sweep". This involved driving a vehicle from Berlin (Checkpoint Bravo) to Helmstedt (Checkpoint Alpha) in the morning and then to return in the evening. Although this might appear to have been a simple task, it was actually quite demanding and involved transit through the Soviet checkpoints and travel though East Germany (German Democratic Republic) Officially this was a simple routine transit trip but unofficially it often provided support and an escort to other British military and sponsored travellers. I can remember travelling on my first occasion from Helmstedt to Berlin as a passenger in the sweep vehicle. At this time all of the vehicles used by the Military Police in Berlin were German models and in view of the fact that the German Government (Berlin Senate) picked up the entire bill, it should have been no real surprise. The vehicle normally used for the "sweep"at that time was the Volkswagen rear engined, air cooled 1600 variant. I must say that this has to be one of the best cars I have ever driven. It was fast, comfortable, economical and incredibly reliable. These cars were used every day by different drivers and driven hard in virtually every weather condition.

The East German roads were also in poor condition with plenty of potholes. I personally undertook over forty autobahn sweep duties using the variant and never experienced a single breakdown. These cars possessed every quality demanded. I started in Berlin in May and after completing forty seven consecutive return trips on the Berlin Helmstedt autobahn sweep I asked for a change of role. Following this request I undertook wall patrols between the British sector and east sector of the city and wire patrols between the outer perimeter of West Berlin and East Germany the GDR.

Those who have undertaken the wire patrol will recall the large amount of wild life particularly deer and pigs which thrived in the restricted area approaching the zonal border.

Duties in Berlin were very different to standard Military Police duties in the Republic of Germany. The three western allies remained in Berlin as occupying forces and this status remained in place until after 1970 when the British Army became a protective force. In addition to the Autobahn sweep, there was a patrol of the wall and wire boundaries, checkpoint Bravo and Charlie and the Tiergarten at the Soviet war memorial. All of these duties attracted extra duty pay in the form of subsistence allowance this was a very lucrative income and as the money was paid in cash deutsche marks it was very welcome. The wall patrol involved patrolling the stretch of wall, about eight miles between the East and West Berlin from it's boundary with the French sector in the North and the American sector in the South. The wall patrol area included some of the most significant building and tourist destinations. These included, The Brandenburg gate, Checkpoint Charlie, the Reichstag and the Soviet war memorial in the Tiergarten. Potsdamer platz was probably the site which had been the definitive centre of pre war Berlin and the site of the Hitler Bunker very close to where the Reich chancellery had stood on the Wilhelm Strasse. This location was a virtual terminus for the tourist buses and there was a continuous stream of visitors particularly from the USA, Japan, South Africa and Rhodesia as well as from Australia and New Zealand.

Although the summer months were the busiest the process of tourists visiting continued all year round even during the coldest Berlin winters.

The wire patrol was entirely different and involved patrolling the Zonal boundary between west Berlin and East Germany beyond the East Berlin boundary. This was no tourist area and in fact there was a one kilometre exclusion boundary to prevent all unauthorised approach. There was a hard track suitable for most light wheeled vehicles along the entire length of the Border and tall watchtowers as well as official border huts at strategic locations. The border was also patrolled by other British military units and German border police. Under the terms of the post war occupation of Berlin the Germans were not officially permitted an Army in the city but it was plain for anybody to see that the police force was an army in all but name and uniform.

The wire patrol was a fairly comfortable duty throughout the year although very, very cold during the winter and very hot in high summer. It included a location which had been swapped with the Russians and formed a small enclave surrounded by East Germany, "The Eiskellar". The area close to the border was a virtual nature reserve and was exceptionally well stocked with wildlife. There were hundreds of wild pigs and deer as well as foxes and game birds.

I can remember that the weather was fantastic when I arrived in the city and as summer approached it became very, hot. It was quite incredible that in Berlin at the height of the summer the sun was shining brightly around 0300hrs. This was particularly apparent if you had stayed out at one of the many local nightspots till early morning. My favourite place was the old Eden salon, where there was a large scale train set circumnavigating the ground floor bar and where all of the other parts of the club were decorated and arranged as school classrooms. The new Eden was a contrast to this and was much more "sophisticated" with corresponding higher prices. Stuttgarter platz was also a much favoured location with a whole row of rather unsavoury bars. For the late night or early morning hungry diners on the corner of the Stuttgarter Platz and the kant strasse there was a caravan selling the best bouletten in the city, a significant feature was that the two men operating the business managed to do so whilst holding hands.!!

Travel on the east west "corridor" between Belin and Helmstedt was fairly straightforward although there were some travellers who seemed to be ill prepared or overawed by the prospect of some contact with soviet soldiers at the soviet checkpoints.

Despite the many trips I made I was only involved in one serious and at the time scary incident. During a return trip from Helmstedt to Berlin there were about seven travellers one of whom was making his first trip in a brand new Hillman Imp. He was clearly more anxious than most and he received a double briefing before setting off.

I explained to him that on the approach to Berlin I would overtake his car and he could then watch my car and follow me through the checkpoint.

Things did not go entirely as planned and instead of being behind me he had succeeded in getting front. When I stopped at the checkpoint he was just leaving.

I entered the checkpoint building with my documents as he drove off. Out of my sight he approached a barrier which was operated by the East German Border guards. The guards were instructed to operate this barrier to allow allied vehicles to proceed and at the same time to temporarily halt any other traffic.

Unfortunately instead of stopping at the barrier as instructed several times the driver negotiated around the barrier and drove away. The East German guards activated the alarm and as the Hillman imp with me close behind drove towards the West sector a massive concrete barrier rolled across the road to block our escape.

A soviet officer eventually arrived and siezed our travel documents. We then continued our journey and the following morning accompanied by the Military police staff officer and Russian speaker returned to the checkpoint to retrieve my travel documents.

All Berlin duties except for the local police patrol and the control room attracted the extra duty pay in the form of a very generous subsistence allowance which was paid in Deutsche Marks in cash. The WRAC NCO's were generally only employed on these paid duties. Autobahn sweep, checkpoint Charlie and Bravo. I know that most of them would have made enough money from these duties to enable them to save all of their normal army wages. In 1967 the British Army in Berlin was still issuing soldiers pay in the form of BAFSV (British Armed Forces Special Vouchers).

These vouchers represented face value pounds sterling and were introduced in 1945 as the official Army grading currency.

I never really understood why these had been retained and nobody else really seemed to know either.

It was not until a few years later that I discovered that the vouchers had been introduced in 1945 at the same time as the NAAFI had been appointed as the official only trading organisation for the Army. I would also appear to be the case that when the German Banks were established and the vouchers deposited as legal tender they were credited the DM exchange rate that was in place in 1945 circa DM 45 to £1 sterling!!!!

Berlin is without question an incredible city and I was really sad to leave, all good things must, as is often said come to an end. Strangely and to my everlasting joy I would return on a regular posting just four years later.

I eventually left my Berlin secondment in August 1967 and after a short period of leave in the UK for the purpose of celebrating my 21st Birthday I returned to Osnabruck. Around this time I met a new arrival (Dave Coates) who was a married man waiting to be allocated a married quarter and for his wife to arrive. Dave introduced me to the game of squash this was historically a sport reserved for Officers and as a consequence it was necessary to book the courts at the most unsocial times, after 2000 hrs. During one of my squash court visits I met the officer commanding who had spent some time watching and then complimented me on some parts of my game. I well remember him advising me to spend more time knocking up before any match or game and that he had noticed how my game improved after I had been on the court for a while and when under pressure.

A few weeks later I was invited to take on the job as orderly room post clerk and moved into the world of "employed" staff.

This new job was not as simple or basic as the title suggested. I worked hard, undertook the responsibilities for post and a range of other administrative tasks and was included in the world of confidential information sharing. I was also free from the routine garrison duties and the dreadful admin fatigues, gardening and vehicle cleaning. Most rewarding however was the fact that my postal duties enabled me to escape the morning muster parade which I was able to justify by the fact that in order to ensure an efficient post collection I needed to be at the field post office before 0730 hours. The senior management and in particular the officer commanding 2 Div Pro Coy. Major Martin Young liked this idea as I was able to ensure that the mail was on his desk ready for him to scan when he arrived around 0830. This enabled him to plan his day and if as it became clear, he was happy there would be no interference from other quarters.

Although I was not to realise it at the time, 1967 was to be my last Christmas in Osnabruck, I had already taken leave in the UK this year for my birthday and had not intended or planned to do what I had done in 65 and 66 and make the annual almost obligatory pilgrimage to see my parents before Christmas.

During the year there was an urgent directive from HQ BAOR that required all RMP NCO's to be tested regarding their ability to reverse a land-rover with a two wheeled trailer of the type used by RMP on Field training. Although I was not involved in the planning or preparation of this event I knew in advance that it was to take place. The annoying part of this was that it was a Saturday and as usual I had already been to the post office to collect mail. All junior ranks were instructed to parade outside the motor transport garages where a short wheel based land-rover with trailer attached was already parked. I noticed that both sides of the rear canopy of the land rover had been rolled up to make the exercise even easier The MT sergeant explained that all nco's were to reverse the trailer from where it was parked into the garage where a space was reserved. One of the senior corporals was assigned to demonstrate the process. After watching his very amateur efforts for several minutes he managed to get the trailer inside the garage but hardly anywhere near to where it should have been, I could not help myself from commenting and in the face of some fairly harsh words from another senior corporal who commented. That it must be very difficult as corporal Collins was finding it hard to do. If I thought I could do any better!!.

I could hardly wait; I jumped into the vehicle and with arm draped over the rear of the seat provided a perfect demonstration of how it should be done. It took me only seconds to put the trailer in precisely the centre of the parking space and left land-rover and trailer in a perfectly straight line. There was I am proud to say a real hush around the assembled onlookers and from some a look of wonder and even amusement..

What my colleagues would not have known and therefore failed to appreciate was the fact that I had been driving, and reversing tractors and every other kind of vehicle and trailers since I was thirteen years old and was effectively a real expert, not only with single axle but also with the much more difficult twin axle four wheeled trailers. I don't think that following my perfect demonstration my offer to reverse two trailers attached one behind the other was really appreciated and might have been considered as a bit of a show off exercise.

My reversing skills with land-rover and trailer had already been well demonstrated during field training exercises, one senior officer from Brigade headquarters was incensed when he saw me reversing my trailer into a small space because he had to help his driver unhook and manhandle his trailer into position. During the exercise I gained a few points by taking the time to teach his driver the basic process but he would have needed to get in a good deal of practise before he came anywhere near to my level.

I can remember that Christmas 1967 was for me and I suppose all of the single men, an exceptionally good time. There was plenty of time off and I made several trips into town to eat out, there was a really great corporals mess prize draw and a good all ranks party in the barracks annex.

There was the single men's dinner served by the officers and seniors and to the great relief of the married men they did not have to attend and instead of Christmas day it was so far as I can recall on the evening of the 23rd.

1968 Farewell to Germany

1968 STARTED AS I RECALL with some exceptionally cold weather and heavy snowfalls. Fortunately for me I was fairly well protected from this as a result of my employed position in the orderly room.

One of my tasks was to collect mail for dispatch and collect from the post office, I managed a petty cash account for the sale of stamps and undertook all of the office filing. I assisted with other admin tasks and was of course included in the confidential chat that was not shared outside of the office.

An additional task was the collection and collating of correspondence such as applications from juniors to the officers and normally in response to advertised opportunities and vacancies. Although there had been an advertised vacancy for a nine month emergency tour in Hong Kong the previous year I had not seen this, I may also have overlooked the fact that there was another detachment on offer and I was really only aware of this when I collected the pile of applications submitted and which I would as part of my duties place in the officer commanding mail in tray. I have to admit that purely on impulse I quickly wrote out a short application and left this on top of the others when I placed the tray in the OC 's office.

I guess that I was a bit surprised when it came back to me endorsed, "you will like Hong Kong " and application approved, the only occasion when I have been in the right place and at the right time.

During my tenure as postal clerk a corporal arrived from the 6 Infantry Brigade Provost Unit at Munster, I had met him a few times during my 1966 " punishment posting"

6 Infantry Brigade Pro Unit was the second of the two Brigade elements of the second division and for command and disciplinary purposes would report to the officer commanding 2 Div Pro Coy

As a matter of routine I asked him what he was doing in Osnabruck, he replied that he had been experiencing marital problems and that he had been sent to Osnabruck for a few days to allow things to settle down. Such situations were not unheard of and I had no reason to disbelieve him. I was certainly not so interested that I should make any enquiries. After reporting to the RSM he was marched in to see the officer commanding, this was also a perfectly normal procedure.

He was later accommodated in the single men's accommodation but instead of being included on the normal duty rota was assigned to the M T section and spent his days cleaning land rovers and carrying out other admin tasks..

A number of the single men were naturally curious about him and asked me what I knew, of course I could not share any information and in any event I only knew what he had told me. I would have suspected that had he been asked by anybody else he would have told them what he told me.

I did not actually know anything about him and I had not seen any documentation regarding his temporary transfer. To the best of my recollection, a few days later a copy of a pt 2 order arrived from Munster but this referred only to his temporary posting without any reasons or explanation being given. This was also a routine admin process and the order would have been displayed for anybody to read.

Although I had no reason to disbelieve his explanation; a few days later I was to have sight of documentation that caused me to be both surprised and a little shocked to discover that in fact his explanation was inaccurate and that he was facing a District Court Martial on charges of "Behaviour of an outrageous nature"

Although the true reasons for his presence in Osnabruck were never revealed by me and although I was able to read the entire case portfolio of case papers that passed through the orderly room office, the true fact emerged probably as a result of the details being publicly posted at the Court Martial Centre in Roberts Barracks.

This man came to me the day before the Courts Martial and offered a full explanation of what had happened and how the children involved had made a mistake in their accounts. He also told me that he intended to continue with his not guilty plea but that he expected to be convicted and sent to prison.

I never told him that I had read the witness, victim statements and I personally thought that his chances were slim to zero once the statements were read out in court and if the witnesses attended in person to give evidence his chances would be less than zero.

The night before the Court Martial as is the normal procedure the man was placed under close arrest and from then until his attendance at Court he was under the escort of two RMP corporals who were responsible for his safety and security until he was escorted to his Court Martial.

He might have considered himself more fortunate than other soldiers of equivalent rank in that he was only restricted to the rear of the RMP duty room and not a guardroom cell that would have been the case for a soldier from any other military unit.

I had planned to attend the court martial and on that day ensured that I completed the morning postal run earlier than normal.

I recall that the trial was scheduled to commence at 1000hrs and although I can't remember how I actually found out, the proceedings were shortened when the man decided to plead guilty.

I suspect that if he had not already done so previously, he had taken advantage of his early morning start and read the witness statements and taken advice from his defending officer. If this was in fact the case he would have seen that his fate was sealed.

I also think that it was his change of plea that saved him from a custodial sentence he was very lucky and escaped with being sentenced to being reduced to the ranks and a dishonourable discharge.

Although it was introduced in 1967 the new drink driving law RSA 67 was not Implemented in BAOR until 1968. This was a consequence of the fact that the new law required police officers as constables (for the first time Military police were included in this definition) to be in uniform. This legislation also conferred a statutory power of arrest not affected by the constraints of Military Law.

When the full details were made clear there was a clamour from the RMP special investigation Branch who decided that they could not take on drink driving if it meant that they would have to wear uniform. The powers of constable which allowed this procedure to be carried out was quite clear, no uniform no authority. As a result the implementation process was delayed until the uniformed branch could attend the relevant training with the alcotest breathaliser and a full briefing on the procedures. I think that the SIB really did not want to take on any officer who was caught drink driving and would rather the helmets in uniform had that problem The power of arrest was by virtue of an act of parliament and was applicable to all ranks including commissioned officers. In addition to the reaction from the SIB The second issue was the commissioned officers outrage at what they considered to be a totally unacceptable power granted to Military Police NCO's. Under this legislation Military Police NCO's would (at least in theory and protected by the law) no longer require the authority of a provost officer to actually arrest any officer suspected of driving whilst under the influence of alcohol. The delay in implementation also allowed the Army on behalf of commissioned ranks to challenge the law but without success. Initially the legislation using alcotest breathalyser was relatively straightforward with a mere seven requests offers or warnings but as time progressed offenders attempted to challenge virtually every case for a variety of reasons which often included allegations of the NCO' not wearing the correct uniform. Bizarre as it may seem the examples included, not wearing Headdress, white, belt, armband or even whistle chain. Many of those attending Courts martial instructed civilian barristers who attempted to dissect dress regulations in order to avoid a conviction on the flimsiest of technicalities.

I recall my very first case in April 68 involving a land-rover driver from 7 Field ambulance who crashed on the tank road towards Dodesheide. I remember taking a urine sample and thinking how much more simple the process was compared to the 1961 RTA procedure. I attended the Court Martial in Roberts barracks when the driver pleaded guilty and received a £50.00 fine.

This year also saw the introduction of a commercial radio system for the RMP vehicles, although I was no longer included on the normal police duty rota I was certainly made aware of how unreliable the system was, still it was better than nothing and over time it did get better.

Military police duties involved policing the garrison twenty 24 hours a day and 365 days a year. Most of the calls made were in respect of soldiers but dependant, wives and children were also involved from time to time. Service dependants are subject to sections of Military Law as well as the laws of the host country. The German laws are certainly more robust in certain areas than in Britain and in particular the regulations involving road traffic, property and social behaviour. Unlike the British Highway Code which is actually only a recommended course of action for drivers and road users, the German Traffic Ordinance is part of the Federal Law.

Military police provide support to the Army during both war and peace operations although some of the tasks differ considerably.

Service dependants, such as wives and children as well as a range of civilians such as schoolteachers are subject to military law when serving overseas although the occasions on which the Military or host nation claim jurisdiction are dependant on the nature and severity of the case as well as the terms of any Anglo /host agreement.

Peacetime duties for Military police are generally similar to and involve most of the type of incidents and offences that the civilian police would undertake in the UK Traffic accidents, theft, assaults just about everything else.

The wartime role is entirely different and may involve a significant contribution to traffic management, dealing with refugees, looters and prisoners of war. Nuclear, biological and chemical warfare tasks also form an important part of the military police role.

In 1965 the Royal Military Police were required to undertake both roles although the priorities were prone to some confusion and conflict due to inconsistent command decisions. It was quite normal to be instructed to concentrate on operational issues and disregard peacetime garrison police duties when operational deployment was pending but the priorities would inevitably alter and police matters would then become the priority on return to peace-time activities.

From the beginning of the basic training it was made clear to all recruits that in spite of the specialist training and the importance of the Peace Time policing role of the Military Police they should be clear that they were operational soldiers first and foremost and that their peacetime role was of secondary importance.

This argument was rather redundant when there was a court martial matter in progress or when the civil authorities and in particular the German police were waiting for reports that might have been delayed due to the relevant investigating NCO being deployed on operations (Exercise)

As a military policeman in BAOR the peacetime role was virtually identical regardless of which unit and Town he might be based in. The operational role however could be much different and would be largely dependent on the status of the Military formation to which he was assigned.

At Army and Corps level the headquarters would be a considerable distance from the front and this would generally mean that the military police would be engaged in duties similar to those in a static peacetime location, security and police type investigations. There would also be the responsibility for prisoners of war and escorts for senior officers.

At corps level the role would not change much from that undertaken at Army headquarters.

At Division the role would start to change dramatically with the headquarters getting closer to the front and in particular the RMP would be busy with traffic control and the movement of formations via signed axial and lateral military routes.

At Brigade level the RMP could expect to be very close to any battlefront and probably moving location frequently together with and in support of the brigade headquarters and at short notice. It would be normal for Brigade troops to move in response to the progress of any hostilities closer to the front or back towards the rear. Routes would need to be signed and there would be more involvement with prisoners of war, stragglers, refugees and deserters.

Police Work

EVERY RMP INVESTIGATION REQUIRED A substantial amount of paperwork and there was a statutory requirement to produce and submit reports and statements in accordance with all of the legal policies and protocols in place. In overseas theatres such as in BAOR such investigations were complicated by the fact that the investigator would need to take account of British legislation, Military Law and German laws. Many soldiers failed to fully appreciate for example that the German traffic regulations were Law. There was no mitigation and no such thing as due care, it is a case of being in the right or being wrong. German drivers simply expect that drivers comply with the law and in particular the rule of " Vorfahrt " priority. They do not need to look left for example at an unmarked crossing because they have priority.

The majority of the routine calls to military police involved road traffic accidents or disputes in bars and nightclubs over unpaid or contested bills. Alcohol related disagreements over non- payment of taxi fares were all too frequent. In the majority of cases, requests for Military Police assistance at bars and other facilities the matter would have been resolved prior to arrival or the alleged offender had left and that peace had returned. To avoid false alarm requests the general instruction was that we should respond only to calls made via the military exchange operators.

There were however some exceptions to the trivial calls and I can recall an occasion when a call was received via the military telephone exchange operator reporting a fight at the Capri bar in Iburger Strasse central Osnabruck.

Based on previous experience of similar calls and being a bit cynical I have to say that I did not treat this call with any more urgency than any other previous call. I suspected that this call was no more genuine any others which had resulted in wasted time and effort. Accompanied by another NCO (Ricky Parry) I set off at a fairly leisurely pace although I had not expected what followed next. I vividly recall turning right at the Rosenplatz expecting the normally quiet street to be deserted only to be confronted with what was effectively a mass brawl with people spread across the whole street exchanging blows.

It should be worth noting that in those days military police patrols had no means of communicating other than by landline and were not routinely permitted to carry either handcuffs or the totally ineffective official wooden truncheon.

As I pulled up close to the bar I saw a number of German civil police officers and as best I can recall at least four police cars. The situation certainly appeared to be completely out of control and there was no disguising the totally unrestrained exchange of punches by both the police and civilians. Before I had time to consider stepping out of the land rover I was approached by two young men who quickly identified themselves as officers from the Royal fusiliers, one of the resident infantry Battalions based in Osnabruck.

They hurriedly explained that they had been attacked along with their soldiers by a gang of very hostile German civilians and police officers. It seemed to me at the time that there was little chance of any constructive negotiation and rightly or not I concluded that a fast tactical exit was required. I completed a rapid turn round in the road whilst the whole group of soldiers leapt in to the rear of the land rover after which I drove away as quickly as possible. The German police who by now were clearly even more enraged decided to engage in a pursuit in several marked police cars. Several officers had batons drawn when we arrived on the scene and did not seem to be in any kind of mood for any discussion. Although it might appear now to be exaggerating the risk, at the time I was actually concerned or even afraid that it would not be too long before a gun was drawn and shots fired. I drove as quickly as possible towards Belfast Barracks with several marked police cars and a number of other cars following closely behind. One of the police car drivers actually attempted to overtake me and block my route but fortunately must have thought better of this as a collision between a 3/4 ton land-rover and a Volkswagen beetle could have only one outcome. I had little doubt at the time that had I stopped, both Ricky Parry and I along with the group of soldiers would have been at serious risk of being attacked and possibly shot. I was not in any hurry to put this to the test. During the journey to Belfast barracks which must have taken about fifteen minutes the police cars followed, swerving across the road with blue lights and two tone horns. On arrival at Belfast barracks fortune smiled on us when the gate sentry immediately recognised one of our officer passengers who was squeezed into the front of the land-rover and opened the gate in a real hurry. The gate was closed behind us and the very hostile group of about twelve uniformed police officers and a similar number of men in civilian clothing locked out whilst demanding entry and for the group of soldiers to be surrendered to them.

A senior Royal Fusiliers officer attended and the Royal Military Police RSM and commanding officer were informed.

The entire compliment of soldiers on guard duty were turned out and provided additional security at the main barracks gate to prevent any attempt by the German police or their civilian associates to enter. At the time I never gave a single thought to any Anglo German legal obligations and it was clear that the Royal Fusiliers were in no mood to open the gates under any circumstances.

In the safety of the barracks I was able to establish what had taken place. The Royal fusiliers had that day returned from the army boxing championships in Berlin and were celebrating their success in the company of their outgoing platoon commander and his replacement. During the evening a young German lady who had apparently been the worse for wear due to drink had, as it later emerged erroneously, although possibly not maliciously accused one of the soldiers of stealing her handbag. One of her male companions had then taken it upon himself to deal with the matter and had launched a surprise and unprovoked assault on one of the soldiers suspected to have taken the bag. The two platoon officers had tried to remonstrate peaceably and after paying the bar bill, with some difficulty had then attempted to escort their men from the premises. At this point the entire civilian entourage from the bar who were by this time also reinforced by the German civil police joined in an attack on the soldiers who were obliged to defend themselves despite being seriously outnumbered. Once the soldiers and customers were outside the Bar the situation continued to worsen rapidly following the arrival of more police cars. By this time there were at least twelve police officers and a number of them had drawn and were using their traditional black leather batons against the soldiers.

After about an hour of waiting outside the Barracks the German Police and their followers decided to leave and at this point Rick and I decided it was safe to return to the RMP duty room..

I can recall that the duty interpreter was taking calls from the German Police who were outraged at what they described as serious criminal behaviour by the soldiers and the illegal act of the Military police who they alleged had assisted the criminals to flee the scene in order to avoid arrest. Again I never gave much thought to any potential consequence and when through the medium of the RMP duty interpreter, the German police vehemently denied even drawing their truncheons I was even more confident that our actions were fully justified.

During the remainder of the evening we produced a fairly comprehensive and accurate report which was submitted to the RMP officer commanding. Together with supporting statements from the officers and soldiers involved as well as a medical report on the soldiers injuries a high level meeting took place the following morning with the local chief of police and Military Police Commander.

The civil police officers again vehemently denied using batons and were highly critical of the Military Police who they claimed had assisted the soldiers by leaving a crime scene and who should be arrested and face criminal proceedings.

The police officers also denied collaborating with the civilian customers and claimed that in fact the attack was launched by the soldiers against the police who had arrived to deal with the allegation and had been overwhelmed.

They also claimed that it was at this point the civilian customers had exercised their legal responsibility in assisting the police who were being overwhelmed by the attack from the soldiers.

This incident was a great shock to me and very disappointing, relations between civilian and military police had always been very positive although the police station closest to the Capri Bar had the reputation of being the least friendly towards the British and in particular the Military police.

I understood at the time that considerable efforts were made at the highest level to minimise the negative political fallout and to ensure that Anglo German relations were not damaged. It was however absolutely clear from the evidence of the Military police, the statements of the officers and soldiers and the medical report that the German Police account of the incident was misleading and flawed. Although I was never provided with the exact details I understand that a number of Police officers were disciplined. I think that the risk of having me and Ricky Parry along with the officers and soldiers appearing in person at any sort of tribunal or Court hearing must have motivated the police authorities to deal quickly with what could have been a serious public relations disaster.

Following this incident my attitude towards any call relating to bar disturbances changed dramatically and although I remained somewhat cautious I was always better prepared for the unexpected. The incident simply blew over and to the best of my recollection I never met any of the police officers again. I was also confident that no lasting damage had been caused between Military and Civilian police and I was never called to the Capri bar again.

Any account of the British Army in Osnabruck and the military police could not avoid reference to the murder of the taxi driver Felix Reese by a soldier from the Royal Fusiliers. I was on duty the night of the murder together with another Military policeman (Chris Marsh) when we were sent to the Scarborough Barracks for an incident of an unknown nature. We subsequently discovered that a taxi driver later identified as Felix Reese had been found dead inside his taxi.

Although there was no immediate association or evidence to connect any British soldier to the incident, which quickly emerged as a murder probably motivated by Robbery ; the Osnabruck taxi drivers had no such doubts. Within a short time virtually every taxi in Osnabruck had been driven from the murder scene to the Belfast Barracks on Sedan Strasse and were effectively blockading the barracks, where the 1st Battalion Royal Fusiliers, City of London Regiment were based demanding that the culprit be given up.

The military part of the murder investigation led by the late Warrant Officer 1 Stan Upton produced a swift arrest which resulted in lance corporal Lesley Grantham who it emerged had shot and killed the taxi driver with a .22 pistol, convicted and imprisoned for the murder. Yet another irony was that during the investigation whilst under arrest the lance corporal was kept in Military Police accommodation for his own safety before being transferred elsewhere.

Funny looking back

S<small>UMMARY PUNISHMENT AND INTERNAL MILITARY</small> sanctions were normally reserved for individual indiscretions such as being late or absent from duty, dirty boots or equipment. Occasionally actions were taken against a group and although after many years such treatment can be laughed off, at the time they might have been seen as funny.

There was always a substantial demarcation between junior and senior ranks embedded in service life and tradition and this is best demonstrated by the separate Corporals and sergeants messes.

On one particular occasion the Osnabruck RMP sergeant's mess had planned an evening function which included a menu of roast half chicken and chips. The sergeant's mess was located on the first floor of the main administrative building and with easy access to and from the duty room on the ground floor.

When the time came for the meal to be served it was discovered that a portion of chicken was missing; believed stolen. The RSM was apparently enraged by this serious crime particularly as there was only the exact number of portions required for the number of mess members attending.

As part of an attempt to identify the person responsible as well as punishing every junior, the RSM ordered all junior NCOs living in Barracks to parade at 0600 hours the following morning in full field order for a ten mile route march.

As expected Sergeant Ray Pleasance was the back up support; following the group in a land rover in case of any casualties.

I really have no idea if the chicken theft actually took place, or if it was a mistake by the cook or the RSM. I certainly never had any idea who might have stolen the goods!!

If there was a theft and if the culprit had been identified I have no idea what action might have been taken, he might have been allowed to continue his military career or even court martialled. Although I am not condoning his actions I can't condemn him for remaining silent, even though I did not enjoy the route march.

On another occasion during the warm summer months a number of juniors, me included were working in the garden at the front of the main office building, some of whom had taken advantage of the sun by removing their shirts.

Whilst this work was taking place the Divisional Deputy assistant provost marshal (Major Houlton Hart) arrived on an unexpected and what was most probably an unannounced as well as unobserved visit.

The men undertaking the gardening work were totally engrossed in their tasks and would have therefore been most unlikely to have even noticed the DAPM;s arrival by land rover. Even if the vehicle had been noticed the occupants would not have been recognised, very few NCO's had ever met the DAPM and bizarre as it may sound he was a little quirky and may well have been wearing his service greatcoat. Despite this the DAPM complained to the RSM that the men had neglected to salute him and that this could not pass without some sanction.

In the very best example of gratuitous revenge punishment just a few minutes later the whole group of us were removed from our gardening duties and after being paraded as was usual in three ranks were then ordered to take part in marching drill supervised by the duty sergeant (Tony Stanley) which continued until we witnessed the departure of the DAPM which we marked with a squad salute on the march.

The corporals mess was subject to a combination of formal and traditional protocols, collar and tie except for rare occasions, ladies first to the buffet and a last minute hopeful smash and grab for the single men. The mess was for a time at least a form of something akin to a sanctuary from daily stresses.

New arrivals would not only be expected to observe the rules and niceties but also, albeit with some objections and reluctance, "Drink the Boot"

For many this was a challenge, for some an unwanted humiliation in front of many others with a fire bucket for company. Having to also pay for the privilege was the cause of additional indignation.

Most junior NCO's however became accomplished and seasoned drinkers although any form of conflict or combative encounters either in the mess or after were surprisingly rare.

In addition to the everyday mess activity we were able to enjoy Saturday evening functions, church parade, regimental " Corp Day" activities, usually and most popular in the form of "Curry Lunches. Also there was the inevitable all ranks Christmas function which together with its huge logistical implications invariably took place at a venue outside of the limited corporals or sergeants mess capacity. These were happy times and an opportunity for the single men to meet families and wives. There was always a serious shortage of eligible single girls, these were days before the regular deployment of WRAC and the children, daughters of soldiers would not have reached their teens. There were a few German girls but the competition was fierce and inevitably most of the single men allowed the evenings to degenerate into ad hoc drinking contests.

In Osnabruck as was the case for the whole of Germany there was a completely different attitude to public holidays. Easter is clearly the most important celebration on the German religious calendar whilst Christmas managed to combine all the best aspects of tradition and progress. There are a number of other celebration days such as May Day traditionally enjoyed in Germany as well as Rosenmontag and Weiberfastnacht not understood or undertaken in the United Kingdom. Christmas inevitably focussed on families. In 1965, my first RMP Osnabruck Christmas all junior NCO's married and single were required to attend for a traditional Christmas dinner on Christmas day and in uniform whether they liked it or not being served by the seniors, officers, warrant officers and sergeants. This dinner was published on the daily detail as a "parade" and failing to turn up and on time could have resulted in disciplinary action.

Despite the fact that the dinner was free it was most unlikely that the married men really appreciated this intrusion into their family life, most single men were probably the worse for wear in any event and had almost certainly been drinking for most of the day preceding their dinner.

The generosity of married NCO's however normally resulted in single men invited to married service homes for a brief and welcome interlude of social normality.

For most of us single men, in our personal lives sickness and death were virtual strangers, very few were ever ill, injuries rare and we were probably convinced that we were very much invincible.

As part of our military police duties in the garrison and during operational field training exercises we were frequently involved with victims and casualties from road traffic accidents, violent assaults and exercise incidents. Although as the uniformed branch we would often be the first Military presence on the scene of any traffic accident the German Civil police would in most cases have arrived before us and alerted any other emergency service. Communication was always a real problem and it's hard to believe that we had no radios and would generally have to find the nearest landline telephone in order to call up for any reinforcements or for the SIB in the case of serious incidents. I do not recall a single occasion when the on duty supervisor orderly sergeant ever attended to provide support. Domestic disputes at the homes of enlisted soldiers were not uncommon and were usually the consequence of too much alcoholic drink and the rejection of unwelcome or ill-timed amorous advances.

We were also involved in the initial investigation and aftermath of several high profile murders, all of which were highly publicised and in some ways controversial. One of these was the murder of the taxi driver Felix Reese which may have been the single most damaging incident to Osnabruck Anglo German relations, due to the legislation in place at that time and which may not have been welcomed by the German authorities and the local community. Legal jurisdiction was retained by the British Military authorities and at a Court Martial in Bielefeld lance corporal Leslie Grantham was sentenced to life imprisonment for murder and served ten years. The second murder of a soldier from the 9/12th lancers by his wife presented some challenging issues.

As a service dependant the wives of serving soldiers are subject to Military Law and the wife was tried by Court Martial. Following her arrest she was detained at the British Military Hospital in Munster as there was no other suitable female secure accommodation. After being transferred to the UK there was a good deal of media coverage which included photographs of the prisoner and her soldier escort erroneously described as Military Police. So far as I can recall the lady received a fairly modest sentence which was later further reduced on confirmation and the period of remand taken into account.

The incident raised other social issues involving young wives of soldiers serving overseas, separated by an unfamiliar language and culture, estranged from family and friends and simply unable to cope with a totally different environment and life style demand..

Duties and Field Training

Life for single military policemen was rather mundane and predictable, sharing barrack accommodation required a communal domestic commitment and then there was the requirement to be ready for any garrison police duty which was generally known well in advance and published on the daily detail and duty rota. The operational wartime role under the auspices of field training exercises were also published in advance and it was essential that we were ready and prepared.

We could expect to take part in field training exercises several times each year, sometimes for just a few days and sometimes for several weeks.

Field training exercises were part of a regular cycle and specifically named exercises took place at the same time each year and at the same level of involvement.

There were occasionally Training exercise without troops (TEWTS) exercises involving the formation headquarters elements including military police and most importantly the annual corps exercise involving infantry, armour, artillery and all other units.

The main annual 1 BR corps field training exercise which was effectively a war games scenario also took place at the same time each year following the completion of the national and local harvest, mainly sugar beet and corn.

Prior to the main exercise each division, and Brigade would conduct their own training as a warm up for the main show which usually dictated that soldiers would be in the field for about four weeks at a time The really big main war play scenario normally lasting about five days. The Royal Military police role included route signing, traffic control of military convoys and the manning of information (info) posts and traffic posts at key strategic locations along main military routes. It seemed on most occasions that it managed to rain whenever we were to set up location in a forest and for the sun to shine if we were in a built up area.

There is nothing quite like trying to set up location and to camouflage land-rovers, trailers and tents using waterlogged hessian sheets and nets in the pouring rain and whilst dressed in NBC Noddy suits..

In spite of the rain, mud, soaking nets, broken nails and filthy hands and clothes we were generally pleasantly surprised when mealtimes arrived. Army cooks on field exercise always managed to rise to the occasion and produce excellent meals under what might well be described as primitive and challenging conditions.

Sleeping arrangements were always a major challenge, front seats and rear compartments of land-rovers were often the choice however when time allowed and tents were available the universal army camp bed and sleeping bag provided a very satisfactory level of comfort. There were distinct disadvantages to using tents as sleeping accommodation, the main issue was the constant risk of being required to pack up camp and move at very short notice during darkness. Dismantling and packing tents in the dark, often during rain and with a complete black out in force was very challenging and likely to result in either damage or loss of equipment.

Whenever possible the best sleeping arrangements were to be had in barns and outbuildings and in particular where there was a store of hay or straw. Soldiers on field exercise do not expect or receive any guaranteed sleep time and instead have to learn to snatch sleep at every opportunity.

Without any mentoring or guidance I soon learned what became for me the five key components of operational field training.

Assigned task

Maintain weapon

Maintain vehicle

Enjoy every meal opportunity and when every other task or component is completed satisfactorily, Sleep.

In most cases the field training exercises for 12 Brigade would find us deployed with the headquarters and signal squadron, this particularly good for meal times as the squadron adjutant made it his business to chase the cooks and ensure the food was high quality.

News story and social adventures

AN UNUSUAL EVENT TOOK PLACE when one of the few black soldiers in the signal squadron appeared during a stop -over in a rural German village. A fairly large crowd gathered and it was revealed that this was the first black man that the villagers had ever seen, outside of books and movies. The local women and children were totally fascinated and wanted to touch him. The poor unfortunate was bombarded with invitations to virtually every German home and under the guise of fearing for his safety the decision was made by his officers to send him back to barracks in Osnabruck.

One of my black soldier friends from an infantry battalion (1 DWR) took a monthly trip to Denmark to visit his Danish girlfriend. Incredibly he stayed at the parental home and with parental consent shared her bedroom. Never any such providence for me. An event took place around 1975 during my time in Londonderry, a telex message was received from the PM army office confirming that a black soldier had been recruited into the RMP and was currently undergoing training at RMP TC Chichester.

Just a few weeks later he was posted in to Londonderry, history was made.

This was a complete first for RMP and attracted a good deal of publicity. I got to know the NCO very well and it always seemed to me that he felt a bit like an experimental guinea pig. I left Londonderry whilst he was still in post, I have no knowledge of how he fared in his career.

The social adventures in 1966 included my first experience of Amsterdam and the prime example of excessive collective drinking. The Amsterdam trip on this occasion involved the hire of a local regimental (9th/12th Royal Lancers) PRI bus over the May bank holiday period. Practically the entire day prior to our departure was spent in the corporals mess and when we eventually boarded the bus, we were accompanied by several crates of beer, as I recall it was Carlsberg and Becks which were the most popular. On arrival at Amsterdam, after booking into the Youth and Student Hotel Koc we all adjourned to the Amstel Brewery. By some strange arrangement I can also recall that there were a number of Church Army female volunteers serving cheese rolls.

The brewery visit included a tour of the premises and after that it was down to the serious business of excessive and gratuitous drinking. The process involved a group of agile waiters skipping around the huge beer hall in what effectively became a competition, waiters versus drinkers. The entire hall was packed with soldiers from other military units, Dutch, German and British.

I think it safe to conclude that everybody was completely smashed and although it may have started out as a good natured singing contest between the RMP and "others" it inevitably became more offensive and personal. It became something of a battle of wills in deciding who was to leave first. I guess that somebody with a modicum of sense decided that as we were vastly outnumbered we were wise to make the first exit.

Apart from the streets with a girl in every window!!! Amsterdam is not all that interesting, the centre of the city was relatively small, of course there are canals everywhere and plenty of eating and drinking places. I guess that the first day was fairly subdued mainly as a result of the excessive drinking and I can recall that on the following morning we found that our hotel breakfast was seriously short of what had been expected. Most of the group ended up taking a trip on the canal and a meal. I have no idea who may have visited any of the ladies in the windows, it was certainly a very tempting opportunity but not for me!!!

Unlike our modern counterparts and something that appears almost beyond comprehension we carried out our mobile patrols in the most unsuitable vehicles, right hand drive land-rovers fitted with desert tyres, no cab heaters and no radios until early 1968. Drink driving cases under the 1961 RTA legislation were dealt with by the SIB, hard to believe and this was the case until the RSA 67(Alcotest) legislation. This legislation was delayed and only introduced into BAOR in March 1968. Unsurprisingly there were those who wanted to challenge the powers of arrest and the SIB needed time to abdicate the task in favour of uniform. There were a number of briefing sessions held all over Germany and it would come as no surprise that the trainers invited a number of trainees to enjoy a drink at lunchtime to enable a proper test of the alchotest device. The first local client subject to the RSA procedure was a land-rover driver based with the 7 Field ambulance. He was court martialled and received a £50.00 fine.

Whilst on garrison patrol duties we had no radio communication system, no handcuffs or truncheons. Truncheons and handcuffs were safely secured in the duty room clean and polished. As I recall, it required an officers authority to even issue these items and this could not happen without a prior examination of each item and comparison against the entries describing each and every blemish truncheon. I was never issued a truncheon except when assigned pay escort duty but can well recall the process. I was never issued with handcuffs which required a similar examination process. I'm sure that a polished wooden truncheon would have deterred all but the most determined gunman.

There was however always time for sport and in particular the Stanley cup football competition and the cricket Swindon cup. The unit also provided a team to take part in the Nimegen marches but so far as I can recall nothing beyond those. On a less energetic level the corporals mess fielded a successful team in the highly competitive world of darts matches.

The RMP fielded a darts team as part of the Garrison Cpls' s clubs league, there were of course rules and regulations and it was the responsibility of the host team to provide suitable refreshments for the visitors. The RMP always provided a decent buffet sufficient for both home and visiting teams as well as any supporters.

On one occasion I was part of the team away to another corporals club. When our team captain (Brian Jones) asked his opposite number what time would the refreshments be available he was informed that no such arrangements for food had been made.

Brian made it clear that if this was to be the case the host team would forfeit the match and may well be excluded from future fixtures.

The result was that the hosting team captain went to the Junior ranks (private soldiers) bar and bought up every meat pie, sausage roll on sale and left the soldiers with nothing to eat. It was not the type of buffet that we would have wished for but it was desperate measures. The most alarming aspect was that when the soldiers turned up for their pies!!! There were none and I guess that when being told that they had all been sold to the RMP it was all they needed to start a mini riot by shouting, swearing and banging on the walls adjoining the corporals club where we were throwing our darts. We certainly had to be careful when leaving as tempers were very frayed and several soldiers were; or at least it seemed at the time ready to exact some revenge on us for hijacking their food.

Discipline

One aspect of service life that affected not everybody but which would have been noticed by all was the recourse for summary punishment proceedings.

OC's ORDERS!!!!

For a whole range of alleged misdemeanours the RSM would normally and quite properly personally inform the unfortunate that he was on Orders and told the date on which this event was to take place. Orders took place as a consequence of a formal charge produced on a AFB 252 (charge report)

The vast majority of such minor indiscretions would have been the most generic charge, under the provisions of section 69 of the Army Act, "Contrary to good order and military discipline" either committed or omitted something which fitted perfectly into this description.

It was no coincidence that the vast majority of these orders events occurred on an individual's rest day or immediately following a night duty. There was a sound reason for this, the added punishment of effectively losing a rest day as well as the reduced capability for rational and effective resistance after a night without sleep, It was also generally accepted that the out-come of any charge would have already been decided prior to any formal hearing an d the process itself was built around humiliation and threat. One of my friends had been on leave in the United Kingdom and had managed to get himself arrested by the civil police after drinking too much, he was subsequently charged and fined at Magistrates court for being drunk and disorderly. Some weeks later a copy of the court papers arrived in Osnabruck and the NCO was warned for OC's

Orders and charged with having committed a civil offence under section 70 of the Army Act 1955.

When the incumbent CSM for 12 Brigade Pro Unit passed the papers to the officer commanding the outcome of the proceedings had already been written up.

By some means not clear to me, the NCO who was subject to the charge discovered what had happened and disregarding any of the normal service protocols or respect for rank he directly challenged the CSM to continue with the orders hearing. The gauntlet was down and confronted with the discovery of this illegal and immoral action the CSM had really no choice other than to withdraw the charge. I have no idea how the NCO discovered what had been planned or if the Officer commanding had any prior knowledge.

Whatever, I guess that the OC and CSM would have had some post cock up conversation!!

1968 countdown

THE SPRING OF 1968 STARTED much like my three previous German years 1965, 1966 and 1967. The difference was now that I was full corporal with a responsible and fairly comfortable job. I was confident that I was now an experienced and competent Military Policeman and that I enjoyed a reasonable level of respect from my seniors and my junior colleagues. Outside of my daily work and the occasional police duty I had no other responsibilities other than to myself and of course the communal tasks of shared living quarters. I had no debt and I was solvent with enough money to enjoy a fairly modest but comfortable lifestyle. Of course there was something missing from the single soldier's life, young females!! With over three years completed service I was much more self aware, confident and comfortable when out of my familiar surroundings. I had moved away from the routine "bar life" and together with one of my friends we had become much more adventurous in our choice of eating and drinking venues. We were sharp dressers and it was unthinkable that we would go out for the evening without wearing a smart suit, collar and tie. I had been working on my spoken German and was now much better with the routine social engagements in shops and restaurants. Umbrellas had also become a regular accoutrement. Life was good and I was very happy and contented. I had never thought about postings or moving on and at the age of 21 years I was not in the least concerned about marriage or the future.

Events in other sunnier climes would conspire to change my life and in early 1968 volunteers were invited to fill vacancies in the Colony of

Hong Kong at 48 Gurkha Infantry Brigade for a secondment of 9 months in support of the RMP unit and the internal security duties.

My application was entirely impulsive and only generated when I saw a number of other applications submitted by my junior colleagues. My application was granted and I was posted to 48 Brigade Provost Unit via the RMP Training Centre to where I was instructed to report in May 1968.

I guess that for a while I had mixed feelings about the move, I had a number of friends in Osnabruck and I think that with hindsight I was more apprehensive than excited.

There was no shortage of advice about life and work in Hong Kong from NCO's who had been there before.

In any event as for all juniors I was given a decent corporals mess send off and a German Beir Stein as a leaving gift. I have treasured this and kept it safe for the past 50 years.

Eventually I said my farewell and waved my good bye to Osnabruck, I was sad to leave and I can recall saying good bye to the two lady kitchen helps, Irma and Maria who had given me the pet name of "paulchen". Both of them told me that I should stay in Osnabruck and find a nice German Fraulein.

The Orient and life as I was to know it

DURING THE 1960's IN THE British Crown Colony of Hong Kong there was some unrest which was a direct consequence of the major changes taking place in the People's Republic of China and the cultural Revolution.

Hong Kong is actually a group of Islands located in the south China sea, the most important of which is Hong Kong Island (Capital Victoria) and which is the closest to the mainland, Kowloon Peninsula..

The island territory was originally ceded to Great Britain on 29th August 1842 under the provisions of the Treaty of Nanking. The island was selected because of its strategic trade location and its natural deep harbour. On 18th October 1860 the territory of Kowloon as far north as Boundary street was ceded to Great Britain following the convention of Peking. On 1st July 1898 at the second convention of Peking the New Territories including "new Kowloon" was leased to Great Britain for 99 years. The worst event in it's colonial history must be the invasion and occupation of Hong Kong by the Japanese on 23rd December 1941 until 15th August 1945.

In the spring of 1966 the Star Ferry operators applied to the Hong Kong government for permission to increase the Ferry prices, the resulting 25% increase generated unrest and riots. This was not only against the fare increases but also in protest at the unfair treatment of much of the population and the rampant corruption of the police and other officials.

The unrest in Hong Kong and what was probably viewed as a serious risk to British control generated the need for RMP reinforcements and as a result applications were invited to undertake a 9 month emergency tour. Following my successful application or the posting to Hong Kong the tenure was amended from the original nine month emergency tour to a regular thirty months accompanied posting. Naturally as I was not married this made no difference to me in the least but all the same I accepted the offer and in March 1968 I left Osnabruck with the first stop the RMP training centre where I would join up with a group of other NCO's for a short stay in Chichester and some training for our new deployment. I reported to the RMP training centre in April to complete a basic course of internal security, duties, brushing up on our weapons handling and receiving a briefing on Hong Kong, China and the Chinese. The group was a very mixed lot which included a newly promoted sergeant, several senior corporals and a batch of lance corporals. For some of the men this Hong Kong posting was a return to the Far East but for most, like me this was yet another new experience and a journey into the unknown.

I recall that one of the younger, married lance corporals had for some bizarre reason either not been told or had not realised that his posting was accompanied and was under the impression that he had said good bye to his wife for the next 30 months.

Fortunately for him, this was sorted out.

Due to an administrative error during which a number of vaccination certificates had been lost and without which we were not permitted to travel, I was obliged to remain in Chichester with three of my colleagues until the issue was sorted out. As a result our departure for Hong Kong was delayed until the 30th September. Stuck in the RMP training centre for two months with virtually nothing to do all day was not a particularly pleasant summer although with every evening free we at least managed some very pleasant social drinking trips. The boredom was relived somewhat when we volunteered to take up regimental duties at the centre duty room.

Our documents were eventually sorted out and on the afternoon of 29th September we travelled by train to the transit centre at RAF Brize Norton from where we would board the RAF support command VC10 flight to Hong Kong.

Our plane took off at 0700 hours on 30th September and I recall that although it was early autumn it was a rather cold and. I was dressed for the cold climate, cavalry twill trousers, corduroy jacket, heavy leather shoes and collar and tie.

I was never a really keen flier and would normally look forward to a couple of brandies to settle the nerves. Unfortunately RAF flights were 100% "dry" so we had to settle for orange juice or tea.

So far as I can recall our flight took us over the French alps and then what (when looking at any atlas) was a really circuitous route. First stop Akrotiri in Cyprus, refuel and change of crew then straight off to Bahrein. I recall that when we landed at Bahrein the captain warned us as we left the aircraft for a short break that it was very warm outside and he was not kidding. My clothes were totally unsuitable and along with the entire compliment of passengers I made a dash for the airport lounge. It was obvious that our arrival was well announced and that the bar staff were experienced The bar was literally stacked with pints of beer from end to end and this was my first taste of Tiger.

Sadly we were not able to manage too much and just as we were hoping to sink another pint it was time to board the plane for the next stage. The next stop was the tiny island of Gan in the middle of the Indian Ocean. I understand that this was no more than a staging and refuelling post and an unaccompanied 12 months posting. The only social contact for the soldiers based there was the weekly air trooping flight.

After another short break with the aircraft refuelled we set off for the next stage, Singapore.

After a short break in Singapore we again boarded the aircraft, take off was aborted, so far as I can recall at least three times due to a fault with the air-conditioning. As repairs were going to take some time we all adjourned to the transit post restaurant I recall that the meal was rather poor and it was clear that the staff were both unprepared for such a situation and there was no contingency plan in place.

We eventually took off about 8 hours late and it was not until we were airborne that the crew informed us that the in-flight meal had not been loaded because of the mechanical problem with the refrigerator system..

We arrived at Hong Kong Kai-Tak about 1030 pm and eventually located a RMP driver who was clearly pissed off having been required to wait for the late arrival and as a result we boarded the land rover for the journey to Sek Kong in the New Territories. We had not eaten a proper meal since breakfast over 36 hours earlier and we were very hungry and tired.

It was a unhappy introduction to Hong Kong made even worse by the fact the driver who had been well aware, chose to not tell us that the RAF had set up a meal for us at RAF Kai-Tak.

I remember that the sergeant on duty at the RMP unit in Sek Kong appeared totally indifferent to our troubled trip and there were no facilities or refreshments available we couldn't even get a cup of coffee. The unit bar was also closed so we couldn't get a drink of any kind. One of the men on duty offered to take us into the nearest place we could get a drink and perhaps something to eat. Just after midnight we made our very first excursion into the local village of Kam Tin where we managed at least to get a beer and to my great surprise an egg sandwich which was to be a regular life saver in the quaintly named Moonshine bar.

We all fell into our beds around 0200 hrs and in between being eaten by mosquitoes and the unfamiliar warmth of the night we managed some sleep.

I recall being rudely awoken about 0630 and being told to be dressed in OG duty order for 0700 and then being asked the most important question, "what sport do you play? Do you play rugby?

The uniform was a real problem as these had not been tailored as required and as a result me and my fellow new arrivals appeared in front of our new and clearly incensed officer commanding in civilian clothes. I thought at the time that it was a bit rich that we should be receiving a bollocking from our officer for not having our uniform ready whilst he was sitting in civilian shorts and shirt and the fact that the senior NCO in the unit who was a Ssgt, (I never managed to extract an explanation as to why as is the case for Brigade Provost Units there was no WO2 CSM) was also in civilian clothes.

The daily routine for juniors in Sek Kong was so far removed from any organised military regime as to be laughable. Duties were detailed from 0830 till 1800 and the night shift from 1800 until 0830 the following day. The remainder of the juniors were expected to appear at 0700 hrs and work until 1300 hours during summer routine. Volley ball was compulsory between 1300 and 1400. In summer order the dress was PE shorts, boots and PE shirt, patrol duties wore OG shorts and shirts until 1800 hours when OG long trousers were worn.

There was no appreciation of the fact that the service dining room meal time was 1230, just another example of how poorly the juniors were treated.

In reality there was very little to do apart from vehicle cleaning and I struggle to recall what we actually did during the hours we were supposed to be working other than on duty. For some unfathomable reason we were also expected to work on Saturday mornings but without any clear plan or direction as to what we should be doing.

We were to discover that the unit senior NCO spent just about every evening propping up the bars in Kam Tin and slept in his office. Apparently his wife who occupied service married quarters in Sek Kong was under the distinct impression that he was far too busy and important tasks prevented him from going home.

I'm not sure if it was down to indifference or incompetence but there was no instruction or advice given about meals and the resident juniors indicated that they used the local char wallah. Incredible as it seem, some of the men who had been in the unit for the past two years claimed to have never eaten a meal at any army facility and had existed on meals from the char wallah.

Whatever the reason it was clear to me that this was sheer abdication of responsibility and demonstrated the attitude of if "it don't affect me why should I care"

The regular char wallah was a gentleman from what in 1968 was West Pakistan and I was to later learn that as was the case for many Muslims he had several wives who remained in Pakistan. He also admitted to retaining a local Chinese girlfriend although we never saw her and I guess the relationship was covert and discrete. Ben and his father and grandfather had been "camp followers" Char Wallahs with different regiments of the British Army both in Hong Kong and other countries for their entire lives. I have no idea how old Ben might have been, probably over 50 years, he travelled around by bicycle and certainly didn't appear to spend any money so I guess he must have been securing a fortune for his retirement.

Business was always brisk at the char wallahs shed and at times it seemed that it would be impossible for Ben to record details of every sale. Any hope that he might miss something was forlorn as he must have possessed a computer brain and succeeded in recording every single transaction for every single customer on the exact date including precise details of what had been sold.

Apart from the char wallah, there was also brisk business for the dobi (laundry) wallah and the boot boy. The dobi wallah would make your bed, change your sheets and then collect and launder all of your clothing. This was very handy in the summer when OG uniform was worn, shorts during the day and long trousers after 1800 hours.

The boot boy would polish your boots, blanco your belt and shine up the brasses for the belt and RMP brass shoulder titles.

These services were all very helpful and saved a lot of time but they had to be paid for.

It came as no surprise to me that many of the single RMP living in Barracks who had engaged these services during the whole of their tour would be leaving Hong Kong after 30 months, virtually bankrupt. One of the longer serving corporals had apparently been taken ill at some time and it became clear that he had not been eating properly, it wouldn't take a genius to realise that a char wallah diet comprising a mixture of egg and cheese sandwiches was not healthy. I would not wish to appear too critical but the facilities used by the char wallah were not exactly clean and in addition I can never recall ever seeing the char wallah wash his hands or in particular the tomatoes which were a regular ingredient for his sandwiches. I suspect that the metal mugs in which he served the tea, coffee and milo were never properly washed.

I have to say that it took me a couple of days to discover the catering facilities which involved either a short drive or a fifteen minute walk across the

Sek Kong airstrip from Sek kong Camp South to Camp North. The facilities for Military police junior ranks comprised a sectioned off part of the main soldiers dining room of the resident Royal Artillery regiment. The food available at every meal was excellent and most certainly worth the modest effort involved in travel.

Although, as I was later to discover a substantial number of soldiers from the Regiment would find themselves arrested by RMP there was a total lack of any animosity or bad feeling by the soldiers towards us. It seemed to me that for many of the young soldiers the more times they were arrested the more their street credibility increased. One significant difference for the soldiers in the North Camp was the fact that their accommodation was better than that for the RMP and in addition they were close to a range of facilities, gymnasium, medical, NAAFI and other shops.

The facilities for single military police in Sek Kong was nothing short of miserable, there were no proper toilets or shower facilities, the accommodation was plagued with mosquitoes and even the electricity supply was barely sufficient to drive the single ceiling fan in each shared barrack room.

Following the rather insensitive, negative and unjustly critical initial interview with our Officer commanding officer and the belated preparation of our OG (olive green) uniforms we were ready to take on our garrison and internal security duties. By the time of our arrival in the colony in October 1968 the internal security situation was all but over although as we were to discover there were still some criminal elements active and as a consequence there were some duties still in place to counter any potential terrorist threat.

Normal garrison duties were in effect not quite normal, there was very little to do. Apart from the odd traffic accident, we were to undertake the rather archaic task of static speed checks which tended to last most of the day on well used routes..

One of the senior corporals who I must say was not renowned for his friendly approach was employed as unit store man from whom we would collect whatever equipment we needed. Field telephones, stop watches, ready reckoner and reels of D10 cable. I remember that we would take this cable out on each occasion and simply leave it in situ when we packed up.

It came as a bit of a surprise when we were told that the cable had to be recovered as it was effectively an accountable item and we then spent about a whole week searching the speed check areas salvaging some cable and then trying to rejoin it to fill the cable reels.

Drink driving cases were rare and involved the old RTA 61 procedure; RTA 67 had not migrated to the colony. Any more serious offences such as assault were usually hijacked by the small SIB detachment, I recall that this was a single SIB Ssgt and an attached uniformed junior NCO.

The duty desk NCO was based at the RMP duty room located at the entrance to the Brigade headquarters (Sek Kong Camp North) and the joint Army and Royal Hong Kong Police (POLMIL) control room. The officer commanding, the unit staff sergeant and the orderly room and chief clerk were based at Sek Kong South.

Apart from the normal task of maintaining the RMP daily occurrence book the RMP duty NCO was responsible for security access to the head-quarters. Strange as it may seem the duty NCO was expected to remain stand-ing outside the main entrance during the morning "rush hour" and check the identity of everybody wanting to enter.

This arrangement failed to provide any suggestion as to how the same NCO was supposed to answer the telephone or carry out any other duties.

For soldiers in the New territories there was essentially only one social activity and that was drinking. Although there were on base barracks bars and clubs including the RMP all ranks bar there were a number of other places frequented by soldiers. The nearest was in the village of Kam Tin where there were to the best of my knowledge about six bar, restaurants, I can recall, the Ying Wah, The Kwon Yick and the Moonshine which was the most popular amongst the soldiers.

In addition to Kam Tin there were two more bars located at Pat Heung close to the local Police Station. The owner of these two bars liked to be known as "Taffy" although he never quite managed to explain just how this name originated.

Taffy was clearly a very wealthy man and often worked in the bar himself, he had a number of other business interests; the most lucrative was his tropical fish breeding farms. Most of the young fish were exported by air to Japan and the USA in sealed plastic containers. Taffy made no secret of his particular dislike of the Japanese and this was based on his experience and harsh treatment at the hands of the Japanese during their occupation of Hong Kong.

Despite this dislike Taffy was quite happy to sell his fish to the Japanese but he made sure they paid the top price, after all business is business.

About fifteen miles from Sek Kong was the large town of Fan Ling. There were a number of Bar restaurants, the Roxy, The Fanling Restaurant and at the local railway station the Better Ole. The Better Ole was the most popular and probably closest to a family facility. The Fanling Restaurant was one of the few places declared as "out of bounds" to all soldiers. Although the reason for this was probably the hostility of the staff and their unwillingness to co-operate with the authorities the place was also very dirty and a definite health hazard. The rather bizarre and colloquial sign as I recall "Fanling good eats" should have been more than enough to put anybody off!!

Although the Fanling bars were popular with the RMP it was only the Better Ole that was used to any great level by other soldiers.

A particular feature of the Better Ole was the huge collection, literally hundreds of British Army cap badges mounted behind the bar. Many of the badges would have been from Regiments long disbanded. The Better Ole was opened in 1947 by a retired British Army Sergeant Major but was eventually closed down in 2007 to make way for redevelopment of what was certainly a prime location.

All bars in the new Territories closed at 0200 and for reasons which I could never really fathom the RMP mobile patrols were instructed by the RMP Ssgt to visit each and every bar at least once before midnight and once between midnight and closing time. Due primarily to access and geography it was the generally accepted arrangement that the mobile patrol would arrive at Kamtin around closing time. This was due to the fact that this town had the largest number of bars and was closest to the main concentration of British soldiers from Sek kong camp. Drinking and drunkenness are part of the soldiers social life and it was normally the case that one or two soldiers would find themselves under arrest and taken back to barracks and the guardroom.

Apart from drinking there were occasions when soldiers would find themselves in conflict with some of the local youths. Chinese have a tendency to socialise and act in large groups and to arm themselves with bamboo canes and as a result they acquired the colloquial name of "Bamboo Boys". On one particular occasion a group of these boys almost certainly from outside Kam Tin attacked a smaller group of soldiers but picked the wrong time as the RMP patrol including Terry "Sumo" Capeling appeared on the scene. Although the RMP patrol was unarmed and seriously outnumbered the "bad boys" had really picked the wrong time and place. Terry was a very big man, agile and fearless and it was a very short encounter that saw the boys leave in a great hurry and wishing almost certainly that they had not turned up.

For those people who have never been to the Far East there are some practises that may be hard to accept and believe. Chinese farmers and small holders would normally grow two crops on the same land and at the same time, this intensive use of land requires some substantial introduction of nutrients. The rural Chinese collect human excrement and store this in large storage pots in the corner of their fields, this is used mixed with rain water to fertilise the crops. Such practise certainly demands that All fresh vegetables are washed thoroughly in clean running water unless you want to acquire some serious and horrible illness.

On one warm summer night a young soldier who had drunk a little too much and had spotted a rather attractive young lady some hours earlier had decided to make an uninvited visit to her home. In his inebriated state he stumbled towards the shack in the fields and instead of finding her he was confronted with her parents who promptly set about him with sticks and then joined by a posse of neighbours let loose the dogs.

In what was certainly a blind and drunken panic the soldier set off across the fields and having already been bitten several times plunged headfirst into one of these open cesspits.

Having been alerted to his predicament we eventually located him stumbling along the Kam Tin road towards Sek Kong camp. There was no way he was getting into the RMP land rover and instead he was gently directed by the front of the land rover towards the camp guardroom.

The guard commander was also reluctant to let him into the guardroom and so he was then taken to the vehicle wash point stripped naked and then hosed down. After finding some clean clothes for him the duty medical officer attended and injected him with about a pint of penicillin. He spent the remainder of the night in the guardroom and in view of the fact that no formal complaint was ever received, no further action was taken, he had probably been punished enough.

There were two duties which continued as a legacy of the terrorism which had threatened Hong Kong in 1966 and 1967, these were OP Teaming and the VPP Village penetration patrols. The OP teaming was an armed duty and comprised two double crewed land-rovers. The duty involved a fairly early start around 0800 with a drive to the wharf at Gin Drinkers Bay on the outskirts of Kowloon. We would have to await the arrival of a police launch from stonecutters island which would deliver a consignment of explosives to be used around the construction sites in Kowloon and the New Territories. There was usually time for a Chinese style fantastic egg sandwich and a cup of real coffee. We would later liaise with a truck load of Hong Kong Police and Civil Aid Service, we would then escort them to the building sites where we would leave two RHKP and two CAS. Although we would have been provided with haversack rations before we left Sek Kong these would have long been consigned to the bin and we would always stop off some place for lunch. The most favourite location was the "Shatin Roadhouse" during my time in Hong Kong, Shatin was an insignificant and tiny fishing village and not the sprawling town that it is now.

The roadhouse was simply a wooden hut in the middle of nowhere but it produced the best simple fried rice and bottle of san Miguel beer for about two Hong Kong dollars. These duties were both popular and enjoyable, it was not hard work we got to see a good deal of construction developments in the new territories and Kowloon and it was a good day out. Of course we were well armed and our land-rovers were fitted with C13 HF combat radio although I certainly can't recall if we ever managed to either successfully send or receive any message.

Village penetration patrols (VPP) were a lot more ambitious. Generally the patrols involved at least four RMP and a similar number of Hong Kong Police. On most occasions we were accompanied by a locally enlisted Hong Kong Chinese medic.

These patrols went into the most rural and remote areas of the New Territories, close to the Border with the Peoples Republic of China. Although the patrols were conducted on foot and involved walking some substantial distances there were occasions when we taken to the start point by helicopter or hover craft. Most of the patrols lasted about four or five days and every man had to carry his own personal gear including food and water for the duration. We were also well armed and between us we carried a A13 man pack radio with spare batteries. Some patrols lasted more than a week and some over much greater distances, on some occasions we were supported by the 414 pack transport section, in 1968 this was the last remaining mule transport section in the British Army.

These patrols were very testing, there were a lot of very steep hills and rough ground to negotiate, during the cooler months of the year between December and March it was hard going but during the other months when it was much hotter and the humidity much higher it was bloody hard work. The main objective of the patrols was to improve and develop positive relations with the Chinese rural community close to the Border with the Peoples republic of china. Whatever our intentions we were not welcome in every village and we relied entirely on the Hong Kong police intelligence and advice as to which route we should take and most importantly which village we should select for our overnight stops. Unlike the military, the Hong Kong police seemed to travel very light and to the best of my recollection they did not ever carry any sleeping bag. They obviously managed to find some suitable accommodation with Chinese families.

Some of the villages and communities were downright hostile whilst others were incredibly hospitable and friendly. Unlike the modern areas of Kowloon, Hong Kong and the towns of the new territories, these remote villages were only just beginning to receive the basic utilities services such as running water and electricity. In the centre of the villages where supplies were connected there was generally a single water stand pipe and electricity connected with a central point where there was often a communal television set.

I can recall on one occasion in a particularly friendly village we were invited to share the communal evening dinner which was to be prepared and served at the village leaders home. We all contributed a small donation I think about $5.00 dollars and around 6pm and despite our total lack of knowledge of any Chinese culinary or social skills we all sat down to enjoy the meal. To the best of my recollection the food was served from some huge metal pots, the rice was easily identified but everything else, the meat and vegetables were a complete mystery. I remember that during my very early days in Hong Kong I thought that everything I ate including in the Army dining facility tasted strange and mostly very sweet. By the time of this patrol meal I think that my stomach had got used to the change in diet and felt able to manage the occasion. I recall a huge metal pot containing a combination of what looked like soup and stew but which was actually a number of duck portions floating around.

In between the food there was an ample supply of Chinese green tea and beer, mostly bottles of San Miguel brewed in Hong Kong and a the imported very cheap Chinese brew.

A more deadly brew on offer was rice wine, this potion slides down very well but too much can guarantee a most unwelcome hangover. With the prospect of a long walk carrying our kit the following morning in very hot weather I remember clearly sticking to Chinese tea and a couple of small bottles of San Miguel. After that I took myself off to the village school where we were sleeping that night and tucked myself up in bed.

The following morning, poor "Paddy" who had not only demonstrated how much beer he could drink in a single session had also over imbibed on the rice wine whilst trying to learn the rudiments of maj- jong.

I recall that he was so poorly and hung over that there was some consideration as to whether he could continue. A compromise solution was agreed and he struggled along with a stick and we shared out his kit amongst us until the evening and next overnight stop. I don't think that Paddy was ever quite the same again as regards his views on Village penetration patrols, drinking and walking in hot weather.

In the 1960's when visiting these remote areas there were some quite startling observations as regards the population. There were simply no juveniles, young adults or young parents. Apart from the rare exception and in such cases the very hostile villages where we were not welcome, the villages contained only small children and old people. In short, grandchildren and grandparents. Where was everybody else? they were all working in the towns and cities, Yuen Long, Kowloon and Hong Kong Island.

Most of the villages had no road access and as a result everything had to be carried in by hand. This was no mean feat and it was extraordinary to see the men and women carrying goods up some very steep hills in two baskets suspended on a wooden pole.

Having arrived in Hong Kong in early October when the weather was still very hot, at least to us it was very exhausting and it was only in the cool of late evening that we felt comfortable. Early morning and early evening getting ready for work stepping into the starched OG uniform which was suddenly soaked with sweat. I suppose that it took until late November by which time we had become acclimatised and also the weather was not so hot and the humidity much reduced.

We had become accustomed to the working conditions, sorted out the catering and dining facilities and life was much more comfortable.

Christmas 1968 approached and we had ventured far from the isolation of Sek- Kong, I remember my first trip by bus, the Kowloon Motor Bus route 26 which I was later to identify as the Yuen Long express.

These ancient machines were built by the Albian coach company in great Britain and sold to Hong Kong after a lifetime of service. They started the journey every hour from Yuen Long via Kowloon eventually arriving at Jordan Road Vehicular cross harbour ferry terminal.

These single deck buses carried as I recall about 45 seated passengers and about 30 standing. The seats were hard plastic, there were no doors but a sliding bar operated by the conductor. On most occasions the bus was filled to capacity and rarely complied with the stated passenger limits. The bus was normally driven furiously and when it was loaded, as it normally was; well in excess of any safe capacity it was a real struggle to reach the top of the mountain road, route twisk.

It seemed to me that once he had reached the top and then cruised the short level section; the driver would turn around and face his passengers then start the descent.

Incredibly the drivers often put the transmission into neutral and the bus would be coasting down the mountain road with virtually no real control.

My first trip on this bus was a bit of a surprise and it required in my view a superhuman effort by the driver to keep the bus on the road as it hurtled down and swung violently from side to side. The other passengers were clearly unaffected by the experience and I guess totally oblivious to their risky situation.

My next trip left me more concerned, I now knew what to expect. Although I was to use this same route on many occasions I never lost sight of just how potentially dangerous it was.

A few months after I arrived in Hong Kong an old friend from the training centre and Osnabruck; John Jinx was posted into Hong Kong Island. John kindly organised a room for me at the RMP accommodation in Victoria Barracks on Hong Kong Island.

I used this opportunity to explore the island which was more like central London than the rural isolation of Sek Kong. I recall the joy of not needing to sleep under a mosquito net for the first time since arriving in the Colony without being buzzed and bitten all night.

Back in Sek Kong I was sharing a room with a good friend Mick, our friendship was sorely tested because he was unbelievably untidy and disorganised. He would leave his stuff lying around all over the room and seemed oblivious to my annoyance. It got to the stage where I could simply not cope any longer and whilst he was out for the day I lifted his bed and locker out of the room and left it on the outside veranda.

It was a waste of time really because he seemed unperturbed and just went straight to bed when he returned

As Christmas approached it seemed so strange, particularly after 4 years in Germany that there was a total absence of any form of pending celebration within the local community. Within the armed forces and the police organisation this was however not the case and celebrations proceeded. On a local immediate level the RMP hosted a small lunchtime reception in the all ranks bar for the bar owners, police officers and civilian partners, dobi wallah, char wallah and the extra ordinary "sweeper.

I recall particularly that Ben Razac our indomitable char wallah arrived and out of respect for his religion I offered him the choice of any soft drink.

Ben replied that he would like a brandy, when I questioned this he replied that," at Christmas I am a Christian" Seemed to me that a Brandy was the right drink.

A few days later I was invited to Pat Huen Police station for a lunchtime "cocktail party" I recall that there was a great deal of alcoholic drink and mountains of food and although I had already eaten and drunk far too much I rather foolishly accepted a second invitation to Yuen Long divisional police station. When I arrived I was asked to assist one of the local bar owners, clearly a man of considerable wealth and influence to prepare the celebratory Christmas punch. After some research and debate we concluded that the bath was the only receptacle large enough to accommodate a case of just about every type of spirit available. I reckon that we emptied a case of everything and then topped it up with orange juice.

When Christmas arrived I was simply astonished that the local population were not in the least bit interested and it was normal routine.

Life progressed, duties continued and we changed from summer uniform olive green to the temperate climate no 2 dress. Just before the change I had checked my uniform and found that it was covered in mildew. I took it to the dobi wallah and asked if the uniform could be dry cleaned. I was told that it could be and I handed it over.

Fifteen minutes later no 2 dress tunic and trousers were drying on the line.

The remainder of 1968 passed without any significant event affecting me although there were some significant staff changes. The officer commanding Major Stan Edwards left and was replaced by captain Timothy (Paddy) Obrien.

Staff sergeant Fred Gunner was involved in a fatal traffic accident when his car struck a local Chinese cyclist. Fred was cleared of any blame for this apparently due to the fact that the cyclist had no lights.

Despite the fact that Fred was exonerated! The command message was that the local village of Kamtin was to be off limits to soldiers on recreation until the dust had settled. I suspect that some form of compensation was provided but of course that was well outside of my remit.

The new year 1969 arrived and as we approached the Chinese new year I met the lady I was later to marry in 1970. I had never considered myself the marrying type but views and attitudes clearly change.

In addition to the rather boring and routine duties and the relatively exciting adventures on Village penetration patrols we found time to provide mobile escorts to the squadron of archaic and semi obsolete tanks which were stored at Sek Kong camp. Once a year a party of soldiers would fly out from the UK to drive the tanks and carry out some test firing of their guns at a military range in the new territories. It would have been clear to anybody that these machines did not present a real threat to the people's republic or present any significant defence. They would certainly never have been able to stop any determined invasion. Apart from a small symbolic gesture this was in reality a swan and a trip out to Hong Kong for a selected group of officers and soldiers. I recall the group including HRH the duke of Kent and the explicit instruction to the RMP that under no circumstances were we to stop any of his party of officers whilst they were driving military land rovers regardless of whatever sort of uniform or mixed dress they were wearing.

We also managed to get down to the 25 metre firing ranges to practise our pistol and Sub machine gun skills and we were to learn a new skill and rather devious method of collecting spent cartridges and other shrapnel. The idea was to leave the ranges and to wait an hour or so whilst some of the local kids would descend on the ranges and dig out the scrap, we would then sort of ambush them and confiscate their hard work.

Not a very honourable or welcome outcome for the kids but it saved us a great deal of work.

Prior to the handover from the old to the new officer commanding I received my first annual confidential report as a full corporal. I had worked as hard as any other junior, had never been late or absent, learned a great deal about the history of Hong Kong, kept fit and was always immaculately dressed yet the report described me as immature and lacking knowledge. That's the price for not playing rugby, football or cricket and for not propping up the bar with the in crowd and the "Boss" and for missing lunchtime volleyball in favour of lunch

Such negative reports demonstrate the failing of a system which relies heavily on personal relationships, I had only actually met the Officer commanding on one occasion. during my original induction interview, other times I may have given him a lift from his home to work.

The only other source of information would have been Fred the unit Staff sergeant and I had never given him the slightest reason to report badly on me. Overall a load of absolute rubbish.

There had been some debate regarding the single men living in Barracks and the need to have some idea of their whereabouts when they were off camp. As a result a book was left in the corporals mess and those booking out were required to enter their name and details of their destination. Although it never really bothered me in the slightest it might have appeared to be a bit unfair that married men had no such obligation.

For some reason an anonymous entry was made which I recall was a reference to the stores NCO George (Geordie) Cartwright. The entry was simple and straightforward.

"Cartwright is a c...t! Not very nice not particularly professional but very childish and immature.

I had no idea who was responsible although Ssgt Fred Gunner made it clear that he would make every effort to identify the offender/s.

A few days later I saw that one of the juniors NCO's had sustained substantial injuries to his face which he claimed he had sustained when he had fallen over. It would have been clear that he had been assaulted. The truth was that the two brave souls who had been responsible for the offensive entry in the booking out register had been rumbled and they had concluded that the individual with injuries had reported them. Only they and the injured man will ever know the truth.

A short distance from the RMP unit there was a village school that had a small sports-field and where a group of rather mischievous and probably communist supporters were regularly parking their vans and lorries. This anti -social activity was damaging the field surface and preventing the school children from enjoying this very basic facility. A deal was agreed between the school head-teacher and the RMP and as a result the school purchased a stack of wooden fencing and the RMP juniors carried out the hard work construction, digging the holes, locating the posts and erecting the fence which effectively prevented the vehicles from parking on the field.

This was a job very well done, it was summer and very hot, .there was a lot of sweat but it was all given for the very best of reasons.

Our new officer commanding had settled in and made his mark, we were to discard our lightweight khaki SD caps and in their place to wear the "proper" uniform forage cap. For reasons that were totally unknown the officer commanding decided that the bushes and trees surrounding the unit volley ball pitch and which provided privacy from the outside world! Had to be pulled up and dumped. The OC also decided that this activity provided the perfect opportunity for his lecture on time and motion.

Duties took on a new slant and duty parades became the normal routine as well as freshly spray painted land rovers thanks to the arrival of a new sergeant whose only object in life was to oversee the unit transport despite the fact that it had managed quite well without him for many years.

I managed to keep up my squash playing but this had to be in the evenings because it was simply too hot during the day.

A regular physical training expedition was to climb the mountain close to Sek -Kong camp " Although I have no real idea how it came about the mountain was identified as "Nameless"" this was a hard climb to the summit but well worth the effort, sadly there was not much of a view from the top because of the local smog and low cloud.

This mountain was also the site of the Gurkha annual Khud (Sharp rock) race.

These sturdy soldiers were really custom built for this competition and although when British teams entered and on occasion managed to beat the Gurkhas to the top, the descent was a different matter.

Hong Kong was my first experience of meeting and working with the Gurkhas, I discovered that they are particularly "tribal" and the families stick together. In addition the tribal caste system meant that regardless of military rank homage was paid to higher caste junior soldiers. They are incredibly proud and tough but equally stubborn and on the occasions when we may have had reason to "discipline" them they would be very unhelpful.

I can recall on one occasion whilst on a joint training exercise with the Gurkha soldiers they handed round their "spare" water bottles filled with rum, they could be very generous but unlike British soldiers who would eat anything on offer, they were really quite dependent on their staple diet of rice and ghee. The Gurkha culture does not recognise the need to thank anybody for providing a drink or food and instead expects that if you have something that they need and you share, that's is the thing to do and why should you be thanked.

On another occasion I attended an incident following a fight between a number of soldiers. One of them had sustained a serious laceration to his face and scalp inflicted by the use of a broken glass. Despite his protests he was taken to the nearest medical centre and the medical officer made it clear that he would need several stitches to seal the wound. He was told that he would need a local anaesthetic as the stitching process would be very painful and take at least an hour.

The soldier was reluctant to accept the treatment until the arrival of a senior Gurkha NCO, he then agreed but refused the anaesthetic as there was no way that he intended to lose face or appear weak. I was only watching but I could feel the pain and it did indeed take over an hour. Once the treatment was over, he agreed to an anti-tetanus injection he was taken back to Barracks but refused to provide any details of his assailant which would also perhaps have been an admission of weakness.

On a personal side I had decided that I wanted a motor car and began looking for the model that I had wanted since it first appeared several years ago, the Austin Healey 3000. After several expeditions around the new territories I was rewarded with a call from the owner of the Artland Motors garage in Yuen Long. I took myself off to the location and gazed on this beautiful motor car a metallic blue MK 2 soft top with stunning silver wire wheels. I managed to get the keys and take the car for a test drive.

This was like nothing I had ever experienced, I recall the power and acceleration and the sheer joy. Sadly as I was later to discover was a common fault, the radiator and cooling system was malfunctioning and after about twenty minutes driving the inside of the car was so hot as to be unbearable. I took the car back and tried to haggle a price taking into account the repairs that were needed. After a two week delay I returned to the garage eagerly expecting the car to be repaired and ready only to find that it had been sold to another dealer for spares as the items needed could not be obtained. There was nothing I could do about this and eventually left the garage in possession of a large Austin saloon with a front bench seat and column mounted transmission. I kept this motor for a few months and then traded it in for a Black MG Magnette which I kept until I got married, when I needed every dollar I could lay my hands on.

In early 1969 I developed an acute dose of tonsillitis, not particularly risky in a temperate climate but in Hong Kong there were some pretty virulent strains and as a consequence I was admitted to the local Sek Kong MRS (Medical Reception Station).

This was not a bad experience apart from the daily routine of intra muscular penicillin injections into my backside. After a week or so I was free and returned to normal life.

Around the same time one of our colleagues (Don Stead) became unwell and was eventually admitted first to the MRS and later to BMH (British Military Hospital) Hong Kong. Don was a very strong strapping 6 foot tall man of substantial build but within a few weeks he had lost so much weight that he was almost skeletal.

Our officer commanding (quite rightly) arranged that a RMP patrol was to visit Don each day hoping to cheer him up and contribute to his recovery. Whatever the cause of his illness I think was never really identified, he never fully recovered at the hospital but after several months he was assessed as being well enough to be evacuated to the UK and to a hospital that would be better placed to oversee his recovery.

I had already found my way to what was probably one of the best tailors in the colony, Ah Lee in Sek Kong. The only problem with this tailor was that the quality of his clothes was so good and he was so popular that he was constantly playing catch up with orders and customers including me had to wait for such a long time. My first order was for a super lightweight double breasted pin stripe suit. This must be the best made suit I have ever owned.

I had also discovered a factory fabric outlet and a superb shirt maker in the local town of Sheung Shui where I had a number of shirts made to my own designs.

In side Sek- Kong camp there was another business, Leong Sum Lucky Tailor who held the lucrative army tailoring contract. She was also a good shoemaker. I had a couple of pairs of soft black leather boots made to measure, incredibly comfortable.

Later the same year the military authorities planned a Military Tattoo to take place inside a temporary stadium to be constructed at the end of the Sek Kong airfield. As part of the promotion of this event two RMP NCO's were dispatched to a patch in Kowloon near to the cross harbour ferry terminal to sell tickets. My first reaction was that this was a complete waste of time and that nobody would be in the slightest bit interested. I had to eat my words and I was most surprised that we literally sold out every ticket that we had taken.

The event went ahead and as I recall the first show was on the Thursday with specially invited guests and free places for underprivileged and needy children.

By all accounts the opening night was a huge success and the first all paying show started on Friday. Unlike the western world, Hong Kong and other Asian countries make great use of Bamboo in construction and in this case the seating was affixed to a bamboo frame. Shortly after the opening whilst spectators were making their way into the arena, part of the seating collapsed. This unplanned and unwelcome event was being photographed by the local press. It would have been certain that not all of the reporters and photographers were pro British and may have been able to present a negative and unfavourable account. Whatever the reason, the order was given to eject the press from the stadium and we set about this task with some enthusiasm. Unfortunately some of the RMP got a bit carried away and in addition to ejecting the press took it upon themselves to sieze the press cameras and remove the film.

Whilst the RMP were ejecting the press a platoon of Gurkha soldiers were sent in to chop up the collapsed in order to release any trapped spectators.

Once the emergency which was restricted to a small section of seating was over the show went on and was very successful that evening and on the successive days.

The following morning the local press presented their account of the unnecessary and disproportionate actions of the RMP and a number of complaints were issued.

There had to be an RMP scalp and brave Gerard Egan put his hands up.

I guess that the whole matter could have been toughed out as there were no clear photographs of any individual that could be identified.

Gerry was eventually summoned to the office of the Brigade Major and probably received some words of advice. It was clear that instructions had been given and the actions simply misinterpreted. The matter was then closed.

The obsolete battle tanks held in reserve were stored at the REME workshops in Sek Kong camp. As is the case for all military barracks there was an armed sentry guard deployed for security. One evening the soldiers were amazed to see a number of young men in civilian clothing who must have gained entry to the barracks by climbing the perimeter fence. The sentry was even more amazed when one of the stored tanks started up and was then driven around the barracks. The men ignored the sentry challenge and after the entire guard was summoned the RMP were called to the scene.

Eventually the four young men presented themselves, apparently none the worst for wear but under the impression that the whole escapade was a huge joke. The four young men were identified as junior army officers (lieutenants) and the duty field officer was called out. All four were taken to the officers mess and confined to their rooms. Following a short investigation by the RMP all four found themselves in front of the Brigade major and the commanders chief of staff.

So far as we were able to determine the Brigade commander was initially minded to send all four officers back to the UK in disgrace but was eventually persuaded to allow the chief of staff to deal. My understanding was that for at least the next six months the officers would have had very little free time and found themselves covering the duty officer rota on their own as well as having to make a substantial donation to mess funds.

Moving onto 1969 I became more detached from the RMP single social arena and spent much more time with my future wife and her family. I learned a great deal of the history of Hong Kong and china as well as the complexity of the Chinese people and their diverse cultures.

The biggest change, challenge and self destruct

I HAVE TO MAKE MENTION of one NCO in particular who was employed as chief clerk.

Terry Scrivens who was later commissioned and rose to the rank of Lt Col.

Terry was a totally dedicated, highly motivated and very efficient man. He was also an excellent sportsman and always impeccably dressed. When the newly appointed Officer commanding decided that as part of our FFR (fitness for role) inspection we should demonstrate our foot drill and marching skill there was no question as to who should take the lead on preparing us and once again Terry demonstrated another skill as a first class drill instructor. Every thing that this man did was to the highest level and standard, there was no other way.

One of the administrative matters he put in place for me shortly before he left was my notice and application for marriage.

I had not anticipated any serious issues arising from this as regards security clearance but before my officer commanding discussed this with me I was ordered to his office in respect of my extension to my terms of engagement. I had originally enlisted for six years but understood (correctly) that unless notice was given to execute the terms it was automatically renewed for at least another three years.

The OC told me that he was of the view that I was not suitable for continued service and then presented me with my annual confidential report, this was not good and I realised that my marriage application was at risk. Naturally I asked him what made him form the view that I was unsuitable. It was of course quite easy to use the old favourites, poor turnout, lack of interest, no team spirit and no ambition.

It was quite extraordinary that he should see fit to completely alter the rules to suit his own personal views and then to concoct such a lurid explanation for his views. There could be no reason other than he objected to my pending marriage. After some debate he agreed to my continuing service but I knew that I was a marked man.

My next step was to visit the brigade warrant officer chief clerk and I asked him if I could be pushed off to another location such as Singapore because of my marriage application and what I perceived as a potential objection from my OC.

The good news was that in my case as a full rank substantive corporal, over 21 years and exemplary service record I could not be moved without substantial cause.

My initial concerns were well founded and just a few weeks later I was again ordered to attend when my officer commanding wanted to discuss my marriage application.

Although I did not record verbatim what was said it went something close to the following.

" I have your application for marriage, my experience is that these marriages do not work and never last. I intend to post you to Singapore for six months as soon as this can be arranged" There was no debate, consultation or words of advice just a simple autocratic bullying statement of intention.

I have no idea what if any response from me was expected but I was confident and sure of my rights. I explained respectfully and politely that I had already sought formal advice from the Brigade chief clerk which would most certainly be held on record. In this case I am informed that you are not allowed to post me without reference to Far East Land Forces commander and without exceptional cause.

He would certainly not have been pleased with my response and he may have considered that I was wrong but he did not show any reaction. He simply told me to leave his office. I fully expected to be served with a formal written posting order within a few days as I knew that Paddy was not the man to be cheated of his aims and intentions.

I guess that I knew then that I was a double marked man and he would want to have the last word at some time. I didn't have long to wait.

In January 1970 the unit was involved in a small internal security exercise, as I recall all time off was cancelled. I struggle to accept that the officer commanding was involved in the preparation of the duty rota but it seemed to me that it was hardly fairly organised, to the best of my recollection I was swapped from one duty role to another during a 36 hours period and do not remember ever having any proper rest or meal break. At some time I was sent to Sek Kong camp south and the RMP unit lines.

I was almost certainly totally exhausted by this time and I can hardly remember any details. What is clear that I must have sat down and simply fallen asleep.

It is a strange coincidence that the officer commanding chose to visit the duty room at this time and dispatched a patrol with a sergeant to check upon me. The OC must have been overjoyed, I was charged with sleeping on duty and to make things even worse he decided that he could not potentially punish me enough so referred the matter to his local immediate superior the Major DAQ at Brigade Headquarters.

I appeared about a month before I was to be married and the fact that I had been on duty for virtually 36 hours without a break was not considered worthy of any mitigation. I was minded to elect for Court Martial but basically just gave up and took the £25.00 fine. I suspect that my OC was quietly pleased and I'm sure he would have liked to get rid of me.

He would I'm sure have been content to some degree that he had hit me where it hurt, in the pocket.

Over the next few weeks or so there were a number of new arrivals including two new staff sergeants. This was to accommodate the changes introduced by the introduction of the RMP Platoon system. Our former resident staff sergeant had also left but before he did so he had found himself in a serious cash flow predicament. The main consequence of this was that he had to sell what was probably one of his most cherished possessions; his stamp collection for the princely sum of £75.00. He may have needed this to pay off the char wallah or the tailor I have no idea!

Another much more distressing incident involved one of the junior NCO's who was planning to marry a local girl. Although I am not aware of the precise details I do know however that for some reason the young ladies actual age had been in dispute and although arrangements were well advanced we were only alerted to a serious situation when the Hong Kong Police arrived on the scene in the RMP unit location.

At that time parental consent was required for females under 21 years of age wishing to marry. This consent had not been given and the marriage was effectively abandoned. Although the official legal reason was the lack of parental consent there may some mileage in the claims that the prospective groom (as is the normal Chinese custom) had refused to pay a sum of money (a dowry) to the family of the bride. Such claims would not have been really appreciated by the Groom or anybody else other than the Chinese and was not quite so straightforward as it might have seemed.

Tradition to the Chinese is all important and some proper research by the groom may well have prevented such a serious mishap.

To all Asians and in particular the Chinese, face is all important; in the case of a traditional Chinese marriage there is a considerable cost and even if the marriage is a simple legal registry procedure there are certain matters which can't be overlooked.

Every Chinese bride has to present some image of actual wealth and in tangible and visual terms this generally includes the wearing of gold jewellery, wrist bangles, rings and necklaces. Without these items worn and seen the family and the bride will lose face and this is simply not acceptable. I suspect that it was this failure to understand and to take the necessary steps to meet such requirements that caused the parents to withhold their consent.

In any event the marriage did not take place and Jock (the prospective groom) returned to the UK alone. I have no idea if he or his former Chinese girlfriend ever established contact after his departure.

The two new staff sergeants got on with their jobs although I struggled to see what these might involve or what they actually were. One of them (butch) as I recall was assigned the primary task of overseeing unit administration such as the orderly room and any police work admin, such as it was even though there was already a sergeant chief clerk and a corporal taking care of the other work. The second staff sergeant John was a different person altogether, he not only joined the night duty patrols but he also set out to provide substantial training based on his former experience and the skills acquired from his service with SAS.

Ssgt John set up a substantial training programme based on the Duke of Edinburgh Award scheme for local schoolchildren and rapidly developed a very positive reputation for himself, the RMP and the Army in general.

In late 1970 John organised a unit training scheme to lantau Island. This training expedition started with a trip on a military LCT (Landing Crafty Tanks) and we were then deposited on the Island in pairs, my partner was Brian Caulfield.

We had to carry every single item needed for the week and the normal routine was for John to provide a map reference for a location where we were required to RV with him. Lantau Island was in 1970 largely uninhabited, there were the ruins of some pirate settlements, a few small fishing villages, at least one monastery and a number of drug rehabilitation sites and farming facilities sponsored by the Kadoori agricultural aid society.

The week was hard walking and some rough sleeping in the open air, the weather was fine and although as I recall it was quite warm probably around 18/20c it was not as hot or as humid as it would have been during the summer months.

John was certainly a professional soldier and with extensive navigational skills. One object of the weeks training was to arrive at the next assigned location before him, even though he never set off until we had all left our overnight location he always managed to get to the next stop first. There were some strict rules in place during the training week and the most important to John was the fact that when we left any location we were to ensure that no signs of us having stayed there were evident.

I personally found this an exceptionally sound instruction. It was certainly good military practise by disguising and evidence of our presence and also it demonstrated both a willingness and ability to respect and care for the natural environment.

One of the men taking part during my week was so eager to partake of a pineapple growing on a hillside that instead of taking a knife and slicing it from the growing plant he decided to lie down and bite into it. Not a wise move as he snapped his front dentures and had to manage the rest of the week semi toothless.

During the evenings when we sat around a small fire, John also gave us a series of mini lectures on a range of military skills and in particular navigation options. One of these key areas was astral navigation by use of the stars. Of course this particular skill needed a clear sky and considerable practise. I don't think that for one moment we even came close to being able to put this knowledge into practise but it was certainly of great interest.

The whole week was great fun even if hard work, it was great to sit down in the warm evening under the stars, enjoying a simple meal accompanied by a large brandy (it was worth the extra weight to carry and it got less each day) and a good smoke and It's always good to be close to nature away from the routine and trivia of everyday life.

On the last day we reached our RV at a small village where there was actually a well stocked shop and where we were able to enjoy a few beers before the LCT arrived to take us back to civilisation.

Although an event after my departure, I was to hear that Butch had been awarded a BEM. I also heard that, strange as it might be that Ssgt John was aggrieved that this honour should in fact have gone to him for his work with the deprived young people in the NewTerritories.

Just a few months later I met Butch in Berlin during a cricket match competition that he was umpiring. I asked him what he was awarded the BEM for, he said that he supposed for running the unit.

Anybody who ever knew Paddy Obrien would find this to be highly questionable.

How on earth could such a thing happen?

Perhaps I am being unfair or wrong.

Throughout the remainder of 1970 I managed to keep my head down and the only real situation I had with the OC was when he objected to me wearing a gold neck chain, I suppose I was asking for trouble as it was just about visible, it was not however the serious crime that he made it out to be. This year saw a period of nepotism in the unit that surpassed what had been in place before. The whole place was top heavy with aggressive and combative seniors and selected juniors being given preferential jobs to keep them free of shift work. The MT sergeant (PC) surrounded himself with a band of men who were able to avoid the dreaded desk duties and a general training centre atmosphere which created a huge difference between a section of juniors that had to work and the seniors that had little or nothing to do.

As a consequence of the dreadful Christmas function the previous year, Christmas 1970 was to be an exceptional occasion. Through the good offices and high level networking contacts of Brian and Felicity Caulfield the Christmas function was arranged for the Connaught room at the Hong Kong Mandarin Hotel. This is one of the finest hotels in the world with a fantastic reputation and it certainly lived up to expectations. The evening started with cocktails and a served buffet containing the biggest and best selection of food I had seen and better than anything since. I also recall that the comedian Michael Bentine was appearing at the Hotel and was persuaded to join our party. It was an expensive outing, as well as the cost of the hotel it was a case of Dinner suits and black ties for the men and long dresses for the ladies. It was well worth the cost and the effort as well as what must have been a task to organise

There were from time to time other more interesting work diversions which included the occasional escort duty for soldiers undertaking practise firing their guns into the sea at the Sai Kung Peninsular located on the North of the colony parallel with the Chinese republic Border, this was usually good fun as it was normal to undertake the task on motorcycle.

Another training course took place at Sek Kong airstrip in conjunction with the local army air corps with the Sioux helicopter. This involved such tasks as preparing ad hoc landing sites, marshalling helicopters and undertaking casevac procedures for injured soldiers.

We also received a basic introduction into hard landings and emergency procedures in the event of the pilot becoming a casualty. In spite of the fact that I was never a keen "flyer" I found the experience and the opportunity to take control quite exciting.

The training programme ended with the scariest activity and in turn we were secured to a stretcher attached to the landing skid. This was not the most enjoyable experience, firmly secured unable to move and when it was my turn I took a deep breath and closed my eyes until we had landed.

In February 1970 I was married and I guess that my priorities changed a great deal, I was particularly glad to be out of the single soldiers environment although for the first six months I was living in Kowloon and in order to get to work on time by 0830 hrs I had to catch the very first bus the number 26 Yuen Long express which left the Jordan Road ferry terminal at 0600 hours. This was a very stressful and tiring journey, there was absolutely no guarantee that the bus would depart on time or that it would not break down or arrive in Sek Kong in time for duty. I later managed to secure the tenancy of a house in Fan Ling at Tak Yuen Villa, this was not such a distance to travel to work but I certainly needed to start early as it was often the case that I would have to change buses several times.

Although situated within the Northern Hemisphere and with seasons the same as in the United Kingdom, Hong Kong is sub tropical, it is very hot from April to October With temperatures generally over 30c. It is also exceptionally humid and it is this humidity that is particularly exhausting, one of the side effects of the heat and humidity is the unpleasant and quite debilitating prickly heat rash. I was afflicted with this, it targets the groin region the stomach and under the arms. I was prescribed several different types of medication but nothing worked. Fortunately my newly acquired mother in law came to my rescue with a Chinese $1.00 box of prickly heat powder and within a week the ailment had vanished and never returned.

Hong Kong was also afflicted by a range of tropical storms and Typhoons which could cause havoc and considerable damage. There was a local system of warnings normally displayed at Police stations and government buildings.

For some bizarre reason the RMP had been assigned what was a potentially dangerous task and when the first typhoon warning was issued a RMP patrol was to be dispatched to a site close to the summit of the Taimo Shan mountain and report on any potential or actual landslide.

The fact that if there was a landslide the RMP land rover and the patrol might be swept away seemed to have been overlooked.

There are deadly snakes in Hong Kong and these appeared from time to time along with several that were probably harmless.

One afternoon the son of one RMP sergeant phoned his father to say that there was a large snake in the kitchen of their service married quarter in Sek Kong village. Several of us drove out to the house and although we had suspected this to be a false alarm we were taken aback when we saw a huge hooded cobra erect and very active on the kitchen floor.

A decision was made to contact the local police station and request the duty "snake catcher" to attend. This gentleman arrived about thirty minutes later and after looking through the kitchen window, he declared that the snake was too dangerous for him to deal with. He also added that the cobra would have a partner and this would either be very close by or in a nest and that it would almost certainly come looking for it's mate. The snake catcher suggested that we push the kitchen door open and the snake might decide to leave. As suggested the door was pushed open and the snake started to slither out. The sergeant rather foolishly and bravely swung a garden rake at the snake and it became impaled. The outcome of this was that the snake was killed and John had himself a mounted snake skin. The snake catcher also warned that cobra's form lifelong partnerships and it was almost certain that the surviving snake would be hunting for it's partner.

Several days later there was a reported sighting of a large snake in the Sek Kong village. In the company of SSGT John F and some others we managed to track it down to a storm drain and trap it by pushing a pile of oil and petrol soak rags into the drain. When the snake made it's escape John manages to beat and kill it with a large stick.

In 1970 the population of Hong Kong was around five million squeezed into an area, including the new territories circa 425 square miles. It was very crowded!!

Public transport was crucial to movement around the colony and apart from the Kowloon Motor Bus company double deckers and single deckers there were hundreds of dual purpose vehicles known colloquially as "dollar taxi's" these taxi's were available around the colony day and night. The drivers were usually accompanied by a tout who would stand outside the taxi's soliciting customers. Travel between Hong Kong island and the Kowloon peninsular was provided by two ferry services. The Star Ferry located at the end of Nathan Road provided a passenger only service to the island, first, second or even third class. The Jordan Road ferry provided a passenger and vehicular service between the Island and Kowloon. It was the actions of the star ferry owners in 1966 who raised the cost of passenger travel by 5 cents in each class which precipitated a major riot and civil disturbance.

In summer 1970 the laws regarding the dual purpose vans was changed and instead of the often garish, rusty and scruffy vans the colony was presented with the Public light bus painted red and yellow.

The rules for these buses were much more strict, they had to comply with local safety regulations, the drivers were subject to more rigorous checks and the fares had to be displayed inside the buses. Workers in Hong particularly drivers as was the case for any other Asian country were resentful of change and to allow the new process to settle a period of grace was allowed.

One Saturday afternoon I was on my way to the beach at castle peak with my wife, we had stopped at Yuen Long and my wife was inside a shop. I was watching the world go by when I saw an incident develop involving the driver of a public light bus and a police officer. Although I could not hear what was said I watched as the police officer pulled the driver from his cab, I was later to discover that he had been asked for his drivers' licence. For whatever reason there was a disagreement and the police officer who had already drawn his truncheon struck the driver across his head. The police officer was immediately joined by several others, whistles were blown and other taxi drivers joined the crowd which quickly became very hostile I decided it was time to leave. Staff from the communist sourced shop came into the street and gave first aid to the injured driver. Later that evening when we tried to return home to Fan Ling via Yuen Long we were unable to do so. A large section of the local community were rioting and the roads were blocked. The situation was not resolved until a company of Hong Kong police from the Fan Ling frontier division were sent in to disperse the crowd. I recall sometime later reading the newspaper report that the injured driver had been arrested, charged and convicted for driving without a licence.

Since I had married I had visited a number of rather exclusive Chinese restaurants including the Deep Bay (Lau Fau Shan) where customers select their live fish and other delicacies and hand them over to restaurant staff for cooking, this put a whole new complexion on fresh food. Unlike some traditional ideas I had an excellent relationship with my mother in law who was incredibly smart, witty and multi lingual.

The three of us regularly ate out and I was introduced to the diverse range of regional foods. Each Sunday morning we would visit the Shamrock Hotel in Nathan road for some of the best dim sum in Hong Kong.

One of the phrases I had heard before I was married was the "gone native" I think that this was a very flippant and insensitive assault by the ignorant group who had scant appreciation of any culture outside their own.

However! I must say that being married into a different culture was enlightening.

I had not really appreciated just how inhospitable the English were until I started to understand the Chinese.

In the last few weeks before we left Hong Kong I was able to meet several members of my wife's extended family although I was not quite sure what they expected of me or how they thought I might behave.

The last meal was at a very traditional and exclusive Shanghainese restaurant on an invitation from my Mother in laws sister and her husband. There were some other family members expected to attend including of course my own mother in law, my brother in law and his wife. To the best of my recollection there were to be about twenty guests in total. My wife was well aware of the possible developments and acting on her advice I made sure that I took a large wad of Dollars, actually just about every cent that I had. My wife told me that my Brother in law was also intending to take a load of cash. This outing was to be a sound lesson in one-upmanship (face) as demonstrated by Chinese. On arrival at the restaurant we were shown to a large round table on the first floor which I was to learn was visible to virtually every diner. This was the owner's personal prestigious table reserved for very special guests. The waiter placed the cups and the green tea on the table and then placed a set of chopsticks in front of everybody at my table except for me and instead placed a knife fork and spoon. I pushed these away and was able to ask in Chinese for chopsticks (Round one to Paul)

The waiter then placed several small porcelain dishes in the centre of the table containing some tasty delicacies. These included peanuts in oil and small pieces of pickled cabbage.

I was able to pick up these items with my chopsticks which was probably something the staff and other guests had not expected. I made a deliberate show of passing some to my wife. I suspect that all eyes were on me. "hoping that I might drop them" I didn't !!! round two to Paul.

The meal began and it was certainly the most impressive meal I had ever enjoyed. During the meal my wife's uncle explained that in addition to his teaching role he was also a professional traditional artist and as a personal friend of the owner had designed and painted all of the pictures that were displayed in the restaurant. I was then given a guided tour by the owner after which I returned to our table. I was literally bursting at the seams having eaten far too much and perhaps I had drunk far too much Brandy, I thought the meal was over.

The table was cleared and then the waiter placed a small dish in front of every diner together with, to my surprise a spoon.

At this point the waiter presented a huge dish of rice decorated with a range of sweet items in the shape of a large butterfly. Once everybody at the table had taken a good look my wife's uncle then proceeded to mix the dish and serve it to every guest.

Once the remains of the "desert" had been removed and after a couple more glasses of Brandy I really did think that the meal was over. I had already taken my money from my pocket and I saw that my Brother in law was in the process of doing the same. The owner then appeared and placed the bill on the table in front of my wife's uncle.

Without even looking at it he simply initialled the bill and handed it to the waiter.

The substance of this was clear, my wife's uncle was held in such high regard that his signature was all that was needed in that restaurant and that he was good for any visit without having to pay at the time.

I may have gained a bit of face at the start but this outcome could never be topped.

Leaving Hong Kong was a very sad day, a last dinner with my Mother in law and then a dash to the RAF desk at the Airport at Kai Tak. We were late booking in For our flight and then found that we were well overweight with our luggage.

Worse was to come as we were suddenly greeted with a crowd of my wife's friends who had come to say good bye, in typical Chinese style they had all brought gifts.

There I was repacking suitcases and deciding what to throw away and then packing the gifts.

Eventually we had to say goodbye and we boarded the VC10 back to UK.

The flight route had been changed since 1968 and Singapore was now deleted. This of course meant a longer first leg to the island of Gan in the Indian Ocean then on to Bahrein, Cyprus and finally RAF Brize Norton. I remember also the two ghastly children in the seats behind us who whined and cried all the way.

I had only taken one weeks leave during my tour of Hong Kong and the accumulated time added to embarkation and disembarkation meant that I would have time off until the end of June.

In early July 1971 I moved to Berlin where I would remain until 1974.

Berlin The divided City

I HAD BEEN TO BERLIN on a previous occasion in 1967 and so I was familiar with the general political and military situation as well as the local places of interest and the duties as unique to Berlin.

During the high summer months June thru August it is very hot with long days and very short nights.

As I was to discover, the duty platoons rota system was almost set in stone and worked on the routine of day duty, night duty, rest day after night and day off. The routine was so certain that it was possible to plan a year ahead. It was only in exceptional circumstances that this would change

Unlike my previous time in Berlin when the German DKW Auto Union jeep-type vehicles were used on wall and wire patrol and the VW variant for the autobahn sweep there had been a change and now the short wheel base land-rover was used for border duties and long-wheel base used for the daily autobahn "sweep" from Berlin to Helmstedt

Other duties included normal garrison patrols, Tier-Garten soviet war memorial, check point Charlie and Bravo and RMP control room.

All RMP vehicles as well as a number of other military vehicles were fitted with German FUG 7B UHF radios and the radio net was controlled via the RMP control room. Communication was always excellent and at a range of over 100 miles, another unique quality of this radio was that it could be lifted easily out of the vehicle and connected to a mains AC electrical system for use in a static location.

Berlin was divided into four sectors, a legacy of the Allied collaboration during the 1939-45 war. The Soviet sector was of course the east of the city and in terms of area was the largest by far, the other three sectors, USA to the South, UK in the centre and the French in the north. The French were not originally included in the partition of the city and the USSR insisted that any allocation to the French would have to be from the area given to the USA and UK and that's how it was divided. The three western sectors eastern boundaries extended from the wall up to the zonal border between Berlin and the DDR (German Democratic republic).

The whole of Berlin was surrounded by east German security forces although technically the DDR was not formally recognised as a legitimate government.

Travel for the western allied personnel between Berlin and the Federal republic was restricted to the road between Berlin and Helmstedt or the rail link from Berlin Charlottenberg to Braunsweig. The road was open every day of the year and the British train ran every day except for Christmas day. In 1971 Allied air travel was from RAF Gatow for the British, Tempelhof for then USA and Tegel for the French.

Civilian travel was from Tegel and restricted to BEA, Air France and Pan Am.

Despite the passage of 25 years since the end of the 1939-45 war there was still evidence of the destruction of the city and there were still many partly destroyed buildings both inside the Western sector and on the border. Berlin was not legally part of the Federal Republic and was effectively governed by the largely independent Berlin Senate although this was funded by the Federal German Government.

Under the terms of the post war agreement, West Berlin was not allowed to retain an army. This rule was effectively circumnavigated by means of a very large and well equipped civilian police force which was an Army in all but name.

Berlin was still technically an occupied city and in terms of authority and responsibility the German police force was subordinate to the Military Police in each of the three sectors. This generally worked very well but I don't think that the German police were always happy with being obliged to defer their local police actions involving Military personnel to the service police. We were particularly fortunate that we had a team of excellent translators who knew the rules very well and in particular the former RMP sergeant, Mr Frank Page.

Travel to East Berlin was permitted although servicemen were required to travel in uniform. Dependants, wives, children and civilians were also allowed to travel but were required to show their passports at the window of the vehicle in which they were travelling. Officially, according to DDR laws and the British Military regulations there were restrictions on what could be purchased in East Berlin and in addition East German currency (Ost marks) had to be purchased at the official exchange bureaux and a receipt obtained. Of course this regulation was totally ignored and Ost marks could be freely purchased in West Berlin, the rate fluctuated but generally the rate was circa DM 1 to Ost Mark 6. Naturally this made purchases in east Berlin much more of a bargain. There were however some very strict rules regarding what could and could not be bought in East Berlin, no object' art, no postage stamps, no children's clothing and a few more. It was also forbidden to exchange West German currency for east in West Berlin at the very lucrative exchange rate available.

I don't think that these rules were complied with although there was something of an enforcement process established which required the RMP to search service shoppers returning from the East. This eventually died out as a result of the many unresolvable issues and the overall legality. This could have caused some something of an issue as the RMP were probably the most frequent East Berlin shoppers.

In addition to the British trading facility the NAAFI, all allied forces in Berlin were granted reciprocal shopping rights at each others facilities. This specifically included the American Post Exchange (PX) and the French economat.

The British army as well as the British Military Government and a range of other non military organisations were located within the 1936 Olympic stadium complex. This included the indoor Olympic swimming pool and the indoor boxing stadium.

Travel around Berlin was particularly well provided for. There was a very good German bus service, the U bahn underground administered by the West Berlin authorities and the S Bahn over ground service administered by the East German authorities. The Army also ran a useful bus service between all service quarters, barracks and shopping destinations, in addition every unit had a team of civilian recreational drivers provided with Volkswagen mini buses. Berlin really was a rare example of being able to manage quite well without a private motor car.

There were many perks to life in Berlin not available in the Federal Republic. One in particular; a legacy of the Berlin airlift was the British FRIS (Families Ration Issue Service) service.

FRIS was set up to provide a regular turnover of the massive food stocks held in Berlin against any potential recurrence of the supply problems experienced during the Air Lift. Each family was provided (according to rank and status) with a ration order book listing about 70 different food items including virtually every basic food item needed. The rations would be delivered to service quarters in a plastic box each week and the new order sheet collected. Most of the items were of good quality and in fact it was perfectly possible for married servicemen to survive without ever having to make any additional food purchases. It was of course quite normal that there were substantial differences between what items junior enlisted soldiers were able to order and what was available to officers. This would probably have included a better selection of meat cuts as well as a difference in general quality.

One advantage was the fact that single soldiers in Barracks would receive exactly the same food as their married colleagues.

Medical facilities were generally excellent and there were a number of local clinics for soldiers and their dependants as well as other UK based civilians, British Military government and schoolteachers. There was also an exceptionally well equipped Military Hospital just a short distance from the military headquarters and in the centre of the main service married quarters area.

In 1972 there was a particularly distressing incident involving a servicemen and his family. The Soldiers wife was pregnant with her second child and her husband had arranged some time off to look after their first child whilst his wife was in hospital.

At the same that his wife was in labour the soldier was taken ill, he arranged an emergency baby sitter and he found himself in hospital, he died very soon afterwards and around the same time that his wife was giving birth.

One of the locally employed German civilian interpreters disclosed whilst accompanying me to an incident that he would not travel in the rear of the RMP mini bus if the incident resulted in the use of emergency warning devices such as blue light and two tone horns.

He then explained that he had been a rear passenger in a mini bus which had crashed on Christmas day 1966 when two RMP NCO's were killed in a road traffic accident. This incident occurred during extremely cold weather following heavy snow falls.

The RMP vehicle was driven through red traffic lights and was struck by a Mercedes car. Apparently the driver of the Mercedes was listening to his radio, had the heater blower on full, he did not hear the RMP warning two tone horns and did not see the mini bus until it was too late to avoid a collision.

In 1973 whilst on mobile patrol and accompanied by a number of other RMP NCO's I attended the Edinburgh House where a large number of soldiers had been seen hanging around and drinking. I recall that a decision was made to simply take the soldiers back to Barracks, they had not caused any trouble and they were both good natured and totally compliant. To the best of my recollection there were 5 or 6 soldiers in the rear of my vehicle seated on one side of a small table. I recall that the RMP driver seemed to be taking the longest possible route back to the barracks in Spandau and I turned from watching the noisy soldiers to look forward through the front windscreen, it took me a few moments to adjust my eyesight and then as I turned my head back towards the soldiers I saw a sudden flash of movement, a small fist direct into my face, just below my left eye. All of the soldiers were small in stature and for the life of me I still don't understand how such a small man could hit so hard.

As the blow landed I felt myself slipping into unconsciousness and at the same time being dragged by my feet towards the soldiers. As this was happening I could feel a flurry of kicks and punches landing on my body. By this time the Vehicle had stopped but I had no idea where the driver was. My legs had turned to jelly and although I tried hard I could not stand up. I have no idea how or when but I suddenly found myself on my knees outside the vehicle trying desperately to stand up. In reality I was totally defenceless. Luckily for me I was effectively rescued by the crew of the following RMP patrol and all of the soldiers arrested. I sustained injuries to my face and left eye but eventually made a complete recovery. Without any doubt the soldier who first struck me had a real powerful punch. I was careless and dropped my guard when I should not have done even though at the time there was no compelling reason to stay particularly alert. I learned from the experience and made sure that I never took my eye off the ball again.

There were plenty of BFES Junior and primary schools to cater for the service children although secondary education was not available. The majority of those dependants of secondary age were boarded at the BFES school at Hamm although many more would have been educated and boarded privately in the UK.

Apart from the major military facility inside the Olympic stadium there were several barracks which accommodated the resident Regiments and Battalions and all named after British Army former generals, Alexander, Brooke, Montgomery, Wavell and Smuts. There were also other military units unique to Berlin such as the BRIXMIS (The British Military Mission to the Soviet Commander in Chief) although their main operational base and for access to the East was actually located at Potsdam a few miles north of Berlin.

Another unique facility was the Spandau Prison where some of the Nazi heirachy had been incarcerated following the Nuremberg war trials. Hitler's deputy was still in Spandau and had in fact been sentenced to a whole life sentence. The three western Allies were more or less in agreement that he might be released at some time but this was always rigorously vetoed by the Soviet Union.

Security guard duties at the prison were undertaken by all of the four powers, USA, UK, France and the USSR on a monthly rotation basis.

The original four power meeting facility was located at the Allied Komandatura building, originally the headquarters of a major German insurance business.

The general idea was that the four allies, USA, UK France and the USSR would meet and agree on policies and actions to put in place for the City of Berlin. Following a rather belligerent verbal assault by the Soviet representative against the absent USA officer the four power collaboration effectively ended.

An incident was relayed to me during the French tour of duty at Spandau prison a party was taking place at the nearby British Brooke barracks. It appears that a French officer visited the British Barracks to complain about the noise which was preventing his soldiers from sleeping. A British officer explained that the regiment was celebrating a past Battle victory, the French as always enjoy their battles and such celebrations but when asked which battle, he was told Waterloo, it seems that he left in a bit of a hurry with no further comment.

British forces in Berlin undertook some low level intelligence trips around East Berlin under the Guise of Flag Tours, normally a group of 3 or 4 soldiers in uniform. Naturally the soviets enjoyed the same rights and were frequently seen driving around in West Berlin in a range of motor cars with a different registration plates. The soviets were also granted access to the British NAAFI shops but I never saw any such visit.

Eating out in Berlin was a special experience although to try and list every venue would in itself require a whole book. The Kurfustendam (Qdam) was probably the most famous street for Berlin specialities and was always packed with locals and tourists. From the RMP aspect however I would like to mention two special places. The first was a tiny wooden cabin in the North of the city where the British sector of the wall met the start of the French. This cabin was situated inside a large commercial lorry park and served mini bock wurst with mustard and a slice of dry bread, cold beer and coffee. I have to say that these bockwurst were the best I ever tasted and the beer was always served at the perfect temperature, summer or winter.

On the corner of Kahnt Strasse and Stuttgarter Platz there was a small caravan which opened for business around 10pm. As well as serving Bratwurst and beer this venue served what were almost certainly the best Boulette in Berlin. A unique feature of this stall was that the two men selling and serving the food were usually to be seen holding hands, one of the two taking care of the cooking and the other completing the transactions. This place stayed open until dawn and was always very busy.

There were also so many places to meet and drink in Berlin that it would be impossible to list them. Some were a legacy of the pre war Berlin and some more aligned to more contemporary tastes. There were two particular drinking establishments worthy of particular comment. In the centre of Berlin the Munchener Hofbrauhaus was a real beer hall with half litre and litre glasses of beer served by female waitresses in traditional skirts, blouse and aprons. There was a smart process for sending a message to any young lady. The idea was to purchase a flower from one of the girls with trays and send it to the numbered table, if the girl was interested the idea was that she would join you at your table. This place was constantly crowded and if a table was wanted you needed to get there early.

At the lower end of the scale there was Pullmans bier stuben on the Kant Strasse.

This place opened at 6am and served the cheapest beer in Berlin around 70 pfennig for a half litre. This venue was particularly suitable for seasoned, dedicated and even desperate drinkers. In the best tradition of old style beer drinking bars the floor was sprinkled with sawdust and there were spittoons alongside the main bar.

Berlin was certainly recognised as a particularly socially liberated city and one such aspect was the totally overt availability of prostitutes. It was well known that certain locations were relevant to the "quality" and price of these young ladies and the most public examples were those who plied their trade on the Strasse Des 17 Juni My understanding was that the most expensive girls could be found outside the Woolworths store in central Berlin. Prostitution was perfectly legal in Germany and apart from the girls on the street there were registered brothels in virtually every town and city. Most of these were in well secured locations and always identified by the expected red light.

Berlin attracted millions of visitors from literally all over the world and in particular there were large numbers of young adults who had made the European tour from Australia, New Zealand and South Africa. To the Military Police in Berlin these were know as "Aussie Tours" and very popular because they were totally dominated by young, attractive and liberated females. Whatever the rules might have been the fact is that it was almost a given that these tours would find their way to the RMP corporals mess, it was a chance for them to get a drink at prices far less than they would be paying elsewhere and an even better opportunity for the corporals mess barman to add to his profits.

There were a number of special tourist targets in Berlin and to name just a few, Brandenburg Gate, Checkpoint Charlie, Potsdammer Platz. Pre 1945 Potszdammer Platz was effectively the centre of the city and in 1971 it was one of the most visited sites. This is close to the site of Hitlers wartime bunker and adjacent to the wartime Reich Chancellory on the Wilhelm Strasse.

RMP patrols were frequently photographed at Potzdammer platz and this was made particularly easy as there was a large car and coach parking space. On one occasion however whilst on wall patrol duties along with one of my RMP colleagues we were amazed to see a number of luxury coaches arrive and an absolute army of beautiful young girls debus. It was 1971 and hot pants were very popular, these girls were all incredibly attractive and appeared to represent every nationality. They were accompanied by several photographers and we were, I am pleased to say included in many of the shots. Once I had got my breath back I asked the photographer who the girls were. "All Princesses" was all he would or could tell me. Eventually I discovered that all of the girls were in fact contestants in the Miss Berlin international Beauty competition sponsored by the Berlin Hotel Schweitzenhof.

There were other major events that took place each year, The Allied Forces day parade involving British, USA and French troops this was a celebration and demonstration of unity which took place with marching troops and bands on the 17th June Street, this parade was always very popular with both service personnel and the local population.

The Soviet union had built a spectacular war memorial in Berlin prior to the arrival of the other allies in 1945, when the post war boundaries were confirmed this memorial was in the British Sector. Each year on a number of occasions the Soviet Army held a wreath laying ceremony at the memorial which involved marching troops and bands.

Berlin was also a popular destination for VIP as part of the annual Queens birthday parade held on the stadium Maifeld. In 1972 HRH The Princess Margaret came to Berlin for a whole week of visits around the city and to take the salute at the parade.

I was lucky to be part of the Royal Visit driving the lead RMP escort vehicle.

During the visit the Princess stayed at the official residence of the GOC Berlin the Villa Lem. This was a magnificent building close to RAF Gatow and about ten miles from the city centre. The Princess had a very demanding schedule and of course this meant that we were also very busy escorting her from location to location.

The schedule included a visit to an army primary school. The Military Hospital, a reception at the city Schloss and a drive through the City Centre as well as trips to the Wall, the Soviet Memorial and Brandenburg Gate. The trip through the city centre and the Kurfustendamm was at night and made easier by the fact that the German police were able to stop the traffic at every intersection and it was a straight drive through with no obstructions.

As was the case for all British military formations, Berlin had a system of emergency alert to call out troops and to test their state of readiness. This alert was known as "Exercise Rocking Horse". The message was passed to married soldiers by the RMP who drove around pre planned routes in the service married quarters areas and announced the exercise using the external loudspeakers on the RMP vehicles. The RMP had a number of tasks as part of the exercise which included taking up positions in sight and view of the Zonal Border between West Berlin and East Germany. Although the East German guards appeared to be interested in the extra activities, I was always fairly certain that their Soviet masters would have known about the exercise in advance and would have told their allies. I suspect that we could not risk taking any action that might have seemed provocative.

During my time in Berlin I was able to visit East Berlin on a number of occasions and it would be fair to say that every visit was undertaken with a degree of uneasiness and caution. Although the British authorities did not officially recognise East Germany as a legitimate state it was mandatory when visiting the East to comply with all traffic signs and regulations, officially the British forces were required to comply with the currency regulations. On only one occasion can I recall being asked for my currency exchange certificate when attempting to make a purchase, I made out that I didn't understand what was said and made a measured exit. I realised after this challenging situation that it was wise to avoid the most prominent shops on the Unter Den Linden which were clearly the showpiece shops of East Berlin. There were places to eat out in East Berlin, the most prestigious was in the high level restaurant in the television tower at Alexander Platz, this structure had been know colloquially in West Berlin as Ulbrichts Tower, named after the East German leader, Walter Ulbricht. Also there was the Moskau Restaurant close by and if a quick snack was he answer it was possible to purchase a bockwurst in any of the local bars although the quality was questionable.

Duty at checkpoint Bravo was probably one of the most important tasks undertaken by RMP, this duty involved the responsibility for checking every document relating to British military, BFG registered and other sponsored vehicles travelling to Helmstedt.

There were two types of Document involved, the BTD (Berlin Travel Document) and the Forces Freight Document, each of these needed to be thoroughly checked for the most minute detail and all supporting documents such as passports and service identity cards. The slightest error or difference such as a missing full stop or a incorrect spelling or date would result in the document being rejected at the soviet checkpoint and the traveller forced to return to Bravo. There were occasions when travellers arrived without a BTD and these would be refused travel unless there were serious mitigating circumstances, on occasion servicemen arrived with incorrect documents and technically these should also have been refused. I must confess that I was always reluctant to refuse travel and on several occasions following some contact with the soldiers parent unit I completed a new document to allow travel.

There was a very good system for managing travellers, each was offered a travel briefing and in the rare cases when these were declined or refused the traveller, regardless of rank or status was required to sign a formal disclaimer in order to confirm that they were fully conversant with the route and did not need a briefing.

Each traveller also received a travel pack with maps and sketches of each intersection and instruction on what to do in the event of any problem such as a breakdown.

There were of course occasions when travellers preferred to "follow" the RMP Autobahn Sweep patrol which left Bravo each day (except 25th December) at 0830.

I was aware that a number of RMP NCO's at Bravo had made mistakes or had failed to notice mistakes with travel documents which resulted in rejection by the soviets, it might sound conceited but I never made any such error and never had a single rejection.

Training opportunities were fairly limited in Berlin and during my tenure apart from weapon training at the local firing range I only undertook one formal training course at Chichester. Sports activities were well sponsored and supported and generally it was the case for additional RMP NCO's to be drafted in from BAOR to Berlin to undertake duties in order to allow the Berlin sports teams to compete for example in the competitions taking place outside Berlin.

In early 1974 each of the platoons undertook a short break with some adventurous training in Shleswick Holstein, this was a very long drive virtually up to the German Danish Border, nothing particularly exciting or difficult, some map reading exercises and orienteering some sports and eating out and sleeping in tents. The main objective was simply to escape from what many felt was the claustrophobic atmosphere of Berlin.

This small exercise never got off to the best start when I discovered to my annoyance and indignation that I was expected to act as the driver for another

NCO who was junior to me in terms of seniority. The issue for me was the fact that the roles and tasks had never been discussed and that my vehicle partner had clearly been briefed by the platoon commander. It was no secret that their relationship was more than professional. This was a classic example of cronyism with which I had been forced to contend since my first day in uniform

In 1972 my son was born at the British Military Hospital, Berlin was a good place to have a child and to see them grow up. There was always plenty to see and do, underground trains, over ground railways, plenty of parks and open spaces, plenty of wildlife if you could get close to the border and probably one of the best Zoos in the world.

Along with a whole gang of RMP NCO's in April 1974 I received my posting to 176 Pro Coy in Londonderry Northern Ireland. In the last few months prior to my posting there had been a huge influx of new postings in to Berlin. Many of these new boys were straight from Chichester (the factory) and a number were from Northern Ireland.

What became apparent was that amongst the new arrivals from Northern Ireland there was some conflict due to the fact that some wives were Catholic and some Protestants, this was something in which I never became involved and I had no real knowledge of how strong and deep the problems were.

One particular advantage of service life in Berlin was the existence of a Military sponsored Hotel "Edinburgh House" booking a room at this hotel allowed soldiers to take a bit of a rest before handing over their service quarter prior to leaving the city.

We stayed here for whole week, a minor but traditional procedure was for enlisted men to be allocated rooms on the front "noisy" section and officers to be allocated rooms on the quiet side.

In May 1974 I flew out of Berlin with my wife and son prior to moving to Londonderry.

Londonderry A different life and a very close shave

Prior to leaving Berlin I recall receiving a letter advising me that my travel documents for Northern Ireland would be posted to me at my home (contact) address in the UK.

In June 74 I received a letter from the chief clerk in Londonderry which included a travel warrant from my home for travel via rail and Ferry from Liverpool to Belfast.

I was surprised and pleased that this had actually happened and even more delighted to read that a car would be waiting for me at Belfast.

When the day to travel arrived I set off with my wife and son and eventually arrived in Liverpool, a cabin had been booked for me but I have to say that the ferry trip was the most uncomfortable and probably the slowest I had ever experienced.

We arrived in Belfast and despite the promise of a car to collect me it did not arrive and I was unable to contact anybody at Londonderry.

Reluctantly I boarded the Army R& R bus which I later realised was clumsily disguised in the livery of an Ulster bus and escorted by an armed patrol following in a land rover. It seemed to me that it could not be driven any slower and in addition it also had to contend with every possible delay including having to wait for some servicemen following in their own private cars. The bus eventually arrived in Londonderry about 2pm, some 3 hours later than expected.

I made my way to the military police building and after some enquiries I was told that my service quarter was located in Bally Kelly which we had passed earlier and that the service quarter had been taken over on my behalf. The keys to my house had been left for me. I managed to procure a lift and was driven to Bally kelly where we arrived about 5pm. When I first entered the house I just could not believe how small it was.

Once we started looking around we discovered so many faults with the place that had I had the opportunity to be present when the quarter was presented I would never have accepted it. Marooned with a wife and young child in a new and strange location has it's own unique difficulties and effectively we were stuck.

Over the next few months we managed to get the house in good order with many repairs being carried out. During our first winter the second bedroom was found to be so cold and damp that our son had to be moved into our bedroom.

We had been prepared for a long wet summer but to our surprise and delight the entire summer was the hottest on record for over forty years.

After three years being spoiled in Berlin, now being reduced to living in a substandard house, in a remote location almost twenty miles from my workplace was almost akin to a punishment. There was worse to come, living in service married quarters in Germany included a deduction from wages to cover the cost of fuel and light charges.

In Northern Ireland, electricity charges were made direct to service occupants and even worse, such charges were circa 15% higher than the rest of the United Kingdom.

The married quarters in Ballykelly had been built to service the now obsolete RAF station in the early 1950's and had electric fires installed in each room. I was not going to be caught in this trap and never used the electric fires, I also carefully managed our use of electricity and calculated our pending bill. When the bills were handed out, they were all posted en- bloc ours was virtually spot on to our calculations and quite reasonable. Many of my colleagues however were shocked to find that their electricity bills exceeded their monthly wages. I heard one account of a soldier who received his bill and who then went to report to his regimental pay office that he could not pay the bill which was much more than his total wages. The soldier had a major shock coming and when the pay staff checked the soldiers account they discovered that although he had been in married quarters in Ballykelly for almost 18 months, for some reason he had not been charged for his service quarters.

Duties in Londonderry were varied, I commenced my tour as a member of the operations room and arrests and finds team. We were based in a series of portakabins located on Police Court Street next to the RUC Victoria Barracks. This was a great job receiving prisoners from the army, processing them and passing them on to the RUC. We were also involved in attending raids and incidents and recovering arms and ammunitions.

The primary legislation used was the Emergency Provision act (Northern Ireland)

Section ten, Suspicion of being a terrorist and section 12 suspicion of committing a criminal offence.

These were the days before computers and emails and as part of the collective reporting process it was necessary to type a record of all arrests and other incidents on to a stencil (skin) that could be printed out on the ancient mechanical gestetener.

This completed document was always given the highest priority and had to be in the main RMP office by 0900 hours each day. The Ops room was located on the West of the River Foyle whilst the RMP man office was located on the East side.

On one occasion due to a serious disturbance which had blocked the Craigavon Bridge and the only road route between locations. I had to call up the Royal Engineers for a lift across the River by rubber dingy. The Foyle usually looked calm and slow but being paddled across against the tide flow was a bit of a scary experience. The most important item was of course the stencilled daily report.

In addition to the routine of processing prisoners and arms finds there was time to undertake mobile patrols in the reasonably secure city centre.

In addition to the infantry battalions based in Londonderry there were also other branches of the service on short tours from BAOR. In particular

18 Light Regt Royal Artillery who were responsible for security duties in the City. The Regiment had their Headquarters in the RUC Station in Victoria Barracks Police Court Street which was conveniently next to the RMP ops room. In addition to the headquarters the Regiment had also based their cookhouse and dining room close by. Unlike other military locations the Army budget for food in Northern Ireland was very generous and not subject to over scrutiny. The consequence of this is that the food available was excellent and virtually around the clock. I was absolutely delighted when on my first visit I discovered that it was possible to have real German Bratwurst along with other delicacies that were regularly flown over from Germany..

A task normally carried out by the ops team was to convey the specialist " mug shotter" to the VCP (Vehicle check point) at letterkenny. Normally the RMP crew would call at the military Bridge camp and obtain an escort, usually an armoured Humber (Pig) or another land rover., the soldiers in these vehicles would be better armed with rifles against our pistols and SMG. Due to expanded commitments the army had been unable to provide escorts every day and acting on satisfactory intelligence and provided we carried at least one rifle we were permitted to proceed without an escort to the VCP. On one such occasion the VCP NCO was in the rear of the land-rover armed with a rifle. Also on this occasion we had been joined by an RAF Police corporal and was accompanying us for his first ever duty. I had decided to drive with the RAF corporal in the front with me and my third crew member in the rear. The route taken passed the Brandywell estate adjacent to the infamous Bogside and overlooked by the Creggan.

I noted that contrary to normal routine the groups of children in the street did not hurl bricks and milk bottles at us and then as I passed a row of terraced houses I heard an almighty bang and caught the distinct smell of cordite. My initial reaction was that one of the NCO's in the rear of the vehicle had discharged a round. Almost immediately the Mug Shotter called out that we were under fire, I called contact on the radio and put my foot down heading for the check point. I also managed to turn round and could see the third member of my crew with blood pouring from his face.

The mug shotter had also opened fire with his rifle. As I arrived at the checkpoint a well armed patrol in a saracen armoured car was already in hot pursuit having seen and heard the exchange of fire and with the target in sight fleeing the scene.

The mug shotter had already applied a field dressing to the injured mans' face and moments later an armoured ambulance arrived. It was a case of in the ambulance and then out as the wound was found to be a fairly minor cut to the cheek a couple of stitches and it was normal service resumed.

The terrorist rifleman managed to escape but in doing so abandoned his Armalite AR 15. The injured RMP NCO made a complete recovery and was no worse for his experience. On the plus side he was later interviewed and received a modest amount of compensation for the injury received.

Although it took a while we eventually discovered how the injury had been caused.

A single round fired at the vehicle had entered the open rear doors of the land-rover, luckily missing both men and had then struck the centre of the spare wheel mounted behind the front seats. The round had drilled a small hole in the wheel and then the remnant of the force had exploded behind the front seats.

This was certainly a very lucky escape for everybody on board the vehicle, just a couple of inches in any direction may well have had serious or even fatal consequences and I might not be writing this book.

Some weeks later a young man aged 18 years was arrested by the Army and handed over to the RMP, there was evidence to indicate that he had probably been responsible for the ambush on my land rover and during the short process he vigorously denied any wrongdoing and claimed that he was being fitted up. I felt sure that he was in fact responsible and reminded him that the British Army and the Military Police had in fact been sent to Northern Ireland mainly to protect the Catholic population and that I had never wished him any harm so why would he wish to harm me? I don't suppose that it made any difference to him but at least I felt a bit better.

In the early days of my tour I was fortunate to at long last find myself in a supervisory role if only to cover for the absence of the team seniors. On one occasion I had to visit the Coy Stores to collect such items as were needed, this included the range of stationery items and Polaroid film, bulbs and batteries. I was somewhat taken aback when I was asked how many men were in the three ops room teams for their chocolate ration. I was to discover that some time earlier a meeting at RMP Headquarters had become embroiled in a discussion about how best to allocate a certain fund that would ensure equal distribution for all ranks. After a number of options were dismissed a junior RMP Officer had one of the greatest ever brainwaves, as he quite rightly explained, just about everybody buys a bar of chocolate at some time so let's save them some money. That's how it came about and as I recall the fund provided for three bars of chocolate every week for every single rank of RMP in Northern Ireland.

Away from the Ops room and arrests and finds team there was a joint RMP RUC initiative so far as I recall this was 19 SPG (Special Patrol Group) based in the relatively secure facility at Shackleton Barracks Bally Kelly. This was to be my next assignment however it was not all sweet and smiley. Patrols were made up from RMP NCO's and RUC constables in both RMP and RUC vehicles. Then RMP used the Austin 1800 which was an incredible workhorse able to carry four well equipped and well- armed men in safety and comfort. The RUC used an upgraded 6 cylinder Macrolon armoured land-rover. Whatever the make up of the patrols the RUC officer was always in charge and this was not always best appreciated.

Shift hours were from 10 am to 6pm and then from 10 pm to 2am although these hours were flexible to take account of operational needs.

The day shift commenced with an intelligence briefing and allocation of crews, on most occasions the next step was to stop off for Breakfast, the most popular location for normal patrols was Mary's restaurant in Limavady for a traditional Ulster fry up.

After breakfast the patrols resumed and a high priority was where to stop for lunch, this was normally at other major police facilities.

Although I enjoyed the assignment it may have been the case that I was perceived to prefer to be elsewhere. There were matters that I had issue with, the first was certainly

The question of who was in charge. In itself this was not an issue but RMP views and opinions were never considered and when I declined and then bluntly refused to work overtime I was effectively ostracised by most of the RUC officers. My main objection to overtime working was that the RUC officers were well compensated and overtime for them was a very lucrative financial option. If they worked a late shift with overtime they could have a lie in the following morning. RMP received no benefits. I did not participate in their breakfast activity and it was also a sore point that the amount of subsistence allowance paid to the RUC was more than sufficient to pay for eating out whilst that paid to RMP was totally inadequate.

Although I was ever mindful of the fact that the RUC undertook a very dangerous job I was never comfortable with the general discriminatory attitude towards Catholics even though there were Catholic RUC officers. It was always my perception that the RMP were simply passengers with no constructive contribution other than an additional armed presence.

I actually enjoyed some of the work undertaken and was fortunate to have travelled extensively around the province often in support of other local forces particularly in Belfast.

On occasions when working with female officers I found that the conversation and comments directed to the females by some of the male officers was not only particularly rude and offensive but under current legislation could well have resulted in disciplinary or even criminal proceedings. I was never comfortable with this and when I attempted to intervene I was simply ignored.

After about four months of what was supposed to be a twelve month tenure I was removed at the request of the RUC and returned to normal RMP duties. I still have mixed views about this, I was totally committed to my role with the SPG and at no time did I act in any way to cause or give offence. On my return to RMP and after discussing the issue with the then CSM WO 2 Bernie Wallis he was in total agreement with my account of the experience and was adamant that it would not compromise my future career prospects.

I later commenced duties working out of Rosemount Police station where I remained for about nine months. This was a great place to work and involved a combination of mobile and foot patrols. We had a virtual monopoly on policing in the area where the RUC would only venture when supported by a substantial Army presence. On most occasions RMP patrols would liaise with the infantry platoon based at the police station and operate on a parallel support role, it was always good to know that a hard hitting patrol was not far away.

The Rosemount area was sandwiched between the staunchly Catholic/ Republican Creggan/Bogside and the mainly Protestant/ Loyalist area. I made several visits to homes in the area but was also asked not to revisit some homes in case of retribution against the residents. It was however of great interest to hear real accounts of life in Northern Ireland from many Catholics with personal experience of the harsh discrimination against Catholics applying for jobs. In common with the vast majority of RMP I had no personal issue with either Catholic or Protestant and I remain convinced that if not for a few hardliners on both sides and some serious errors on the part of the British Government (1972 internment) the troubles might have been much better managed and would not have attracted such public support. It has to be remembered that the internment operation was largely an intelligence disaster that generated sympathy and support for the republican cause to such a level that would not have occurred otherwise.

During my tenure at Rosemount Police station there were a number of incidents and developments which included some attempts to implement a "truce" or declared cessation of hostilities between the IRA and the security forces. During a visit by the officer commanding and in view of the fact that things had been quiet for some time and as a demonstration of our faith and confidence in the truce continuing he suggested that we consider "unarmed" foot patrols subject to parallel infantry patrols providing armed cover. I may have compromised my career prospects by insisting that this was impossible and I would simply never agree and suggested that even if ordered I may have refused. I may have been lucky that just about everybody else shared my sentiments and the idea was shelved. We later managed to reach a compromise by wearing covert body armour under our jackets which may have presented a more confident and relaxed image.

A short distance from the Police station and the city Centre was the Strand Road, this was mainly a commercial area and was often covered by RMP foot patrols. On one occasion two RMP NCO's were attacked by a group of 4 or 5 young men armed with pistols. Both RMP were struck and one fell to the ground. The second NCO was able to return fire using his pistol and the group ran off. Two pistols were recovered close to the scene. Soldiers from the city security Regiment came to the assistance of the RMP having heard what they though was automatic gun-fire. The two men were taken to hospital and as was the normal procedure for any member of the SF interviewed by RMP SIB. My understanding is that when asked by the SIB how many rounds he had fired the NCO freely admitted that he had emptied two full magazines, a total of 20 rounds. He was then reported for having been in possession of excess ammunition and reminded that he had only been issued with ten rounds at the start of his duty.

Although it may have been the case that formal disciplinary action was not initiated my understanding is that NCO who returned fire was never commended or recognised for his cool action despite the fact that had he not acted he and his colleague may well have been killed.

Normal duty parades did not take place at Rosemount police station simply because the duty commenced at Ebrington Barracks where vehicles were collected and weapons issued. One newly promoted sergeant for reasons known only to himself decided to parade the duties in the police station yard and to inspect weapons.

One young NCO who may have been a bit agitated by this unusual activity made a simple error and instead of allowing the working parts of his pistol to slide forward and then replace the magazine and squeeze the trigger replaced the magazine, released working parts, squeezed the trigger and fired a round/.

This could have easily been a fatal friendly fire incident, I was standing immediately to his right and it was fortunate for me and everybody else that he had held his pistol pointing to the ground. An expensive mistake that cost him £80.00 and a second lucky escape for me.

It was a strange irony that the very same sergeant supervising the parade later mislaid his briefcase at Ebrington Barracks outside the headquarters armoury. The case was later blown up by the ATO much to the amusement of several juniors.

The resident infantry battalion for Rosemount and the Creggan estate was the 1st Bn The Staffordshire Regiment. These were very professional, hard and efficient soldiers.

As is the case for just about every major unit the Staffords had adopted a regimental Pin up, she was afforded the title of Miss Pompadour. This incredibly beautiful young lady Beverly Pilkington was an established but "conservative" glamour model who had appeared in the sun newspaper page 3.

Miss Pilkington arrived at the Police station and I agreed for the RMP to man the soldiers posts whilst she took part in a PR photo shoot with the soldiers. She later visited the RMP office and very graciously agreed to have her photograph taken with the entire RMP Rosemount team.

It is also worth noting that civilians were arrested by the Army, processed by RMP and RUC then often interrogated by the Army specialists and in many cases they were then incarcerated under the provisions of an Interim Custody Order authorised by the secretary of state,. This order could be renewed and the individual could find himself in an internment centre for six months with no charge and no trial

There were many deaths and injuries during my tenure and I guess that many RMP personnel will have had much closer and more personal involvement.

I will mention two of the incidents that I was closely associated with and which affected me. The Staffordshire regiment was responsible for the hard republican areas of the Creggan and Shantallow estates and it was always a pleasure and a privilege to work with soldiers from that Regiment. Close to the end of their tour of duty a very young subaltern from the regiment arrived to join his soldiers. It was my understanding that he did so from choice and could just have easily remained in Germany where the regiment was based. The officer had only been in the city for a few days when he was shot by a sniper using what was subsequently identified as a Garrand rifle firing an armoured piercing round. The round struck him in the stomach and although he was evacuated quickly and treated at what was probably one of the best and most experienced gunshot wounds hospitals in the world, he could not be saved.

I met some of his soldiers shortly afterwards, the officer was barely out of his teens, he was a well liked and respected officer and his life was simply cut short.

As part of the follow up action the Staffords searched the estate and as well as taking a number of suspects into custody literally dismantled the local community centre looking for the rifle.

Another soldier with one of the Artillery regiments had also volunteered to join his comrades even though he had been eligible for discharge having completed his period of service. He was assigned the task of documenting the vehicles wishing to enter the secured city of Londonderry and worked from a small wooden office. At some time a terrorist explosive device was dropped and detonated on the roof of the building and the soldier was killed.

Sadly there were occasions when soldiers were hoodwinked and an example of this was in the City Centre where military checkpoints had been established. The normal crew would be at least one soldier armed with a rifle, one soldier armed with a pistol and one female WRAC. Everybody entering the secure area was subject to search, on one occasion two young females are believed to have entered the city and may have not been searched as well as they should have been. They were followed by two young men who were probably more carefully searched, it would appear that the two females had carried in pistols, probably concealed in an intimate body space, they had then been passed to the men who had simply walked back into the checkpoint and shot the two soldiers dead and then run off.

Although Police court street was supposedly secure it was not really difficult to gain access, I was quite shocked when I first joined the team and to note that the RMP would normally get into their land rovers parked in the street and drive away without even a cursory check.

Over the course of time one particular RMP Corporal had attracted a deal of criticism because he simply could not stay awake when it was his turn to ride (shotgun) in the rear of the RMP patrol vehicle. In a move to give him the opportunity to undertake less arduous duties he was transferred to work with the RUC from the Waterside station. Unfortunately whilst on such a patrol the NCO was in the rear of an RUC patrol car and somehow managed to negligently discharge two rounds from his sub machine gun. Needless to say and although the two rounds passed through the side of the rear door and the RUC officers were unharmed they had a real scare and the NCO was again moved to other duties, following an expensive appointment with the officer commanding.

It is only with hindsight that I think about how lax some of the procedures were regarding soldiers and weapons. The routine for soldiers undertaking armed duties was to report to the Armoury in a secure area of Ebrington Barracks there were no checks for identity or authority, this was perhaps aggravated by the fact that when drawing weapons; the necessary ammunition was also issued.

A serious consequence of this was an incident involving a young soldier who had apparently received a "Dear John" letter from his wife, one of probably many who may have been left alone and were struggling to cope. This letter contained an ultimatum to the effect that unless the soldier returned home she might not be able to stay faithful. I have no way of knowing if this soldier had confided in any of his friends or supervisors or if he had sought advice. The outcome however was fatal, he reported to the armoury, signed for a rifle and twenty rounds and then promptly shot himself with the barrel in his mouth. The poor armourer would not normally be expected to stand and watch the soldier or indeed question him as to why he wanted the rifle, he was never required to undertake the duty again but to the best of my memory the procedure was not changed.

Safe handling of weapons was always a priority, in particular when leaving or entering any secure facility or building the loading and unloading of weapons was to take place at outdoor unloading bays.

What to me was always a sense of amusement was the fact that the RMP Austin 1800 cars as well as having MOD registration number plates were used in civilian mode with Northern Ireland plates fitted. Although intended as a safe covert use it must have been the simplest task for anybody to note the cars leaving the barracks and come up with a list of the obvious.

I recall that the new RMP WO2 took it upon himself to visit the Rosemount Police station on his own driving one of the civilianised cars. On his arrival I pointed him in the direction of the station unloading bay and politely reminded him that no loaded weapons were permitted in the station. I was more than a little shocked when he told me that he had not loaded his pistol. How fortunate that he had not been ambushed as he may well have had a serious situation.

Negligent discharges were actually fairly rare but sanctions and punishment was assured and a substantial fine applied regardless of rank.

I recall a very young high flying warrant officer from an armoured regiment who took the trouble to introduce himself to the RMP ops room in his role of intelligence officer. Unfortunately for him it would seem that his weapon handling skills were flawed and when he left the Ops room and then ran up the stairs inside the RUC police station he succeeded in discharging a round from his pistol and shot himself in the foot.

As was the case for most juniors in their final few weeks I was removed from operational duties about six weeks before the end of my tour after I had received a posting order to 102 Provost Company located in Moenchen Gladback.

In my case I elected to undertake security duties at Altnagelvin Hospital.

This was a very easy number undertaken in civilian clothing. The object was to provide some security for any RMP patient and support when any other soldier was admitted. Meals were taken in the staff nurses canteen and although it was a case of staying alert and keeping out of the way during the daytime, at night I was able to help out making tea and toast for the nurses.

The Army R&R bus made the daily trip from Ebrington Barracks in Londonderry using a winding route via Ballykelly, Limavady, Coleraine and other service married quarters enclaves before completing the journey to Belfast docks.

As is the case for all British Army Regiments a number of Battle Honour trophy figures are displayed outside the guardrooms. On one occasion the guardroom sergeant at Shackleton Barracks Ballykelly noticed that some of the Regimental figures were missing..

The RMP were called and the R&R bus was followed and stopped before it reached Belfast. A very large brass elephant and a number of other figures were located and were escorted to Belfast pending the arrival of a spare land-rover to return them to the Barracks. I was amazed at the initiative and daring of the soldiers who had managed somehow to take the figures which were extremely heavy undetected and onto the bus. It would have been virtually impossible, without a confession to identify the culprits. Any attempt at arrests would most probably have resulted in something akin to a riot or mutiny and in reality it provided the best laugh that the RMP had enjoyed in a long time. The battle honours were recovered and secured and eventually found their way home.

Northern Ireland was an enjoyable time for me, I learned a great deal about the troubles and the mistakes made by Government and the Army. I made some good friends and most importantly learned how warm and hospitable the Irish people are. In May 1976 I left Londonderry for the last time and after a short period of leave I flew to RAF Bruggen en- route to my new unit in Germany.

Back to BAOR and
a Belgian disaster

AFTER FLYING FROM LUTON AND landing at RAF Bruggen in Germany I remember a bit of a shock when I handed over some pounds sterling and received my Deutsche marks in return I could not believe the low exchange rate and at first thought that the staff had made a mistake.

I arrived in the unit only to find that it was in fact a German public Holiday and there was nobody at work, I had to find myself someplace to sleep but at least the dining room and kitchen was open so I managed to eat.

At my initial welcome interview the following day I was asked why I had become such a senior corporal and had not been promoted. I didn't really have an answer for that although it was a question I had been asking for the past few years. Other than that I hoped that the next promotion board would seek to address my misfortune and change my status.

In any event I settled down and took on a few duties at the RMP Duty room known as the Joint headquarters police station located inside the Rheindahlen Garrison.

Sadly I was to meet a newly promoted WO2 who I had known in the latter stages of my Hong Kong tenure and it soon emerged that he had put in a "bad word" for me almost certainly to the RSM and officer commanding. One of the sergeants that I had known for several years confided that the WO2 had told him that "Torr" needed watching. A fine example of crude and mischievous nonsense.

About two weeks after my arrival I was ordered to attend an interview and instructed to move to the RMP detachment at Emblem in Belgium. I resisted this move as I wanted to remain in Rheindahlen and also the fact that I had secured a married quarter and the flight for my wife to join me was confirmed. Despite my objections I moved to Emblem in June 1976, I was accompanied by another corporal who had as I was to find out applied because he had thought that he might be promoted to acting sergeant rank when the incumbent detachment commander left. I was also to meet another corporal who had already moved to Emblem in order to cover for the sergeant detachment commander but had failed to make a positive impression and had almost certainly realised that the acting position was not to be his. I also suspected that the management minds had been corrupted by the resident WO2 that I had known in Hong Kong and a decision was made to get me out of the way.

The detachment was commanded by a sergeant with supposedly a full time establishment of six juniors, most of these were not the best of the bunch. There was an interpreter, a clerk and a cleaner. During the major military Exercise season the numbers would be expected to be reinforced from unit headquarters in Rheindahlen or by other units. I was soon to learn that this in fact seldom happened and in most cases the men loaned were either the least experienced. The two senior corporals dispatched to Emblem just before me were not without problems. The first several weeks earlier and whose temporary experience as detachment commander had proved to be unsatisfactory and the second whose financial affairs were such that he thought that the allocation of the disturbance allowance resulting from a move from Rheindahlen would relieve the pressure.

It was also clear that the possibility of the sergeant rank and detachment commander status was an incentive particularly as the incumbent sergeant was due posting.

All military convoys were legally required to be escorted through Belgium to the Dutch border at Venlo from the coastal ports of Oostende and Zeebrugge as well as Berth 326 at Antwerp.

The detachment commander in post when I arrived was I soon discovered totally indifferent to the needs of the juniors. During the main

BAOR training period there were so many escorts on a daily regular basis that the juniors would effectively never have a clear day off that had not been preceded by a night duty and even these were at risk. On many occasions the men who had been on night duty would be required to report to one of the ports early in the morning and have to leave before dawn. In contrast the sergeant detachment commander worked only Monday to Friday 0900 1700 and undertook no other duties. Some of the long (100 ton) escort routes were so arduous and demanding that they could last the entire day from an early morning start to late evening. There were also the routine RMP duties to take care of and an all ranks bar which opened each lunchtime and evening.

Apart from the convoy escort duties and the rare routine police incident the most common task for the RMP was the management of British servicemen in transit and in distress travelling from the United Kingdom to Germany via Belgium and then Holland.

It was a criminal offence under Belgian Law to be unable to pay for any expenses such as breakdown recovery and also an offence to run out of fuel or to fail to be in possession of items including, warning triangle, first aid kit and fire extinguisher.

The RMP worked closely with a local garage contractor and were able to navigate any difficulties by arranging breakdown recovery and then organising recovery of payment via the soldiers own unit.

As is the case for soldiers anywhere, excess alcohol and bad behaviour occasionally took place. The most usual location for any problems was the Town of Lier and the most prevalent offence was the interference with National and international flags and emblems. The Belgian authorities. Proscribed a definitive list of the 15 most serious offences. Of course this includes such offences as Murder and treason right at the top but surprisingly for some people the offence of interference with flags rated vey high about halfway down the list right next to speeding on the Belgian highways in excess of the national limit. Any British soldier or dependant could easily find themselves arrested and taken to court, the fines imposed by British Courts would seem very small compared to those imposed by the Belgian Courts.

Belgium is effectively divided in to two separate social and political regions,; the Northern area of Flanders including Antwerp where Flemish is spoken and the Southern area including Brussels where French is the primary language.

Belgium is a relatively new country and the Belgians are probably the world's most accomplished linguists. English is spoken by the vast majority of the Belgian population in the North of the country and many of those from the French speaking South.

Policing is generally divided into two separate organisations, the National Police Gendarmerie and the local Town police the "Polite". The National Police have authority throughout the country but the authority of the local "Town Police " is restricted to the town boundaries.

The Belgian Military Police are closely modelled on the RMP however they have much more of a statutory policing role in support of the national government.

Belgium is a very rich country and the population very much enjoys the "good life" property is expensive and trappings of wealth are very much overt and well publicised. Eating out and drinking is very popular particularly during the summer months.

Apart from any other free time or social activities there are two sports which are supported by the vast majority of the population. It would be no surprise to learn that one of these is cycling and the other pigeon racing.

There was a particularly good relationship with the Belgian Military Police and one particular advantage of this was the supply of very good boots, similar to the Boots combat which would be introduced into the British Army in 1983 following the adverse performance of the DMS boot in the Falkands. In addition to the boots the Belgian army was able to supply some very nice shirts similar to no 2 dress and which were worn by just about every soldier in Emblem.

During my first week at Emblem I purchased two of these shirts and after collecting them from the tailor I hung them in my room in the detachment building. It may have been some kind of omen about what was to follow but when I returned to my room one of the shirts had been removed (Stolen).

242

Although I had my suspicions about who may have been responsible, there were only four RMP suspects it would have been difficult to prove. I suppose that in hindsight I could have carried out a more sophisticated investigation but I simply put it aside because of my workload and also the fact that I had secured a service married quarter and needed to travel to the UK in order to fetch my wife and son.

On reflection this omission may have been my first mistake as Detachment commander and one which may have contributed to what for me was a personal disaster and which was to seriously derail my career progression.

At the time I did not want to believe that one of my RMP colleagues had stolen a shirt, I could have checked with the Belgian Military police and the tailor to establish who had or who had not acquired such shirts legitimately and then to have searched every room. There were only 4 other RMP NCO's besides me and the chances or likelihood of any casual entry by any unauthorised person was much too unlikely. I would probably have identified the culprit and he would have been arrested and my Emblem History may have been much different.

As detachment commander I set out to ease the workload for the juniors and as a first step I deleted the duty of day desk NCO/lunchtime barman and although it was sometimes a real struggle I took on this duty myself.

In July 1976 I fetched my wife and son from England and settled down to live in Herentals about 15 miles from Emblem camp.

My son started pre school in Herentals I had a beautiful house and garden and the Town itself was a real joy to visit and explore. In November I collected my New car from the local Ford dealership so on the personal front life was good.

I worked hard to secure RMP reinforcements from the Coy Headquarters in Rheindahlen and because of the unreliability, established good contacts with the Belgian Military Police and the Gendarmerie with an assurance of continuing and enhanced support for the convoy escort duties to take some of the pressure from my men.

I arranged a complete redecoration of the RMP accommodation, the Bar, offices kitchen and men's accommodation.

I made a monthly trip to JHQ NAAFI to stock up on items that were in short supply in Belgium. I took time to explore the local area and made regular excursions into neighbouring Holland.

I recovered the discarded collection of vintage headdress including the obsolete Belgian Kepi's donated by the local police and visiting soldiers and procured a fine display cabinet mounted in the all ranks bar.

In February 1977 my daughter was born at RAF Hospital Wegberg and my son started at his first school Emblem primary.

As the transit season got under way I was able to secure support with convoy duties and this enabled me to ensure that my men were able to have regular days off, something that had never happened before.

Although I can't remember the exact date, one of our honorary mess members from the RCT had managed to secure redundancy and had asked me if he could have a small celebration in the bar. I of course agreed and later that week he and his wife attended along with a number of others guests and most of the RMP.

One of the RMP team, Ken Wood and his wife arrived quite late and shared a bottle of blue nun wine. I remember that Ken took only a sip from his glass whilst his wife drank only a small amount. They could only have been present for about 15 minutes when they said their goodbyes and left. A short while later everybody else left and I cleaned up and closed the bar. I was covering the night duty so that the maximum number of my men could enjoy a drink and I had decided to sleep in the office rather than drive home.

I had retained only one other NCO as a duty driver and I sent him off to bed.

A short while later I received a telephone call from the operator who said that he was calling to tell me that Ken Wood had passed away. I was a bit confused and asked the operator if he understood what "passed away" meant. He went on to explain that Mr Wood had been taken to Hospital In Herentals and had passed away.

I woke the duty driver and instructed him to go to the hospital and find Mrs Wood and hopefully find out what had happened. I contacted the senior

RMP Officer DAPM British Forces Antwerp and then had to wait for the call from my duty driver.

About an hour later I received a call from Mrs Wood who told me that she had taken my duty driver home and sent him to bed because he was so distressed. I was pretty much confused, however Mrs Wood explained that her husband had died following a road traffic accident.

The whole episode was a terrible shock and to this day I suspect that we will never know exactly what happened. The facts are that only a short distance from his home with his wife a passenger in his right hand drive car he struck a roadside lamp post. The post fell onto the roof of the car and Ken was struck on the head causing fatal injury.

I can particularly recall the following morning I was advised that the NCO I had sent to check on Mrs Wood had taken to his bed suffering from acute migraine and another of the juniors was apparently so distressed by the death of Corporal Wood that he was unlikely to be fit for his next duty.

I guess that my perceived detached attitude to this tragic death was even more ammunition for the two of them disliking me. I never could understand how they could both claim to be so affected when they had never been friends and when after all they should have been fairly professional as Military Police and might reasonably be expected to deal with such incidents on a regular basis.

Aside from the routine convoy duties there were occasionally other tasks requiring RMP action. On one such occasion I received a call from a Military unit in Paderborn Germany regarding a soldier from the unit who had "beaten up" the guardroom staff and had escaped custody, he was believed to be driving a motor car heading for the UK via the Belgian Port of Oostende. The regimental officer also added that the soldier was particularly dangerous and should be restrained with handcuffs on his wrists and legs.

I organised the details to be passed to the Belgian port authorities and later that afternoon a call was received con firming that the soldier was in custody at Blankenberg police station.

Accompanied by another NCO I travelled to the Police station and was shown to a cell. I had read the description of the soldier but it must have been about ten years out of date and totally inaccurate. The soldier stood up, he was well over 6 feet tall with a body builder physique. I confirmed his identity and explained that he was to be handcuffed. I also explained that in view of the long journey back to Emblem I would apply the cuffs to the front if he gave an assurance that he would behave properly.

He was polite and totally compliant and agreed without any hesitation.

The journey back to Emblem took about three hours, although he was not questioned he freely disclosed what had happened, he had wanted some home leave and had been refused several times although by his account he had been given no legitimate reason. He had got into an argument with his sergeant who had then placed him under close arrest. Whilst being escorted to the guardroom he had in his words been wound up by the guard who had decided to take the piss, He had in his words then "lost it" beaten them up and done a runner.

He had collected his suitcase and driven off in his own car.

He had however retained a sense of humour and had laughed when he explained that as he was waiting in line to board the Ferry, two Belgian police officers had approached him and said good afternoon Mr "Jones" we have a message for you. They then detained him and placed him in a police station holding cell.

Throughout our journey he remained polite and compliant. On arrival at Emblem, where there is not normally a full complement of soldiers on guard a number of soldiers had been called in for the duty, some of them from home and it was clear that they were not best pleased.

The soldier was to be detained over night to await his own unit escort the following morning, I released him from the handcuffs and left him in what I hoped would be good hands but with a note of caution to the guard commander.

He has no issues except with his own unit so just keep an eye on him without too much pressure and he should be ok.

The following morning his escort arrived in two land rovers, no less than a sergeant and six soldiers, that was the last I heard of him.

In May 1977 I was eventually promoted sergeant and I received a posting order for 111 Pro Coy in Sennelager. Some weeks earlier I had been advised that the detachment commander post was to be upgraded to that of staff sergeant, I suppose that with hindsight this may have strengthened the gap between juniors and the man in charge but in my view it would not fix the manpower shortage which became so critical during the convoy escort season.

The logic behind this was that the detachment should be upgraded to support an RMP platoon and it would make sense to have the platoon commander in post.

In any event my replacement, SSGT arrived and I prepared to move on to new pastures. Although I had made substantial improvement to the quality of life for my juniors I had found it necessary to remind one NCO of his responsibilities regarding duty rota when on several occasions he asked one of the single men to undertake his duty without consulting me.

In addition he had failed to comply with civilian traffic regulations after he had been caught speeding on the motorway in a borrowed motor car, it also became clear that he was almost certainly not properly insured to drive the borrowed car.

Exceeding the national speed limit in Belgium by more than 20 kilometers per hour was one of the most serious traffic violations and could be punished by a very substantial fine.

I had no powers to intervene with any police action and in any event I would not have considered it proper even to consider trying to. I warned him that he may well face prosecution. I was later alerted to the fact that the NCO had appealed to my interpreter to liaise with the local police with a view to avoiding formal proceedings. I had no idea if any kind of inducement was offered but I suspect that this may have been the case although I was never to have any evidence.

Whatever agreement or debate took place was never made clear to me, all that I know is that formal proceedings were dropped and the matter forgotten. Although the detachment interpreter was something of a personal friend I made it clear that if he had acted improperly and had in fact intervened and had I been remaining in post I may have considered disciplinary action regarding his actions and that of the RMP NCO. The most distressing part of this was that I had considered the interpreter as a friend and I had visited his home on a number of occasions As it was I left a briefing for my replacement SSGT and so far as I was concerned the matter was closed.

Shortly before I left Emblem I was asked to organise a bus for the men to attend a social as a welcome event for my replacement.

Foolishly I went one better and I agreed to drive the bus for the evening and save the cost of a driver, I had not intended to attend the social in any event as I had considered it as a welcome event for my successor.

I collected the men and their wives and dropped them off at the Mess. Rather than drive home and return I decided to remain in the unit until the event closed and in the event anybody to leave early I would be available to take them home.

About 2230 I was sitting in one of the side offices reading a newspaper, one of the juniors clearly quite drunk entered the room and started to moan about me and that he had just about had enough of me. I was totally confused as I had no idea that he had any issues with me other than he had probably hoped to have inherited the detachment commander position a year earlier. In any event as I stood up he struck out and landed a blow to my head I could see that there were two other men standing outside the door, one of them a close friend of my attacker and the other a bit of a simple follower.

I suspect that my attacker had expected to get the better of me but it didn't work out that way and I had him securely restrained against the office wall. That might have been the end of the matter except moments later I felt a massive blow to the back of my head and a searing pain. I put my hand to the back of my head which was already covered in blood, I could by now see my second attacker holding a RMP issue wooden truncheon which he had used to strike a blow to my head. The third man had left the corridor and was nowhere to be seen. My recollection of the events after this are simply too vague however it would appear that I lifted a wooden chair and smashed this on the desk. I can only assume that I did this after the attack but I could never be certain.

I have no clear memory of what happened next except finding myself in the Lier Town Hospital with a suspected fractured skull. I was later to receive several stitches to the back of my head and then spend a week in the hospital.

I recovered from the physical injuries albeit with a sore head for some time afterwards, what I have probably never recovered from is the sense of anger and dismay that these men had for some reason generated such a grudge that they felt it necessary to behave as they did.

It was a lesson to me, I had treated them well during my tenure as detachment commander. I had certainly made their working life easier and substantially reduced their duties. I had secured the support of the Belgian Military Police and the National Gendarmerie to assist with convoy escorts which allowed the men to actually have real days off.

I had secured a substantial grant to completely redecorate our accommodation and offices and totally refurbish the "all ranks" mess.

What ever motivated them will always remain a mystery to me.

I do know that the two attackers must have spun a good story and tried hard to make out that I "started" the problem. A few days later when I made my farewell visit to my OC at Rheindahlen he had clearly already decided that I had started the fight. My understanding is that the first attacker had claimed to have gone into the office to wish me good luck and goodbye and that I had insulted him, told him to piss off and then smashed the chair in order to attack him. The second assailant had struck me in self defence of his good friend. I suspect the third man had simply denied all knowledge or involvement although it would have been quite clear that he had been acting as lookout..

Whatever views anybody had the two men were tried by Court Martial, the first assailant was fortunate to escape with a severe reprimand which to me was a total let off and the second man who had struck me with the truncheon reduced to the ranks and discharged from the service.

The third man appears to have wriggled out of the plot although I know for certain that he was present and I can recall seeing him scurrying away from the scene when I was wrestling the man who started the whole incident.

Prior to the Court Martial I left Belgium and a few weeks later I had arrived in Sennelager and 110 Provost Company.

The real consequences from this incident were to follow me and as I was to discover there was nothing I could do to avoid my fate.

Sennelager Dead man Walking

ON MY ARRIVAL IN SENNELAGER I reported for initial interview with my new Officer Comanding Major Richard (Dickie Poole) BEM. At first the interview was cordial and I was made to feel very welcome. At some point the incident in Belgium was mentioned and I replied that I had been advised not to comment as the matter was still under investigation pending Court Martial. At this point the mood changed drastically and Maj Poole told me in no uncertain terms that he would not tolerate any bullying by punchy sergeants. I made an effort to defend myself against such a scurrilous accusation but this was clearly a waste of time, I was a marked man!

Within a few days I had secured a married quarter in Schloss Neuhauss and collected my wife and children. My wife was to be my only refuge and defence against a total breakdown.

My duties commenced as duty room section sergeant, during the day this task was subject to continuous overbearing scrutiny and it seemed that both the OC and the RSM had one single object in mind, to criticise and abuse the duty sergeant, specifically me.

There was never any opportunity to take a break and the sheer volume of tasks to be routinely completed was staggering. If the day duty was testing the night duty and its aftermath was simply demoralising.

At 0600m hours the duty sergeant was required to telephone the OC with a full sitrep of the nights incidents and any actions taken or pending. At the same time or often much earlier the RSM would arrive and demand the occurrence book and all other duty room records, unbelievably this process would often commence as early as 0500 hours

The RSM would retain these books until the OC arrived and they would examine every entry. It was quite normal to have to wait until after 1000 hours for the books to be returned and then of course the handover certificate had to be entered after the oncoming sergeant had read all of the previous entries. If lucky it might be possible to leave the duty room by 1030 or 1100 and then to return for the next duty at 1700 hours.

During the following weeks and months I was subjected to a concentrated campaign of aggressive humiliation, bullying and public rebuke.

I was assigned the task of completing the Paderborn route signing project which I could only undertake between normal duties on my supposed rest days. I was also assigned the task for developing the Company map store also during free time, the idea behind this was that I was to provide a comprehensive catalogue to allow anybody to obtain a map of anywhere in the Federal Republic at instant demand.

For an enlisted soldier under the spotlight it was impossible to escape scrutiny and there was simply no defence. It was also unfortunate for me that the duty system was such that I followed another sergeant who was in the spotlight and also subject to a similar level of scrutiny.

I have here produced a list of some of the incidents and events which contributed to my downfall.

In addition to being instructed to pass a sitrep to the OC each morning it was also necessary to ensure that the daily newspapers (the previous days) were collected and delivered to the OC at his home address every morning. I received a strong rebuke from the RSM for not delivering the papers. I was due to attend a senior promotion course in August but this was cancelled by the Officer commanding, allegedly in consideration of operational matters but in reality to allow him more opportunity to pursue and bully me. It would seem obvious that my future had already been decided and that such a course would be totally unnecessary and a waste of time.

Following one of the long delayed duty handovers between me and the oncoming duty sergeant, one of us had omitted to sign one of the certificates and had both been charged under section 69 of the Army Act, contrary to good order and military discipline. We were both awarded a reprimand.

Apart from the formal disciplinary action against me the RSM made a habit of allocating me extra night duties, particularly on a Saturday and guaranteed to take place if there was a Sergeants mess function. The consequence of this was that I never attended the mess on any social occasion, I never had the time or the opportunity.

On one occasion I received a complaint that a RMP land rover had struck a privately owned motor car in a married quarters area. There was only one such RMP vehicle that could have been in the area and when it returned I discovered some damage. I questioned the driver under caution and reported him. When I passed the information to the RSM and OC they accused me of falsifying the report and that there was no evidence to implicate the RMP NCO. I was instructed to send a paint sample for forensic examination before making unsubstantiated allegations.

On another occasion I was asked by the officer commanding to measure a "clay board" I had not the slightest idea what he was talking about and this was yet another opener for rebuke. I was to discover that this item was a wooden board on which the RMP commercial radios were mounted and the boards fitted into the RMP land rovers. They had been designed by the WO2 and were subsequently credited with his name. They were very useful and guaranteed to crack your head on in the event of any collision.

1977 was Jubilee year and the company was responsible for policing the event.

Prior to the actual Royal Visit and parade the company undertook two full dress rehearsals starting at 0300 hours. On the day preceding the actual parade, all seniors were required to stay overnight in the sergeants mess and parade the following morning at 0230. The parade was not scheduled to start until after midday and HM the Queen was not due to arrive until afternoon until circa 1430.

On the day of the actual event following the same early start, I was responsible for supervising three junior NCO's deployed as traffic points-men. The Officer commanding and the RSM were constantly driving around and on one occasion the RSM who was driving a military police liveried car ignored the traffic signals of one NCO and it was only due to the alertness of the driver of another car that an accident was avoided. The RSM then commenced rebuking the NCO and whilst he was doing so the Officer commanding arrived on the scene. When I cautiously tried to intervene on behalf of the totally innocent junior, the Officer commanding threatened that if I opened my mouth again I would be locked up.

About two weeks later I was again charged with failing so ensure that the handover certificate was properly signed, I received another reprimand and placed on a three month warning order. Just prior to this event I had applied for a transfer to the intelligence corps. When I appeared before the OC to answer the charge he referred to my transfer application and added that they would never accept me as a sergeant, when I replied that I would happily transfer as a corporal he replied that he could make sure of that.

Around September the company was deployed on operational field training, the officer commanding spent the entire time being driven around in a German police car driven by a senior police officer. Any hopes that he would keep out of the way were dispelled as he was constantly watching the seniors and delivering rebuke for the slightest reason. By a strange twist I was the only senior not to be singled out for personal rebuke and foolishly I had some notion that I was being let off the hook.

There was never any reason or logic to the outbursts of the officer commanding or the RSM and it seemed to me that there never needed to be. Even if things were going well they would find something to complain about.

Incredibly in between his crazy outbursts the officer commanding presented as an amiable patron and ensured that the seniors were well provided for in terms of catering, our field training meals were nothing short of excellent.

At the end of the training we all returned to Barracks and retribution was to follow.

I was surprised that I was not one of those to face disciplinary charges but one of my colleagues Ssgt "Alex" was charged for failing to stop at the scene of a Road Traffic accident. He received a severe reprimand which effectively derailed his pending promotion to Warrant Officer, when I asked him about the incident he insisted that he was totally innocent and had not even seen any accident.

Back in Barracks, on a later occasion I had warned my platoon commander the same senior staff sergeant who had already been preselected for promotion, and who was on duty as Friday night orderly sergeant that I was to meet the RSM the following day (Saturday) at 0600 hours.

As it happened the RSM arrived at 0500 hours and found the Orderly sergeant with his feet up in the rest room and asleep. He was charged with sleeping on duty and the OC managed to have his promotion revoked.

During the summer it was reported that the RSM had collapsed whilst at home on a day off whilst cutting the grass, the reasons or causes were never revealed however the following morning all of the seniors were called to the OC's office and bawled out. We were accused of being lazy and incompetent and that we had driven the RSM to the point that he was totally worn out covering for us and hiding our inefficiency.

The reality was more likely that he needed a break from constantly looking for reasons to criticise me and others and simply did not have the strength of character to remonstrate with the officer commanding. He was a sad case for the senior enlisted rank who failed to support the seniors and simply took on the willing role of Officer commanding hit man.

I had received an annual confidential report which was pretty poor by any standards, there was one particular comment which demonstrated the depths to which the OC and the RSM would go in order to bully and ridicule. I was accused of being far too familiar with my juniors and in the OC's view because I was so useless as a sergeant.

When I was in his office reading the report I challenged this statement and asked on what basis this was made. He replied that he was tired of listening to me having cosy little chats with wankers like (a named junior)

What he had in fact been doing was accessing the duty room intercom

And listening in to everything that I said.

For the remainder of my stay in Sennelager I did my best to get the work done and keep my head down. It was a forlorn hope, I was constantly rebuked in front of the Juniors, other seniors and visitors. I was awarded extra duties for the most trivial matters such as not ensuring that the duty vehicles were properly cleaned or the papers not arriving at the Oc's house on time.

I had heard of soldiers cracking up under the strain and I was probably close to my limit. I was effectively suffering from peacetime combat stress, I was having to deal with a situation over which I had no control.

I did not have long to wait, shortly before I was to hand over day duty a call was received from the wife of a soldier who claimed that she had been as-saulted. She was unable to attend the duty room and she said that she would not be at home for at least an hour, she also added that she did not want to see the RMP until her husband returned home some hours later.

I handed over my duty with a verbal brief to the oncoming sergeant who I understood would be taking the necessary action and the matter was dealt with. When the incident was reported as part of the daily sitrep the RSM charged me with failing to take any proper action, I again appeared in front of the OC and awarded a severe reprimand. I was also told that he intended to apply for my reduction in rank. I was given 24 hours to submit a letter of mitigation.

I actually completed a comprehensive letter but it was clear that it would have no effect and I would be surprised if it was actually submitted.

There is a strange irony about my experience which supports my theory that the bullying and intimidating campaign against me was planned before I arrived in Sennelager and it most probable that conversations took place be-tween Major Poole and others who had decided that I was to be demolished. There was nothing that I could have done to prevent what was an inevitable outcome. This view was confirmed when during one occasion when I was in the OC's office he stated " I didn't have to take you, I was warned that you were a wanker and a bully"

I rest my case. I never, ever had a chance. I was doomed before I even put one foot in Sennelager.

Whilst in Sennelager I met a RMP sergeant that I had known as a corporal in Hong from 1968 to 1971.

He had come to meet Major Poole and I was to discover that he had been Committed for a Court Martial having been charged with a serious assault on a Junior RMP Officer during a Christmas party. He had asked Major Poole to support him as defending officer. I also understand that Major Poole had used his extensive network of contacts to procure a smart QC to actually present the sergeants defence.

My understanding is that the Court Martial was halted on two occasions when the procedures were challenged by the Defence. It actually took a third attempt and a QC hired by the Army Legal services to successfully undertake the Court Martial.

Taking account of Major Poole's statement to me that he would not tolerate punchy sergeants and the vindictive bullying treatment to which I was subjected hardly seems compatible with his willingness to defend a soldier who was charged with assaulting a fellow albeit junior RMP officer.

Some time after I had left Sennelager it seems that Major Poole's sponsored luck may have run out. I had always suspected that certain senior officers supported him in everything that he did without question and I think that perhaps he had in his own mind become invincible and all powerful. There may be some speculation as to the reasons but at some time it was decided that Major Poole was to be made redundant as one of the four oldest serving RMP officers, my information is that before he could be served with notice, he had been tipped off and resigned.

It would have been a huge blow to his monumental ego to be "sacked" and I guess that his resignation letter or speech would have contained some powerful comments.

In December 1977 I was officially reduced to the rank of corporal and posted immediately to 114 Provost Company in Detmold.

It is impossible for anybody not in the Army and having never been in such a situation to have the slightest appreciation of what I had experienced. There is simply no escape from the merciless attack and of course being subject to Military Law there is no redress.

DETMOLD THE GREAT ESCAPE BUT AT A PRICE

I arrived at Detmold and after meeting the RSM Chick Harding attended an initial interview with the company commander Major David Manger.

I had not expected a particularly gracious welcome but at least it was honest and certainly not intimidating.

I suppose that he had to respond to what he had clearly been told by Dickie Poole.

He made it clear and along the lines of, " If we find that you really are a wanker we will have to deal with that " he also advised me that he had received a letter from the Intelligence corps who had rejected my earlier application.

Apart from the obvious loss and humiliation I was actually relieved to have escaped Sennelager even if the price was high.

I commenced normal police duties and on most occasions found myself undertaking the duties of supervising orderly sergeant. It was a real joy.

I soon secured a new married quarter and within two weeks had collected my wife and children from Schloss Neuhauss (Sennelager)

The Detmold regime was so different to Sennelager and the next two years were certainly some of the best of my entire service. There was no culture of bullying or fear, there was no intimidation or ridicule. The relations with the local police were better than anything I had ever experienced and an example was the regular invites to the police indoor shooting range and as always followed by beer, schnapps and Bockwurst.

The strain of the past six months on my wife was probably something that I had neglected and probably ignored or not understood. Our second child had only been born in February, I had been in a desperately dark place, we had moved house twice in a year and my son only five years old was now starting his third school.

My wife came out of a period of what was probably post natal depression. When I had taken her to see the local SSAFA welfare nurse she was totally unsympathetic and it seemed to me in my fragile state that even though I had escaped Sennelager my wife was to continue suffering the consequences. I realise now that I had been so consumed with my own despair that I had not seen her fragile state.

I settled down and really enjoyed the duties and the unit environment. We had settled into our new home and were able to enjoy and explore the local area. My son liked his new school and was making good progress.

I was able to resume regular running both on my own and as part of the company training programme, I kept myself fit and was enjoying life.

When soldiers and officers move service quarters there is a process to ensure that the cost is debited from their monthly pay. This involves a simple Pt 2 order being published, stop quarters, start quarters.

I had noticed that my pay was not being debited for my service quarter and had advised the pay office. The matter was not resolved for six months and when it was, the money was taken out in a single payment. I received a rather humorous note with my pay slip from the pay sergeant, " don't spend it all at once". My total pay that month was Deutsche Mark 11.00 (circa £4.00)

After about six months in the unit I was asked by the RSM if I would like to take over as the unit MT corporal, it seemed to me that this was a good move and I was very confident that I could do a good job.

I set out to overhaul the company transport fleet and in a relatively short time I had transformed what was a bit of a shambles into an efficient and effective motor transport fleet. I developed excellent relations with local REME and RAOC to ensure that our vehicles received the highest possible priority and that the maximum number of vehicles were always roadworthy.

In November 1978 I attended a motorcycle instructors course at ASMT Leconfield in the UK. I was probably not all that welcome by the bulk of the RCT students who may have considered that an RMP NCO taking up a course allocation normally reserved for RCT was a bit unfair. The course was in two main parts, the basic road-craft in and around Leconfield but with the cross country phase, a whole week in North Yorkshire around the Catterick Garrison. This phase was hard work and very cold. One of the training objectives was negotiating deep mud and when it came to this exercise it was necessary to jump up and down on the ice before we could get to the mud beneath it. We had expected to be training on the new Canam Bombadier but we had to console ourselves with the BSA B40.

On my return to Detmold I was able to set about training as many motor-cyclists as were needed. By this time I could also confidently assure my officer commanding that we had a transport fleet that was entirely and consistently fit for purpose, something that he had never had available before.

I will be ever thankful to him and RSM Harding for having faith and confidence in me, I was now properly "reintegrated" and had regained both my self confidence and self esteem both of which had taken a serious blow in Sennelager.

Although I had left Sennelager and had no contact with anybody from the company an incident took place in Detmold which was a clear example of the Sennelager mentality. During a field training exercise the RSM in Detmold had arranged with his opposite number in Sennelager to provide some men to assist in covering the Detmold duties. Such arrangements were fairly common.

At the same time one of the juniors from Detmold had travelled to Verl for an upgrading course and was using an RMP land rover to make the journey.

By the time he returned it was too late for any food from the unit cook-house and he drove to a local Schnell imbiss, fast food outlet.

A visiting "guest" RMP patrol would have been well aware that this junior was not on duty and when he left the imbiss they stopped him and asked why he was using the land-rover. They then required him to take a roadside breath test which was of course negative. In any event they submitted a report which included the fact that he had been required to undertake a roadside breath-test and that he was using the land-rover for his own personal benefit.

A few days later I was called to the RSM's office and shown the report, I was not at all surprised to see that the RMP corporal from Sennelager who had made the report was one of the men from my Sennelager section and a well known protege of the Sennelager RSM and officer commanding. The report was treated with the contempt it deserved and consigned to the bin although the junior involved was summoned to the RSM who had his own individual method of dealing with minor transgressions.

Although he was quite aware of the mischievous and malicious nature of the report he was aggrieved that the junior had not been smart enough to avoid the engagement.

Another example of the harmonious regime was that the RSM, seniors and juniors all met for breakfast at 1000 in the juniors dining room. Such interaction in Sennelager was utterly unthinkable. The unit professional capability was not in any way compromised and the morale was sky high.

Welfare of the men was clearly a high priority, one of the juniors a young ACC cook had found himself in serious financial difficulties caused by his inability to manage his own affairs. He was married with children and had reached the point where his monthly credit purchase repayments exceeded even his gross monthly wages. .He was a compulsive spender, vulnerable to virtually any invitation to part with his money.

The RSM had been tasked by the OC to sort this out and took over his financial affairs. He organised a repayment scheme to clear the man's debts and provided him with an allowance for him and his family. The man's chequebooks were confiscated and after about a year he was more or less solvent.

Very few officers and RSM's would have taken the time and trouble to take on such a task.

I also attended a four week German Language course in Dortmund, during this period I stayed in the RMP single men's accommodation at Werl and made the daily trip in a shared mini bus each morning to the training centre.

Over the next few months there were a number of changes, a new OC, new 2I/c, new RSM New CQMS and the unit moved into totally refurbished and vastly superior accommodation. I was able to retain my garage area and my own office.

In June 1979 in company with other unit members, RSM Stead, Pete Berry, Steve Wren and a loaned REME fitter I travelled to Pau in the French Pyrenees to take part in the annual Circuit Des Pyrenees, this is a motorcycle competition rally sponsored by the Pau Chamber of commerce and more colloquially known as the "Pau Rally"

This adventure required considerable organisation particularly as we would be travelling as military personnel through France which has a zero tolerance for foreign military intrusion or travel. The documentary and po-litical arrangements were undertaken by Pete Berry and I took care of every other aspect of the planning and logistics. I set out to partially demilitarise our vehicles, a land rover, a Bedford 4 tonner and four BSA B40 motorcycles. I painted these vehicles matt black and silver over the very overt black and green camouflage livery.

I procured a substantial stock of motorcycle and other vehicle spares, compo rations, water cans, jerry cans for petrol and diesel as well as a stock of duty BP coupons that cold be used during the time we were in Germany.

I also packed a stock of cleaning materials and first aid medical supplies, we were taking on a substantial journey and would have to manage without any support from the time we left until our return.

The journey was fairly slow and of course dictated by the speed of our slowest vehicle the Bedford 4 Ton. The route was as dictated by the French authorities, no deviation was permitted.

Our route took us via the SHAPE headquarters for our first overnight stop then via Paris to our second overnight stop at Poitiers where we stayed at the Le Routier truck stop and enjoyed a splendid communal evening dinner.

We continued via Bordeaux where we took a welcome lunch break and then reached Pau on the third day. Our accommodation was absolutely the most primitive I had an officers in training undertaking their parachute train-ing. The only toilets were the squat Asian style, I was later to make good use of my drum of disinfectant and I also cordoned off one section for exclusive RMP use totally respected by our unwilling hosts.

On arrival we were met by Major Honey of the Parachute Regiment who was a fluent French speaker with French wife and appointed as Military Liaison officer.

Pau is a significant French Military training facility providing parachute training for French forces and particularly junior or trainee officers.

The rank structure in the French Army is more similar to that of the USA than the British and includes what is effectively an NCO corps. All ranking enlisted men share the same dining facilities and in Pau we discovered that payment is made at the cash office prior to each meal. I have to say that our first meal was pretty much atrocious but at least the bread and the red wine were plentiful

We spent the next few days getting to know the rally route, enjoying the scenery and sampling the local food particularly the cakes and bread from an abundance of village Boulangerie.

The rally route is not particularly suited to the faint hearted, it includes the highest point the Col Des Solour and the tortuous Col Des Spandelles. Although the sun was very warm it came as a surprise when I began to feel the cold as the road took me above the summer snow line.

Our evenings were mostly spent at the local town and of course enjoying the wine and the favourite speciality, Pastis Grenadine. The local bars were always crowded with young French soldiers, mostly enlisted or conscripts. I guess that the officer cadets from our shared accommodation were simply too knackered to attempt any social outings as they were required to complete five parachute drops each day. They were not treated with any kind of respect during their training and appeared to be subject to gratuitous violence from the instructors.

The day of the rally arrived and I was the last of out three man team to set off, as I recall about 0400 hours. There were a series of checkpoints to reach and an optimum arrival time was printed on the competitors form. The weather had turned and it was cold, misty and raining, the closer to the mountains the worse it was. The Rally involved a morning route of circa 150 kilometres and afternoon of about one hundred.

I managed to get around the morning session without any mishap and was in fact only 15 minutes late, as the competitors were expected to resume within 45 minutes of their ideal morning completion time this allowed me to take 30 minute meal break.

I had invented a new vocabulary for the rally which included to the great amusement of Mrs Honey, the "Boulang" a corruption of the French bakery.

My boulang creation was a bread roll with a compo sausage and probably one of the most delicious outdoor meals available.

After lunch I resumed and was doing quite well until I reached a very steep hill. It was clear that the clutch had failed and I could not engage gear,

the engine and gear box was simply overheated. Although there was a procedure for recovery I wanted to complete the journey. I found a nearby stream
and managed to collect a load of very cold water that I poured over the engine,
I managed to restart the engine but could only manage about 5 miles an hour.
I managed to enlist the help of a passing motorist who towed me to the top of
the hill. Once at the summit I stopped for a smoke allowed the engine to cool
and then coasted down the far side.

I actually managed to complete the route albeit some three hours late.
I got back to our accommodation but had only the briefest rest as we got
dressed for the formal mayoral function the same evening.

I was to discover that neither of my team mates had completed the route
and had in fact both retired with broken motorcycles before the end of the
morning session.

The evening function was also a prize giving ceremony and in recognition
of the fact that I had completed the route and was the only Military rider to
do so I was awarded the winner of 350 cc military class.

It was great to be going back with some reward, in this case a nice Pewter
cup which I retained as a memento and a bottle of Armanac which I gladly
donated to Major David Manger.

I had now been in Detmold for nearly two years it was 1979 and although
I was very happy with both my work and family life I had decided that it was
time to leave the Army. I had received a thoroughly decent confidential report
the previous year but could not see myself making a quick return to sergeant
rank. I had no wish to become a time serving corporal.

In May 79 I had applied for a vacancy with the Cambridgeshire constabu-
lary, I travelled to the UK and after completing the entrance examination underwent a successful medical and personal interview with the Assistant Chief
constable. I later received a confirmation letter with a commencement date of
31st December 1979.

I felt that a great weight had been lifted from me and alough I was enjoying the best job in the best RMP unit I had known I had also secured a lifeline
to a new start. I had made it no secret that I intended to leave the Army and

had in fact given notice to terminate as required. I was close to having completed 15 years service and probably a fairly cynical and disappointed corporal. It was not what I had hoped for and far less than I deserved.

Around September 1979 the whole unit travelled to Vogelsang for unit training, we had a great time, ranges, live firing, orienteering and mobile treasure hunt. This was character and comrade development at it's best. About half way through the training I was summoned by the officer commanding and told that I was to report to the Assistant Provost Marshall Office in Bielefeld the following day.

I was fortunate that I was allowed to attend in civilian clothes and duly arrived at the appointed hour.

I was made most welcome and invited to relax and sit down, this was not what I had expected and for me it was a surreal experience.

The conversation started around the fact that I had given notice and I was asked about what I intended to do after the Army, I was able to share the fact that I had a written offer from the police and that although I was very happy in my post I was looking forward to a new start.

The conversation then moved to my period in Sennelager. We were returning to an unhappy and uncomfortable period. This was not an apology session but the tone was clearly one of recognition of the unfair treatment I had received. For the APM to state " I cant' do anything about what happened in the past, I would think that it would have been something of a relief to have got away from those two" was something of an admission and I have to say that I felt so much better.

The interview continued and I was then offered a sergeants post at Verl to commence in the Autumn. I had not expected this and admitted that I would need time to think it over. The APM was most understanding and agreed with the proviso that he needed to know within three days one way or another. He wished me well, I thanked him and that was the end of the meeting.

It is only now that I can appreciate that this invitation and meeting came after the resignation of Dickie Poole. Although it would be the case in my view that his departure was necessary for the invitation to take place might be contested I think I know best.

I spent that night at home and had to discuss with my wife what I should do, it was a very hard decision to reach. I had an opportunity for a completely fresh start away from the possibility of any future "Sennelager" but in order for this to happen I was leaving the life, and the country that I had grown to love.

In any event I returned to Vogelsang the following day having decided to accept the offer from the APM.

I informed my OC and in due course I received a formal posting order to move to 115 Provost Company in Verl in December 1979.

Detmold under the command of Major David Manger and the unique and irrepressible RSM Chic Harding was a happy place, if I had been fortunate enough to have been posted there from Belgium my career would almost certainly have had a better outcome.

During my time there I got to know the 2 I/C Captain Richard King-Evans. He was a prolific sweet eater and the best map reader I have ever met. I drove him on field training exercise and never ceased to wonder how he could fall asleep in the land-rover then wake up in the dark and know where we were.

Richard was good to me and helped rebuild my shattered career.

David Manger was a real gentleman and judged me from what he saw.

I will always have fond memories of him and be thankful for his honest, constructive and complimentary annual reports.

During my tenure in Detmold I met up with an old colleague from Berlin, corporal Spike Burbank

I had known Spike as a real ladies man, white BMW convertibles and stunning blondes. Spike had two failed marriages but had married again.

Spike visited me at my home and it was obvious that he had found his perfect partner, he was very happy.

Just a few weeks after this visit Spike was cruelly and most tragically killed as a result of a traffic accident whilst on field training.

My Detmold days came to an end, of course I was overjoyed and relieved to be promoted sergeant "again" but sad to leave Detmold, I had made many friends and it although I had been fortunate with some great postings during my fifteen years service Detmold must be the place where I and my family had been the happiest..

Verl and a reincarnation

THE HOME OF 115 PROVOST company at Vittoria Barracks Verl had previously been a Canadian establishment. Although a bit remote it was a well appointed location and next to Albuhera Barracks which at the time of my arrival was occupied by a Scottish infantry battalion.

Verl was also designated as the RMP BAOR training centre location for the upgrading training for the junior lance corporals and although in it's infancy, the venue for the BAOR close protection training overseen by RSM Chick Harding.

The officer commanding and the majority of the headquarters staff were located in Vittoria Barracks and some 20 miles to the West there was a detachment at Dortmund commanded by a Warrant officer 2.

At the time of my arrival the company was deployed on the annual field training exercise and a message had been left for me to undertake some of the routine police duties cover at the Dortmund detachment this lasted for about two weeks and when the unit returned from Exercise and having met the RSM I was told that I was to take on the duties of MT Sergeant.

I should add that I had never sought, obtained or claimed to have any formal MT training and was therefore effectively unqualified. I could however and without appearing to be too big headed demonstrate beyond question a substantial knowledge and had managed to create an effective transport regime out of a total mess.

A combination of my excellent organisational abilities, creative skills and experience enabled me to manage any vehicle fleet. In short there was nothing

I could learn from any formal training course that I didn't already know or that I needed to succeed.

I would add that prior to my posting to Verl I had actually visited the unit on a number of previous occasions, what I had seen and what I had heard from other visitors made it clear that such a job would not be easy as the reputation it had was very poor. I had heard many examples of RMP seeking assistance with transport problems and being given short shrift.

I joined the incumbent MT sergeant for a few days before I took a couple of days to collect my wife and children from Detmold and move them into my new married quarter at Hamm Rhynern about fifteen miles away.

On my return I agreed a date for a handover and on a Friday morning my predecessor moved out of the office to take over a new role.

It was clear to me that the previous post holder a thoroughly decent man had virtually abdicated his responsibilities and the running of the transport section. It was clear to me that the day to day fleet management as well as any decision making had been left with the three REME fitters. The REME staff consisted of one full corporal and two lance corporals. My initial impression was that they didn't care or worry all that much, or else they were not particularly competent. The team also included an RMP corporal although I was not really clear about his role and it seemed the only real task he undertook was the collection of stores. I was determined to get the department running efficiently but wanted to do this with the co-operation of the REME.

Whilst in Detmold I had adopted the policy every Friday afternoon of presenting the officer commanding with a state of vehicle availability, this would enable the OC to respond to any operational request or demand, I was most certainly going to do the same in Verl.

Like it or not things were going to change, life for my newly acquired staff as they knew it was going to change immediately and for the better.

I recall that about 1400 hours on the Friday afternoon the three REME fitters and the RMP corporal appeared to be busy cleaning themselves up and it was at this time I decided to ask the dreaded questions.

What are you doing now? How many vehicles are available?

The first question provided the answer that Friday afternoon was the corporals mess session and it had always been the case that the department would close down and go for a drink.

The response to the second question was nothing short of vague, the REME fitters simply did not know. It was even clearer now than what I had seen earlier, the MT sergeant had simply sat back and allowed the fitters free reign.

I presented the men with the reality of what was going to happen. Before anybody finished work I wanted a complete summary of what vehicles were available and in the case of those not roadworthy I needed a summary of what was required, what was happening and when I could expect them to be available. I also wanted any vehicle that could be fixed now within a reasonable amount of time to be fixed today. If it could not be fixed I wanted to know why.

I handed over a list of the unit vehicles to the REME corporal and then included the fact that at least one of the three REME would be required to check the Duty room vehicle defects book every morning including weekends, starting the next day. At this point I showed them the defects book which I was to leave in the duty room.

I had also discovered the role of the RMP corporal, one of his tasks was to undertake the admin for obtaining spares and equipment for the REME. I instructed him to liaise with the REME corporal and to provide me with an update on any list of awaited spares.

I made it clear that once the tasks had been completed, then and only then would I consider close down and allow them to go for a drink in the mess.

This was not essentially the start that I would have wanted but it was necessary, I had seen the row of land rovers that had not moved for several days and I was aware that the previous management regime was very slack.

Combine this type of vehicle management with slack platoon commanders and the result is and was total chaos, the company could not have deployed on any operation and was effectively not fit for role.

Every RMP unit is a mobile force and without a reliable and efficient transport fleet the unit would be unable to undertake any operational task.

Rather grudgingly the REME corporal got to work with his two men.

Having been presented a vehicle update and a summary of the spares needed as well as which of them would be covering the morning duties start on Saturday and Sunday, it was by now 1600 hours and I allowed them all to leave.

Over the next few days I got to work with the team and they were left under no illusions about the direction we would be taking.

I wanted the team to be happy but there were to be no deals, I was well acquainted with the routine for REME soldiers in other establishments. If they would prefer a large workshop or regimental placement together with such delights as weekend guard duties, fire piquet and other duties I could and would without hesitation easily arrange this.

The company transport fleet was a total mess, there were far too many vehicles that were not roadworthy and the general condition was poor to very poor.

The problem was not at all the responsibility or the fault of the REME. The RMP juniors were lax in carrying out the basic daily checks, the seniors did not supervise and in particular one platoon commander was totally and unbelievably ignorant as to which vehicles were his responsibility, he had even less of an idea if they were roadworthy.

There was a totally complacent, who cares attitude.

As is the case with reality checks, the overall responsibility for operational efficiency lies entirely with the company commander.

Apart from the operational vehicles, the land-rovers there were a small number of patrol cars, a 4 ton Bedford and twelve motorcycles. I recall that there were only 3 or 4 motorcycles available.

I undertook a complete check of every vehicle and trailer and submitted a copy to every senior, every platoon commander, the Officer commanding and the RSM.

One of the REME was instructed to attend the duty room every day and to check the vehicle defects book, it was often the case that the duty NCO's would not check their vehicles and then try to blame the REME for failing to take action. The drivers checks were required to be undertaken at start of duty and any faults reported. The REME would attend and remain until the duties were operational and to examine and sign the defects book. They would be expected to rectify, or at least attempt to rectify any minor faults and if this was not possible it would be the duty platoon commanders responsibility to identify another vehicle.

About a month after I had taken over the MT job my RMP store man was detained by the German civil police for drink driving. He would be losing his licence and I subsequently started a search for a suitable replacement. I regularly monitored the juniors collecting the land rovers for duty and I had spotted one such man (Tony Gratton) who always ensured that he carried out the crucial morning first parade checks.

I caught up with him and confirmed that he would like to join my small team.

The process took a few days and he was to prove to be a really inspired choice.

He was keen, smart, capable and very reliable. He undertook a local ad-hoc RAOC stores accounting familiarisation course and from then on we became an independent self ordering unit. This meant we were able to procure stores and vehicle spares more easily and much quicker.

Within reason and subject to RAOC clearance we were able to obtain vehicle parts not usually available to RMP units and which enabled us to enhance the appearance and security of our vehicles. Tony Gratton was keen to practise his skills and within a very short time he had modified a number of land-rovers, HQ ops and the OC's vehicle with hardtops which quickly became the envy of RMP units everywhere.

The three REME fitters were now well on board, one of them Steve was a keen motorcyclist and he accompanied me on some regular cross country training and the round of Army sponsored Enduro competitions.

I was keeping fit in preparation for my SPC (Senior Promotion course) in June 1980 and was determined to be the fittest student on the course. I was running regularly and a week before I attended the SPC in Chichester I recorded my best ever BFT (Basic fitness test) time of 7 minutes 39 seconds.

I was also improving my squash game and had a new partner who had played a high level whilst stationed at Chichester and been a member of the Combined Services Team. We played every lunchtime and he thrashed me every day for about two months. After this my game had improved and I had also learned his game strategy.

First I took one game from him then a second and after another couple of months I could beat him easily. Not only had my game improved but I was so much fitter and could pick up shots that he would miss.

In June 1980 I attended the RMP Training centre for my SPC and on the Monday morning of the first day the whole course was instructed to parade for BFT.

Prior to being instructed for this course I had set out to get myself very fit in order to comply with the Corps directive. Just a week prior to the course I had completed the BFT in 7 minutes 39n seconds, the best time I had ever recorded. I had also scanned the nominal roll of those nominated to attend and I was more than confident that I could outrun every other candidate.

Early on the Monday morning as instructed we all set off and I activated my wrist stop watch. I clocked my time in at exactly 9 minutes. Somewhat egotistically I had not been trying and there was nobody to challenge me. It came as a surprise to see that the DS (instructors) had recorded my time as 10 minutes. When I challenged this it was initially suggested that I had got my timing wrong, the tune later changed and it was admitted that as the second runner had taken 10 minutes 26 seconds it would be demoralising for the every other student on the course to be so far behind.

Later the same day we received the course induction briefing by the WO 2 in charge, Pete Berry. Pete was a good man who I had known for several years, I knew him to be fair and efficient and so I expected a better deal from the results of my efforts during the course than I actually received. I worked hard during the course and in the spirit of Pete's briefing "leadership is from the front" I pushed myself to do my very best and as syndicate leader throughout the course and during every "exercise" that I took charge of I set out to motivate the men and push them hard always leading by example from the front.

During the field training at Crowborough I led my syndicate against that of the second team (led by Tony Pearson) over the very challenging assault course. This involved the men carrying logs and the females carrying poles. We beat the second team easily and set a new course record. During the classroom phase we were required to deliver two presentations and I had prepared and practised these using acetate slides and OHP (overhead projectors). The classroom feedback was excellent, I thought I had done a brilliant job, timed to perfection contained all relevant information and achieved stated objectives, able to answer any question. I even managed to improve my BFT time and I left the course feeling completely satisfied with my personal performance and confident that I would be rewarded with an excellent course report.

The report when it arrived was factually flawed, totally unrepresentative of my performance and even went so far as to say that I had struggled with the service letter writing. Despite that induction "pep talk" about leading from the front and being fitter than your men, the only positive recognition I received was to say that I was one of the few to pass the BFT first time.

My own OC wanted to make a complaint and to redress the report but as I said " it's typical of the training centre and not worth the trouble" I know the truth and that's all that matters.

Secretly I was angry and pissed off but I had no intention of letting the two clowns masquerading as professional instructors know!

On my return to Verl my work preparing for Exercise Crusader really began. The company would be providing real police duty cover for the exercise which would involve the largest deployment of British and NATO troops into Germany since 1945.

It was crucial that every single vehicle was roadworthy, including the 10 motorcycles.

I am proud to say that due to the hard work of my small team the whole Transport fleet including the twelve Canam motorcycles was able to set off to our exercise location at a disused brick factory in Sarstedt near Hildesheim.

For almost a month I was able to deploy mobile patrols to investigate a wide range of incidents including road traffic accidents and to collaborate with Exercise Damage control staff.

Despite the non stop deployment the unit transport fleet did not suffer a single breakdown or accident. On the day that we returned to Barracks in Verl the autobahns were literally choked with military convoys heading West including many returning to the UK.

It had been my stated aim and ambition that every single vehicle would return undamaged and that we would not sustain a single injury. As part of my plan to supervise our RMP convoy I rode a motorcycle so that I could more easily navigate and control the traffic. I stationed other motor cyclists along the route with clear instructions. Everything was working fine however I left the motorway ahead of the convoy and collected my own car then drove to Barracks. In the moments after I left one of the motorcyclists, our very young but competent lieutenant managed to bump his machine into the side of one of our land rovers and fall off. Nothing too serious in the way of injury but a badly dented motorcycle and my perfect record spoiled.

Overall the exercise and the policing role we had undertaken had been a huge success. Although the exact figures are lost I can recall that the number of road traffic accidents that our unit investigated was in excess of four hundred.

Whilst recognising that other staff made a huge contribution such as our radio communications expert, the key to or success was the fact that I had managed our transport and my staff so successfully that we were able to do what were needed to do.

The fact is that a mobile unit with no reliable transport is doomed to failure.

In any event somebody up there must have liked what we did as our OC was awarded an MBE.

It's a classic example of how the honours and awards system works, the OC may have deserved the medal but I would have at least appreciated a word of thanks which never happened.

Apart from the daily work I managed to stay fit and in addition I applied for, attended and passed a QTO (qualified testing officer) course at the ASMT (Army school of mechanical transport) at Leconfield North Humberside

This was one of the best and hardest courses I had ever attended. When completed I was qualified to conduct driving tests ranging from motorcycle to class 3 HGV

Tests were referred to me by the Divisional Master driver and included soldiers with military vehicle test and dependants, and soldiers in private cars, It was not an easy undertaking which I had to fit in with my normal duties.

It was occasionally funny and sometimes very scary.

Most of the military vehicle tests involved soldiers from the neighbouring barracks and usually involved a group of students from an organised course.

In collaboration with the REME QTO from the regiment i agreed to conduct a series of tests on the last Friday of each month.

The first student was so bad that I had to take action and effectively abort the test. I instructed him to remain in the small canteen at the local YMCA from where we commenced the tests. I started the second test and was horrified by the poor standard of the student. I returned to the start and caught up with the other QTO it was clear that something was wrong and we assembled all of the eight students. When I questioned them it emerged that the two instructors who were nowhere to be seen had been leaving the students at the YMCA and had then been teaching a number of wives to drive in their own cars during Army time. This had resulted in the soldiers receiving a mere fraction of the training required. Every one of the tests was abandoned and the two instructors ended up in the guardroom.

Some three months after I had qualified I started to receive more sensitive tests, these included officers and their wives and children. I understand that some regimental QTO may have felt under pressure to carry out tests of their own officers and their families.

A measure of the difficulty was the fact that the QTO course pass rate was less than 25%, when I qualified and until I left the Army I was the only RMP QTO in the whole of the BAOR and had completed over 200 driving tests.

The Sergeants mess was very active and as part of the social regime we hosted a dinner every month, these alternated between regimental and ladies dinner nights.

These functions were always well attended, as might be expected and even more so because we had some excellent cooks and spent as much money as was needed to ensure a good dinner. We were also very fortunate that our female civilian cook was an ace cake baker and regularly provided such delicacies as Banana bread for our mid morning break.

There were some other functions taking place I competed at the Cop Shoot competition in Hohne, a number of RMP shooting competitions and the BAOR Tetrathlon, comprising Swimming, shooting, motorcycling and cross country running.

Our team didn't win any prizes but we came close and it was good fun.

There were several staff changes, a new OC, a new RSM, CQMS and chief clerk.

The new OC Major Jimmy Graham was keen on field training and we all took part in one of his exercises with emphasis on navigating and map reading, on one occasion he decided to abandon the vehicles and have the whole company march with all their kit to a location some 10 miles away. He set out his frugal survival philosophy when there was some dissent over the fact that the men had not received a proper meal since the previous afternoon and we were now fast approaching midday.

He had no sympathy whatever" Eat cold and drink water" was his only response.

Later that year (1981) the company deployed on the annual field training exercise, although I was the company MT sergeant I took on the platoon commander role but was not amused when the officer commanding implemented a situation simulating that the entire platoon had been wiped out and that another platoon of men would take over our vehicles and our operational tasks. Of course we made a reciprocal move by taking over from the platoon that had "seized" our vehicles.

I liked Jimmy Graham as a person, he was a religious and honest man but some of his ideas as a commander were simply unrealistic and poorly thought out.

This was a real exercise in disaster and one which precipitated such a fall in the general morale of the juniors that I felt compelled to approach the officer commanding with my concerns. To my surprise he actually acknowledged that it was hard for the men but that that they were too soft and in addition some of the seniors appeared to have little idea of coping with unplanned operational challenges and that his plan was to target them more than the juniors.

A few days later after the endex there was a meeting which included the OC 2IC RSM and the seniors including me. The 2ic had prepared the return to barracks plan and again I found myself at odds with what he was proposing and which took no account whatever of how long the men had been away from home, how hard they had worked during the exercise and what sort of work particularly around garrison police duties would be waiting on our return.

Once again I was probably out of line and the OC took a direct involvement when he instructed me to pack up and return to Barracks taking our attached New Zealand senior with me. I was instructed to ensure that the necessary measures were in place to receive the returning soldiers and I was also given licence to organise a "Special" supper and to ensure that the corporals mess was well stocked.

I may have thought that after such engagements I might have compromised my pending confidential report. Although this was initially generated by the 2ic and included the fact that I may on occasion be too outspoken the OC appeared more than happy and the completed report was exceptionally good.

On the transport side our team was performing very well and our new liveried patrol cars were easing the load on our operational vehicles. I had prepared for the coming winter, Verl was expected to receive substantial snowfalls and I had planned for this by procuring a set of wheels fitted with heavy tread winter tyres for all of the cars. The cars had to be well looked after to ensure reliability and I chose to monitor and where necessary exclude some juniors from driving them.

One evening during the winter after there had been an exceptionally heavy snowfall during the day and which was expected to continue I received a telephone call at my home from a newly promoted sergeant who was on duty as the orderly sergeant. He told me that he was sending an RMP patrol to my home to collect the keys to my office so that he could take out the patrol cars as they were fitted with "snow tyres".

This typically idiotic and ridiculous idea got short shrift from me and there was no way on planet earth that he would get his hand on my office keys and even less chance of him or any of the juniors on duty taking my precious cars out in the snow and ice. He must have been mad or stupid to even think about using cars when he had the option of the land-rover the best four wheel drive all weather vehicle in the world. An added inhibitor was the fact that that the sergeant had also contacted my OC to seek permission to take the cars out, that was never going to work either. The chances of my OC choosing to "order" me to release the cars was nonsense and was never going to happen.

Sadly I did not get my own way every time, following a request from another RMP unit, annoyingly not direct to me as they would have anticipated my response for the loan of two of our vehicles fitted with hardtops and insulated. My OC instructed me to release the vehicles on loan for a month to travel to exercise Snow Queen in Sonthofen Bavaria. I could not hide my resistance, I argued against the idea and rejected every reason submitted in support but I was outranked and overruled.

Even the argument that the temporary loss of the two vehicles would compromise our operational capability failed to sway.

The most painful words from my OC were "They are only vehicles." it was this more than anything else that made me realise how little he understood or even appreciated how much work, time and effort had gone into modifying our vehicles.

In early 1982 during the developing Falklands situation the unit was on annual training in Vogelsang. I received a message from one of the juniors who had heard that I was to be posted. Apart from being really pissed off by the fact that here I was, the last to know something that only concerned me and which was already common knowledge I didn't want to move and only two months earlier I had sought and obtained official confirmation that I would be remaining in post for another year.

On the back of this confirmation I had bought a new "tax free" car and of course I assumed quite naturally that my posting was to the Falklands.

Later after I had admonished the initial source of the informant who had taken it upon himself to share this "confidential" information I read the initial warning signal. I was to be posted to the RMP training centre with posting order to follow

I was absolutely astonished to read that I was to assume the role of MT sergeant, this was a job I did not want and in a location that I would never wish to work. When I actually got round to discussing the posting with my OC he told me that I had been specifically selected "head hunted" to go to the training centre as a result of the positive feed back from a variety of sources and that I should be well pleased.

I noted that the posting order contradicted the information that he, the OC had secured for me only 4 months earlier which confirmed I would re-main in post for another twelve months and that I had only purchased a new car on the strength of this information. Although I can't recall the exact dates I can recall that the notice I was given was the absolute minimum and that I needed to be in post at Chichester within three weeks so as to allow for the continuity of a handover takeover.

I was not at all happy, this will be a familiar situation for many, pack up the house, organise removals, re-house the children's pets investigate new schools and organise a place to live in the UK. I was fortunate that I already owned a house in the UK but there would still be work to do to make it fit to live in.

I also had to negotiate with HM customs regarding the payment I would have to make when importing my car. I had no time to arrange for importing the pets and my children were very distressed to lose their rabbits and cage birds. Around 3 months is the minimum to arrange pre checks, import checks and quarantine there is also the significant cost involved.

Sadly I had to leave and everything was arranged although it was impossible to meet the deadline date I had been given.

I had contacted the inland revenue and they had agreed to accept a personal cheque accompanied by a letter from my bank.

When I arrived at the port of Felixstowe and entered the "To Declare" section I introduced myself and the duty officer located the memo reference my earlier contact.

Armed with his copy of the Glasse's Guide he proceeded to give my car the once over.

I had deliberately left it dirty even though it was only three months old. The customs officer was not very confident and was asking my advice regarding the model of my car. He identified a model and the figure to pay was just under £500.00, I was happy with this and was about to write out a cheque when a more senior and clearly wiser!! Official decided to stick his nose in. He looked at the book, looked at the car and unfortunately for me correctly identified the exact model. Result £850.00 to pay.

The next three weeks involved sorting out the house reconnecting the phone and a thousand other tasks. Back to Britain and the general incompetence expected. BT originally quoted a three months wait to reconnect the phone and all they had to do was press a button, I also had to pay but at least they managed to amend their connexion time to a mere two weeks.

Although we all have to pay our way, this posting back to the UK was proving to be very expensive particularly in view of the fact that it was unwanted, unexpected and sudden.

I have done my best to forget but the overall expenditure would have been in the region of £3000.00 within a couple of weeks.

Roussillon A pressed Man, Intrigue and conflict

I ARRIVED AT THE RMP Training centre to take up my new post and contrary to what I had been told, I was to discover that my predecessor had already departed for pastures new on promotion. He had left me a written briefing which suggested that the transport fleet was in very good order and that all documentation was fully up to date.

My initial meeting was with my direct, next in line supervisor the RQMS.

This meeting did not go well and I took serious offence at the " learn your job" and how things are done at the training centre.

I had decided that for the time being I would live in the mess whilst my wife and children remained in our own house. Both children were now established at a new school and I wanted to avoid any more disruption.

Before I could really get to grips with the MT management I needed to undertake an audit of what vehicles were on the books and where they were deployed.

I was astonished to discover that there were so many irregularities that I hardly knew where to start.

The commandants staff car was permanently allocated to his wife and he had permanent use of another pool car, the RQMS was allocated a pool car which he used to travel home at weekends to his home in Southampton. Not only was this a blatant misuse of MOD transport and fuel but he had no access to a secure parking area and this in a part of the country where there was a substantial Irish population and IRA support.

The TAVR land rovers had been improperly deployed to the initial training wing and fitted with dual controls. This had been against the wishes of the WO 2 TAVR and it seriously compromised his operational capability. Although the close protection wing at Longmoore was well established and of great importance I identified a totally cavalier attitude towards the maintenance of the diverse range of non -standard vehicles that they used. Servicing and repairing these vehicles was very expensive and there was no real programme in place to ensure that they were seen as often as needed so as to ensure reliability and safety. I was to discover that all relevant documents were held by the CP staff and they would only present their vehicles when they were suffering serious faults.

I was liking this job less and less every day.

I eventually located the service documents relating to the proper military vehicles and discovered that they had largely been maintained by the civilian fitter.

I was also to find out that I would be expected to undertake regimental duties with the trainees at the Centre Duty room, I actually enjoyed these but a bit annoyed to discover that my predecessor had not undertaken such tasks because he was far too scruffy to mix with the recruits and in addition he did not have a uniform that fitted him simply because he was too fat.

It was inevitable that I would find myself in conflict with the established regime although there were some incidents that were simply unbelievable. At the end of my first month and having located the vehicle record books I discovered that my calculator battery had run out. Quite reasonably I went to the G1098 stores and asked the storeman (another retired RMP warrant officer) for a battery. When I confirmed that I was actually using my own personal calculator (despite using it for official purposes) he told me that a battery could not be provided for use in unofficial equipment and that I would have to buy my own.

Arguing with idiots like these was a total waste of time so I just never bothered and walked out.

I informed the senior driving instructor that I would be recalling the TAVR vehicles from his training fleet and that the dual controls would be removed. He protested loudly and even threatened to go and make a formal complaint to the Centre commandant. My response was to go ahead, after all they were not his vehicles and they have to be available for an operational role first and any secondary role will have to be subject to a satisfactory agreement between the training wing and TAVR. I have no idea if he went to the commandant but I heard no more about it except from the TAVR WO who was now able to undertake training as and when he chose.

As a qualified testing officer I registered with the South East District master driver as soon as I arrived in Chichester. I also offered my services to the senior driving instructor and this included my skills as a qualified motorcycle instructor. When I shared this information with my immediate line manager I was told that I would have to pass any request referral for any driving test to him for approval for the necessary time off. The irony of this is that later on in the year when I received my annual confidential report I was severely criticised for not making myself available for driving tests!!

I was also required to provide a pool car each morning for the Training centre commandant despite the fact that he had his own staff car and allocated driver.

This caused no end of trouble and I could already sense the hostility creeping in.

I failed to see the importance of providing such a car as a few simple enquiries revealed that the additional driver obtained by the commandant was simply undertaking domestic chores and that the commandants wife was using the commandants official car as a personal taxi service.

During the operation regarding the Falklands conflict it was necessary for every military unit which included the training centre to post an availability of personnel and vehicles to MOD in London. The simple process for this would have been a registered package sent from the post office by 1600 hours which would be delivered by 1000 hours the following day. Because the training centre was reluctant to spend the money on postage I had to provide a car to be driven by one of the centre driving instructors assigned the task of delivering the letter each evening to central London and on overtime pay.

During the annual Chichester marches a huge amount of equipment had been delivered to the training centre by commercial freight agencies. At the end of the March and once the equipment had been assembled on the barracks parade ground I was instructed by the Quartermaster to organise the return of the equipment using military resources. This was of course not only impossible to organise as the sheer number of vehicles needed would be beyond the local military capability but also the equipment to be moved was not military and in fact had been hired and delivered under the financial accounts of the Chichester march organisation.

In addition a forklift was required as most of the equipment was so heavy that it would have been impossible to load by hand.

I had no option but to engage the same commercial freight company to remove the stuff that had delivered it several weeks before the Chichester march organisation and would certainly have reduced the overall profit.

The arrangements for the annual RMP Chichester made were completed prior to my arrival and were largely overseen by a march committee. I had not been assigned any particular role however I made myself available during the week leading to the event and undertook a large number of out of hours driving tasks. During the march weekend and the day of the march, I had still not been allocated any specific role. I remained in the barracks ready to assist at any time.

I was however kept rather busy undertaking the task of duty officer, providing access to refuelling for military vehicles and providing support.

I noticed that a number of the permanent staff seniors had found themselves busy at the bars, how convenient

I was a tad annoyed but not really surprised that a few days after the event I was effectively rebuked by the quartermaster who had been told that I had not taken any part in the programme and had allegedly been reprimanded by the RQMS several times. The conspiracy was gaining momentum.

Although I do not know how the idea originated but the training centre commandant had organised a special concert at the Chichester festival

Theatre in order to raise money for the Falklands fund. There were several well known TV and film personalities, John Mills, Petula Clark, Terry Scott and a host of others.

All members of staff and recruits were required to attend in full ceremonial (no 1 dress) and line the aisles between the seats full of paying guests. The concert was a complete sell out but most of the soldiers were unhappy about having to take part in the show with a special rendition of "A policeman's lot is not a happy one "

I could see that many of the soldiers were very nervous and embarrassed. I simply told them to close their eyes and shout out the words of the chorus and it would soon be over.

Apart from the inconvenience and embarrassment it was a good concert and without question in aid of a very worthy cause.

As is the case for most sergeant's messes there were regular mess meetings and in addition to the normal routine business including planning functions and allocating funds there was the almost mandatory moaning and complaining session. There was one particular individual who I found painfully annoying and if my recollection serves me well, he was the chief clerk.

For reasons best known to himself he found it necessary at every meeting to complain about the mess newspapers being removed from the mess and therefore preventing members from reading them.

Because I was travelling home at weekends and to avoid the appalling traffic, I had after several weeks of experimenting decided to leave home at 0400 hrs on Monday morning, with a bit of luck this would get me to Chichester circa 0630, with time for morning hygiene and breakfast before starting work.

You can imagine my surprise when I returned and saw the complainer throw a newspaper into the bin outside my mess bunk, .I had to ask!! Of course he maintained that he didn't know it was my bin and they were old papers from Saturday.

There was never any further mention of newspapers!!!

Some weeks later all mess members received a "corporate" invitation to the Chief Clerk's wedding reception which was being held on the Saturday in the mess.

I did not attend but when I returned on Monday I did ask the mess staff how the "party" went. It would appear that the Bride failed to attend and instead had "eloped" the night before not with another man but another female.

Towards the end of the summer I received my annual confidential report which was the equal worst report I had ever received. It was pure and total fabrication and lies and the following morning after taking advice I submitted a very substantial appeal.

By a strange coincidence I met the RMP officer in charge of the RMP records office whilst I was undertaking one of the tasks of the duty officer and opening the petrol point out of hours.

I was asked how I was getting on and enjoying the training centre. I was never going to waste this opportunity and gave him a complete uninhibited account including my recent confidential report nonsense. He admitted that he was very surprised at what I had told him and responded by telling me that although a number of highly complementary referrals had been made, the posting order from Verl had only been made following assurances from my Officer Commanding that I wanted to move.

He promised to look into the matter for me but realistically I did not expect a great deal and certainly not as quickly as it turned out.

The following morning I was rudely summoned to the commandants office and invited to speak to the officer in charge of records by telephone. In total disbelief I was asked where I wanted to go, I said that I would take the first vacancy in BAOR but that I would not move overnight and would not move before January 1983.

My request was agreed and a few days later I received a posting order to 111 Provost Company to report on 6th January 1983.

The commandant was most unhappy and made it clear that he wanted me out of the training centre immediately, he did not get his way and although I handed over responsibility for the Transport section I had to remain in Chichester for the remainder of 1982, the only vacancy that could be found was as sergeants mess manager and that's what I did.

I was rather annoyed that I was posted to Chichester and particularly by means of deceit, I would never have agreed to such a posting at such short notice, I was never asked. I have no idea who was telling the truth and I have no idea why the Verl officer commanding should have said that I wanted to leave. There can only be two possible explanations. The OC really thought that he was doing me a favour and that a stint in the training centre might enhance my career and promotion prospects.

The other explanation might have been that the OC and the 2IC considered that I was on occasion too outspoken, too precious about my little empire and too big for my boots.

Training bluff and double standards

FORMAL AND LOCAL TRAINING WAS an important part of service life and I was to undertake a number of accredited programmes.

In February 1973 whilst serving in Berlin I was allocated a six weeks regimental signals course at the RMP Training centre. Although it was freezing cold when I flew from Berlin the weather in England remained kind for the duration of the course.

The whole programme was great fun, I got on well with the other students and staff. There was a lot to learn, theory of wavelengths and frequency, antennae, voice procedure and encoding systems.

There was a good deal of outdoor practical work including days out around the country.

The end of the course involved a comprehensive practical and written theory test.

On the last day of the course we were presented with our results.

Paul position on course 1st overall pass mark 79.8% grade C.

I struggled with the .2 and was annoyed that I could not have been raised the full stop to a B grade.

In 1978 I attended a Motorcycle instructors course at the ASMT Leconfield in what was then North Humberside.

The first part of the course took place in and around leconfield and we used the BSA B40 as the replacement Can am bombardier had not yet been deployed.

The second party of the course took place at Catterrick North Yorks, it was very cold and very hard work.

At one point it was so cold that we took to jumping on the ice covered pools to expose the deep mud underneath.

I actually found the course to be very testing and on one occasion after I had completed my training objective delivery I was "asked" to do another high speed run through the deep mud disaster struck and my chain snapped.

The general rule for students was, fix it or push it.

The instructors threw me a new chain, it was getting dark, the bike was covered in mud and I was most unhappy. One of my fellow students helped me out, we replaced the chain and I was on my way.

We eventually returned to Leconfield where we completed the training and cleaned and serviced our machines in preparation for the next course of students.

I was glad to finish and set off back to Germany and home. I had however learned a great deal both about myself my over cautious, riding techniques and maintenance which would help me later with training and competitions.

In 1978 I also attended a 4 weeks German language course in Dortmund, this was great fun and I learned a great deal to improve both my spoken German and my ability to read.

There were two great instructors, one an Army Major and the second a very attractive civilian Swiss lady.

I came away from the course with a good pass mark whilst regretting that I had not done this many years earlier.

In 1980 I attended a six weeks Senior promotion course, July and August at the RMP training Centre Chichester.

I had been mindful of the ongoing hype about leadership and personal fitness which had in recent years become the primary qualities demanded

I was at that time the fittest I had ever been and determined to be at the front from the start

I recall scanning the students nominal roll before I left for Chichester and thinking amongst those that I knew who could give me a run "quite literally" for my money.

The very first day of the course started with an early morning BFT I was a bit surprised when I saw who I had considered to be my only competition struggle to make the mandatory minimum time. He had become overweight with sergeant rank.

Throughout the course I worked hard and demonstrated my superior fitness on each test occasion including the long walk back from Brighton to Chichester over 100 kilometres

The course report hardly reflected what I had achieved, I think that in hindsight this was an omen that the training centre culture and me were incompatible.

In 1984 as part of the deal I had conceded for an extension of tour in Hohne I took over the role as CQMS and attended the 6 weeks RQMS course with the RCT in Aldershot.

This was an entirely theoretical programme and one which required substantial extra study.

The course went well and the students were a good bunch mostly Ssgt or WO2 rank with a couple of sergeants including one Gurkha.

The course concluded with a two days of written examinations one each in the morning and the same each afternoon afternoon.

I was coping very well no problems. The final examination involved the dreaded ammunition account, all of the examinations were based on a scripted scenario and with about an hour to go I had answered every question. I had taken time to review my answers against a copy of the Material Regulationss and decided to hand in my answer papers. I was a bit confused that the other students were still writing and as I shuffled my papers for the last time I glanced at the rear of one of the question papers and was horrified to realise that I had missed three questions.

With about twenty minutes to go I allowed myself a moment of panic and got to work.

I managed to finish on time and later allowed myself a cigar and in the evening as well as a couple of brandies.

What a near disaster, I managed a good pass but it was a near thing.

January 1983 Hohne and Salvation

‿·

On 6TH January 1983 I arrived in Bergen Hohne, home of 111 Provost Company.

I was delighted that a married quarter had been allocated so that I was able to have my wife and children travel with me. We arrived about 8pm, I collected the keys from the duty room, it was a decent flat and Ssgt John Salmons had thoughtfully provided some arrival rations so that were able to have a reasonably decent meal after the very tiring drive. Next morning I went into the unit and this was the start of what was probably the most rewarding posting I had ever had.

Although I was to start as a section sergeant in number four platoon commanded by John Salmons my transport management reputation had preceded me and due to a serious failing in the RMP Hohne transport department I was also assigned the additional task of sorting out the MT and generating an efficient regime.

I had visited Hohne previous to 1983 and although I had never really heard much good about the company or the location I had not had the opportunity to form any particular view.

I was soon to develop a very positive impression, there was a total absence of the intimidating and bullying type of regime that I had feared might be in place and morale was high amongst the juniors.

Bergen Hohne has a long history of Military training although it was the evolvement of the NAZI regime and the need for a large tank and artillery training area that really developed the area.

In 1936 the Wermacht cleared a number of villages and created the modern training area of around 284 square kilometres.

The most infamous association with Hohne is the concentration camp at Belsen close to the town of Bergen, a short distance from the Hohne Garrison.

Despite the fact that Hohne was in the front line of any potential military conflict I was to discover that the men and equipment, including vehicles were far from being ready to go to war.

After only a few weeks I was relieved to find myself promoted to Staff Sergeant and even more delighted when I was informed that I was to remain in post as platoon commander in place of John Salmons who was also to be promoted and posted.

To many it might seem that such a promotion was not all that significant. It was to me and for many reasons. My unhappy period at the Training centre and in particular my serious reverse at Sennelager had compromised my career and promotion prospects and in a moment I had felt vindicated.

Hohne might not have been the most glamorous location but for me it was a reward and as a platoon commander the best job I could ever have been given.

On the personal front, my wife had acquired a part-time job and both children were happy and well settled into their new schools.

The service quarter was fine, the shopping facilities were excellent and access to other towns and places of interest were good. I was more than happy with my job, life was good.

Shortly after arriving in Hohne and whilst driving from my home in Bergen to the Garrsion I spotted a gentleman walking towards the Garrison. I recognised him from his walking style even though I had not seen him since Chichester in 1968.

It was Tony (Paddy Roper) I stopped and I think that he was even more surprised than I was and highly amused to know that had only recognised him from his distinctive walk even after fifteen years.

Tony was no stranger to Hohne as he had served there earlier in his career, he had married a local German girl and after he retired had returned to live in Bergen.

What a small world?

The next year was exceptionally busy, I had by now rectified any deficiencies with the vehicle fleet and had felt confident enough to relinquish responsibility to another senior. I was able to implement the measures I felt necessary to improve the operational efficiency of the platoon although not everybody shared my enthusiasm.

I was able to send the maximum number of newly arrived Juniors on German language courses and to approve the maximum number to attend the Exercise snow queen.

I was also able to complete the Education for Promotion Certificate at the garrison education centre and keep fit with the almost daily and very competitive morning runs.

Operational field training exercises took place and although it gives me no pleasure to admit, it was the juniors who made the exercises successful rather than my seniors who were mostly unable to compete in levels of skills, knowledge and sheer enthusiasm.

I was perhaps fortunate that I had a substantial number of excellent juniors in my platoon although with hindsight I may not have been as vocal in letting them know

One unpopular written instruction I delivered was that once we had deployed on exercise there were to be no visits to shops and in particular any fast food outlet any (schnell imbiss) was 100 % off limits.

I was conscious of the abilities of all of the men under my command and was careful to allocate men who could work well together and in the case of the seniors to ensure that a top notch junior was crewed with them to make good any shortcomings.

Overall I believe that my plans worked well, I wanted the men to be able to eat well and to be able to survive in any environment using the resources provided. As part of our platoon training I had ensured that every man was able to operate the issued cookers and lanterns, was proficient in the use of combat radio and the security systems that would be required.

It may be the case that I did not tell them often enough but the men of my platoon were without question the best in the company and at least as good if not better than any other, anywhere.

I had also made it a routine to personally inspect every mans packed personal equipment and had always invited them to inspect mine before I did so. This offer was never taken up and I know that such inspections really pissed the men off.

Once packed I expected each man to secure his equipment in the platoon store and in the event of any operational deployment, planned or otherwise we all knew that we would not have to go hunting for our kit.

I had no mercy in respect of our platoon vehicles and there could never be any reason or excuse for any NCO to garage any land rover after use without it being cleaned and refuelled. I was determined that my platoon would be ready for immediate deployment at any time. I know that this also pissed off the men but they realised the benefits when we turned out for exercise or emergency (quick train) callout and were literally ready in minutes whilst other platoons were scurrying around in panic and confusion.

I was very busy with undertaking driving tests and also working towards improving the driving skills of the men under my platoon. In addition to some formal activities I had developed a covert method of observing. As part of the platoon and duty officer programme I would cover the 72 hours period for the three night duties when my own platoon was on duty. I would always attend at 1800 hours for the handover takeover and again at 0800 hours the following day. In addition I would visit the duty room around 2200 hours and at any other time that my attendance was requested. My routine was simple I would inform the orderly sergeant the time I was to be collected from my home and he would send a car or land rover to collect me, I was always dressed in duty order. Once again I knew that the men would be pissed off but they had to live with this and I had the opportunity to observe their driving. I suspect that some of them would have tried every dodge to avoid this dreaded collection duty.

I was always confident that apart from the differences due to rank and age!! I was able to enjoy a good relationship with my men, most of them understood my nature and my reasoning. I was particularly keen to allow even the most junior corporals the opportunity to demonstrate their ability and supervisory skills with garrison police duties and on operations.

My reasoning was not shared by other seniors but appreciated by my juniors and I can say that they never let me or themselves down.

On operations I made it a habit to spend some time with each crew and I made it clear to them that part of this was for me to observe their cooking skills and to share a meal with them. I have to say that in this respect I was never disappointed but one crew in particular Messrs (corporals Mcmath and Denison) were always the ace in the pack who produced some excellent meals. Some crews had a lot to learn and I was always at pain to sound positive, never to criticise and to remind them that they could only learn by doing and that if we ever went to war they would have to fend for themselves without bratwurst and chips.

Following our deployment on the major exercise Lion heart in 1984 my platoon received such positive feedback that when a platoon was requested to attend another major FTX in support of another Division my officer commanding agreed to allow me to deploy. Unfortunately I was never properly briefed as to my role and I was simply held in reserve for two weeks, it was clear that those in charge of our host RMP company had little or no operational experience or knowledge and didn't' want me around to observe

Off duty both the sergeants and corporals messes were always busy and board Sailing had become a most popular pastime for the juniors. There was ample time off and I was always willing to grant annual leave and additional days off for any convincing special occasion.

I was also particularly mindful of the need to provide maximum notice of duties and wanted to ensure that when the men finished any duty they would know when they were next required.

I was however intolerant of any lack of punctuality and I enforced my rules regarding vehicles.

Police investigations and reports featured significantly in our daily routine and I personally kept a close watch on every open case file. There was no excuse for any unreasonable delay and every NCO was required to ensure that any live case was either completed or minded by a colleague during any absence on leave or course.

As far as I was concerned, once published the duty rota was to be fully complied with. I would not allow any unauthorised changes, during my tenure as platoon commander there was only one such misdemeanour and this led to the only occasion when I felt it necessary to place one of my juniors (an otherwise outstanding NCO) on report.

I only discovered the change due to my platoon being on duty Christmas day and when I visited the duty room I discovered that my NCO had actually paid a sum of money to the NCO from another platoon to take on his duty so that he could take a trip to the UK.

This was not simply a case of swapping duties, his leave away from his unit was unauthorised, the payment to another man was totally improper and he had demonstrated a complete lack of manners and respect. It was almost certain that had he approached me I would have agreed to his taking leave, one man more or less would not have made such a huge difference.

As a consequence he appeared in front of the officer commanding, admitted his guilt and received a fine.

In 1984 I applied for an extension to my tour in Hohne, there were some who thought that I was mad or taken leave of my senses but they were wrong. I was enjoying my time and had hoped that with that extra bit of luck I might just make WO 2 before I retired at the 22 years point in December 1986.

My request for extension was agreed but only subject to me agreeing to take on the duties of CQMS.

I agreed to take on this new post and prior to attending the six week RQMS/CQMS course at Aldershot I most reluctantly handed over my precious platoon to a new staff sergeant who I hoped would take great care of the whole works.

I duly set off to Aldershot and in the winter discovered it to be the worst barracks I had ever lived in and in short it was a dreadful experience. The RCT sergeants mess in the home of the British Army is a place that I might have expected to be reasonably comfortable. The reality was different, the four storey building accommodated a different course on each floor, in our case twenty students on the third floor. Each of the rooms were so tiny that there was barely room to walk between the bed and the wall, the central heating was totally inadequate and was even unable to prevent the forming of a layer of ice on the inside of the windows.

The worst discovery however was that there was no shower!! And astonishingly only one bath on each floor.

To make matters even worse there was never enough hot water and I eventually took to having a bath at 0400 hours when everybody else was in bed, the bath was the only time that I was warm.

At least the food was good.

It was essential that a couple of hours study was undertaken every night after classes.

It was however so cold in the rooms, I had taken to sleeping in a tracksuit and woolly hat, the only place to be able to study in relative comfort and warmth was in the sergeants mess bar area.

In any event I rather enjoyed the course although the final exams were fairly hard.

I was pleased to see the end of Aldershot and to return to Germany and Hohne.

On my return I was informed that during my absence on course, a board of officers had had taken place comprising the The 2IC, the RSM the Training WO2 and the outgoing CQMS.

The necessary certificates had been prepared for my signature although it was always the case that had I insisted, a new board would have to be convened.

I agreed a compromise, the outgoing CQMS would show me around the stores, I would examine a range of items such as accountable documents, technical instruments, arms and ammunition and the allocation inventories to the platoon commanders.

I had known the outgoing CQMS for a number of years and Hohne had in fact been his first Germany posting. I was of the view that his knowledge and ability as a platoon commander was flawed but hearing him talk about his job I might be forgiven in believing he knew what he was doing as CQMS. Big mistake on my part

Having checked most of the really sensitive items including the Mobilisation stores which I noted contained the full mob issue of NBC suits I saw that each package had been endorsed and signed by each member of the board as having been checked and was correct.

I then selected some random items one of which was sleeping bags.

I was assured that the number held was in excess of the numbers officially held.

This was a major miscalculation and this is how I identified the error.

Each NCO was issued with a sleeping bag and in addition there were some in for dry cleaning, my predecessor had counted those signed for, added those in for dry cleaning and those on the shelf not issued. His result was a surplus.

My calculations were different, count the number of signatures, compare those signatures against the bags in for dry cleaning and deduct from total then add any on the shelf. Result shortage of around ten sleeping bags.

This was not a trivial issue, the basic price of a standard sleeping bag in 1984 was around £ 150.00 plus added VAT.

This was most certainly for my predecessor an unexpected and distressing turn of events and it took a while for the facts to sink in, there was a deficiency of around £2000.00 and somebody had to take responsibility.

I decided to check a few more items but there was nothing of particular concern.

I presented my finding to the officer commanding and we agreed that the hand over could go ahead with the deficiencies recorded, any decision regarding covering the costs would be his decision and in the event that I was unable to arrange something through normal accounting procedures and liaison he would need to exercise his powers of write off, in any event I was not going to be responsible for this deficiency.

In between my CQMS duties I continued to conduct regular driving tests, take part in any fitness programme, organise sergeants mess functions, take a share of duty officer rota and supervise any driving related training including the written BFG matrix (tick tests) for new arrivals.

I needed an assistant that I could trust and rely on but such a post was probably seen as irrelevant and in some cases a backward step. I managed however to persuade Corporal Mario Mianini to join my staff and I was ready to go.

There were many standing tasks to be completed and also some that were involving annual events. The majority of stores required a manual document to be completed and submitted via channels endorsed with the relevant priority and quoting the necessary authority under which the items were being requested.

There were some items that did not require a unit request to be made, these included expendable items such as dry cell batteries, these were reconciled against the equipment held by each unit. A more important item was the NBC (Noddy Suit) and gloves, inner cotton and outer disposable rubber. In the case of the suits new items would be automatically delivered and as part of the stock quality rotation these would be taken into the MOB store and the oldest stock could then be taken from the store and used for training. The suits came in three sizes, naturally; small, medium and large. In a military police unit such as Hohne there would be five suits held in stock for each member of the unit regardless of rank.

A few weeks after my takeover I received my first "Auto Maint" issue of new NBC suits but I was in for a surprise and not a welcome one either. When I opened a box of what was labelled as the oldest stock and checked the contents I found that there was a whole range of expiry dates. I opened a couple more boxes and found the contents to be similar. This was potentially a serious matter and the only option I had was to open each box and separate the contents into date order and with a proper distribution of the three sizes in each box. The unit strength was about 140 plus the usual 10% spare allocation so for ease of accounting here about 150 x 5 = 750 suits.

The operation took me and Mario virtually the whole week and worse was to come as when I checked the contents it became clear that my predecessor and possibly even before him had not understood or had not bothered with the rotation of the suits. Some of them were date expired and older than those in the main store as training items. In any event I repacked every box properly labelled and endorsed with number, sizes and expiry dates. Some of the suits on the training shelf were taken into MOB stores. It was fortunate that had already met up with the Divisional Ordnance Warrant Officer who was able to authorise my urgent request for replacement NBC suits and within a month the stock was correct. I had also taken the opportunity to unpack and check the protective gloves, there are two items. Black rubber over gloves and inner cotton, the rubber gloves have a shelf life of three months but here I was in April 1985 unpacking mob (war time) stock which would have been essential for survival in an NBC environment and which had been taken into stock in 1963. Trying to open the gloves to wear them simply caused them to split open. Ordering gloves was easier than suits and I soon had this matter resolved. I was beginning to regret taking over but I simply had to keep going or else the whole thing could end in disaster. In the event of a real operation the rubber gloves would have been useless and the wearers unprotected.

Further checks revealed that a whole load of specialist tools incorporated into the mobilisation stores had been issued to the REME fitters, more favours of the BOWO in order to replace these items which could only be obtained with his specific authority

What else would I find? I would not have long to find out.

A diary of events had been published for the whole year at both company level and within the CQMS department. One major event was the RMP sponsored Exercise Cop Shoot. This competition involves competitive live firing and the amount of ammunition required exceeds the amount that the company would be able to source from the normal annual training allocation. I had received written confirmation from my predecessor that the ammunition had been ordered via divisional ordnance from central training and that it should be delivered at least a month before the event. Allocation of such an amount of ammunition would of course be beyond the unit training allocation and had to come from the Divisional pool. I did not want to risk anything and decided to follow up for a progress report. To my horror I was informed that no such request had been submitted and that this should in fact have taken place prior to my takeover to enable the Divisional Ordnance staff to assess the annual non standard training entitlement. Normal training ammunition is derived from the rotation of mobilisation stock when new ammunition is taken into store and the oldest released.

Here I was only a few weeks into the job and already into debt to the DOWO. I was obliged to call him again for help and the matter was sorted out.

I was able to help him out not long after when he called me urgently late at night hoping to borrow trailers, shovels, pickaxes, tents and torches. I was only too willing to help him immediately and I must say I felt a lot better and much less in debt.

Life continued much the same each day, cop shoot came and went and then I was hit with the news that I was to receive a visit/inspection from the MOD defence audit inspection team. Fortunately I had previous experience of such visits so I knew what to expect. There were two inspectors and they had allocated five whole days to the visit. On arrival they explained what they wanted to see and I then showed them around my empire. They liked an early start which suited me and it was clear that they were smart, thorough and professional moles. They left nothing undisturbed and had lists of commercial radio equipment for which I was apparently responsible but had never heard of and even less idea of where they might be located. It took a while but we eventually managed to find everything. Most of the "hardware items" such as antennae and rebroadcast had been set up years earlier and had never been seen since.

Over the five days literally every item was inspected including, weapons, ammunition, every item of stores and documents.

On the final day the lead inspector presented a verbal summary to my officer commanding. The overall report was initially graded excellent with two recommendations.

First. During a check of the training ammunition which I had checked days before, the inspector had opened a small number of cloth ammunition (7.62) pouches and when he counted the loose rounds discovered that one of the pouches contained eleven instead of ten rounds. The outcome of this was that there a surplus of one single round over that declared. Accounting in the army is a perfect system and does not allow for any surplus. It's okay to have used ten more than declared but never hold one more

Recommendation That CQMS and duty officer undertake weekly count of ammunition to avoid any surplus held. Substantial quantity of dry cell batteries were issued each month and placed on a range of shelves. These were rotated so as to ensure oldest at front and newest at rear. I was not able to provide a precise number of each type of battery as I had never considered this to be necessary.

My reasoning, The allocation was based on possible wartime use to enable each item of equipment to operate and in fact a number of batteries were for equipment not used during peacetime. The majority of Batteries were disposed of as rubbish and never used. I was also able to add that my representation to RAOC regarding level of stock referred to the potential operational "wartime" needs

This cut no ice with the inspector who recommended that a stock bin card be attached to each shelf section with numbers of each battery held.

My officer commanding asked me to implement the recommendations and that was job done.

A few weeks later I received a personal visit from the BOWO who had also received a copy of the Auditors report. He was most pleased and like me a bit amused at the trivial observations, it showed that the inspector was pretty much happy with what he had seen but needed to be able to provide something for me to action.

Several weeks later I received a call from a CQMS in another major unit which was due an audit inspection in the near future. I told him what the inspectors had been like and specifically mentioned three areas to focus on.

The first was anything that might involve actual money, travel warrants and duty coupons for BP fuel.

Second was the need to ensure accounting of consumables such as dry batteries. Finally I described the counting incident with the ammunition and suggested that he should make sure that he was not showing any kind of surplus over his recorded holding.

Some months later I heard that the CQMS that I had spoken to had been warned for Court Martial. It would appear that as is fairly common even though a serious breach of the rules he had stockpiled a quantity of surplus items of ammunition. After our conversation he had stored the extras in his own car until after the inspection so as to prevent them being discovered. No real problems except that during the inspection his car had broken down and when he had left it in a lay by to get some help in recovering, it had been stolen.

He had dwelled on the matter for a few days and had then reported the whole matter to his officer commanding and this resulted which resulted in him being charged. I didn't want to know any more.

I was due to complete my twenty two years service in December 1986, in 1985 I had applied to join the Thames Valley Police although I was hoping to find a job in Germany either on the local economy or with a long service post.

I had submitted my LSL (long service) application and in addition a replacement for my CQMS post has been allocated. During the next few weeks I received a number of job offers within the UK but I continued to hold out for a post in Germany. LSL posts were much sought after and applications exceeded vacancies many times over.

One offer arrived which did not at first interest me, the sergeant in charge of the clothing store at Rheindahlen Garrison this was really a rubbish job but it was in Germany and in a great location. An added bonus, potential was that I had received two consecutive recommendations for promotion and I was reliably informed that the RQMS post was also to become vacant within weeks of my arrival. When I sought informed advice I was pretty much assured that I would be able to snatch the RQMS post and that would make me very happy indeed.

Acceptance replies had to be submitted literally by return as there were always many others waiting and if I didn't want the job somebody else did.

I submitted my acceptance and was later invited to take up my post on 1st December.

I eventually said my goodbyes to Hohne and RMP with a decent dining out dinner in the borrowed corporals mess. It was a sad day for me and my wife who had given up her job and for my children who would have to change schools yet again.

Extra Time the tainted gravy train

MY FIRST DAY AT RHEINDAHLEN was a bit disappointing, instead of meeting my new boss Lt Col Lambert who was on holiday I met the RQMS and I was not impressed., it was clear that my authority was to be very limited and I was already regretting my move.

Another bit of bad news was that the incumbent RQMS had been granted a twelve months extension and the potential opportunity for my promotion seemed to be virtually doomed A few days later I took over a married quarter in Monchen Gladback and fetched my wife and children from Hohne. We settled down to our new life and sorted out the children's new schools.

My wife was able to secure an interesting and well paid post as batman to one of the Headquarters senior officers, wives of RMP were much sought of for such sensitive posts and they were very scarce in Rheindahlen garrison.

I later met the quarter master Lt colonel Lambert and I got the clear impression that RMP were not his favourite people. As a qualified testing officer I registered with the HQ BAOR master driver who was anxious for me to conduct regular sensitive driving tests. Rheindahlen garrison was awash with senior officers and officer status civilians and there were of course many dependants, wives and school teachers applying for driving tests.

It would probably be no surprise that I was the only Royal Military Police QTO in BAOR and the Rhine area master driver was most pleased that I had arrived and could take on such tests to lessen his workload.

Although there were of course a number of other testing officers it was sometimes awkward for them when drivers failed and there was some fear that such results might!! Compromise the testing officers day job relationship. I was of course more than happy to take on as many tests as were needed. From the start it became clear that Col Lambert did not approve of my QTO status, I suppose that as an RCT officer he felt that such matters as testing drivers should be left to RCT and not RMP.

He was most insistent that I should submit a list of any test requests for him to consider before he could authorise my time out of the office.

After informing the master driver I understand that some conversation took place between Col Lambert and the garrison commander and I was simply asked to advise what days I would be undertaking tests and to restrict these to one day a week.

I was also of the view that he did not approve of my good relationship with the local RMP and the fact that I received regular visits from RMP personnel. I suspect that he may have discussed this with the RQMS who took to examining the clothing issue records, perhaps he thought that I was giving preferential treatment to RMP!!.

The colonel also took issue with the fact that I had a class 1 HGV licence and a permit to drive even the most specialist vehicles of that type which I had gained from putting in time with the MSO (mixed services organisation) at Hamm and their refurbished 1950's vintage Antar tank transporters. I was reluctant to share the fact that I was a RCT trained motorcycle instructor. But I'm sure that he must have checked my records

I was becoming increasingly disenchanted and bored, to counter this I set about reorganising the store making it more customer friendly. I took my share of regimental (night) duties, one each month alternating between security duties at the JHQ (big house) and duty clerk at the garrison. These duties were a welcome diversion and not particularly demanding.

The job I had was a simple enough role except for the fact that I suspect that RCT officers such as the QM were accustomed to applying constant supervision of their subordinates. I recall one incident at a staff meeting when the QM rebuked one of the sergeants for wearing shoes when his regimental barrack dress was technically boots. How trivial and petty.

To assist in the running of my department I retained a WRAC (female) corporal who undertook a good deal of the routine admin work and the tasks of a PA.

On one occasion the QM invited her to go skiing but I made it clear that it was not convenient as I required her to help me with the monthly returns.

I was pretty much incensed when I turned up for work the next morning to find that she had been "ordered" by the QM to join the skiing party.

The real kick however was the fact that the incumbent RQMS had applied for and was granted a twelve month extension in post in order to snatch a posting to Cyprus when it became available, my promotion opportunity was effectively lost.

The garrison sergeants mess was possibly one of the richest in the army and there were regular functions. I was only in the garrison for one Christmas but I was to discover that it was possible particularly in the weeks leading up to the Christmas break to attend several functions every day. I was also part of the 1987 Summer ball organising team, this was a truly huge, very expensive and enjoyable party.

In early 1987 I was asked by the colonel to be part of a QM department Veterans marathon team to take part in Monchengladbach annual marathon. I agreed to take part but wanted to ensure that we would get to regular training runs every day.

The colonel agreed to this and we started out training runs each day at 1330 hours.

About one month into the training the IRA planted a bomb in the garrison visitors mess accommodation I had received no instruction to cancel our training and in effect bomb crime scenes were nothing to do with me. Incidentally I felt the force of the explosion during the night at my home in Monchen Gladback some four miles away.

I waited outside the garrison compound at the normal time ready to set off as soon as the colonel arrived to my surprise and annoyance he leaned out of his office still in uniform and shouted out at me wanting to know how I had the time to go running after the bomb attack.

I was very much pissed off by his attitude I returned to my office and from that day I trained on my own after working hours. The following morning I submitted formal notice to terminate my service. The meeting with the colonel was not very friendly I was angry and upset, my pride was hurt and added to the fact that I did not like my job I allowed my emotions to make the decision that I should perhaps have sat on for a month.

I took part in the marathon but ran on my own instead of with the original team. I was miles ahead of them. I also took part in the annual Rheindahlen garrison marches again running the 40 kilometer route on my own.

In addition to this incident and the lack of any real authority in my job and the feeling of being constantly under scrutiny I just could not stand being micro managed, I just had to go

It was a very distressing time for me and my family and once again my wife would have to leave her job which she really enjoyed, her employer and his children were reluctant to lose her and I was asked through the medium of a third party to withdraw my termination notice. My pride would never allow this.

My wife wanted to remain in Germany and my children did not want to change schools.

Rheindahlen Garrison was a virtual British community town in Germany. Monchen Gladback was a fantastic place to live with easy access to the autobahn, only a fifteen minute drive from the Dutch border, loads of places to shop and explore. I never wanted to leave and neither did my family. I had spent the majority of my service life in Germany, a total of fifteen out of 22 years. My children had hardly any experience of life out of Germany and I had many German friends that I would be sad to leave.

Once I had submitted my notice I just wanted to get away as soon as possible, I also had to consider my children and requested that my departure date could be arranged to coincide with the start of the school summer holiday which would at least make the move a little easier.

Even at this late hour I suppose I could have been persuaded to stay if asked by the right person but I was not. I then had another surprise when I was told that I may well have to stay longer than anticipated because a suitably qualified and experienced replacement could not be identified.

It seemed to me that this was simply a mischievous act to punish me for my exit, I had only been in post for six months and it may have been the case that I should have allowed a bit more time, I could also have tried for a change but the chance of that happening was somewhere between slim and none!

When it looked as though I was going to be prevented from leaving at the time I submitted a letter to the garrison commander. It was also the case that my requested exit date was agreed.

Interestingly under the provisions of the Freedom of Information Act I have recently obtained copies of memos written by garrison staff. Apparently one officer considered that the sooner I left, the better!!Another officer refers to this individual having a dislike for RMP. How nice.

As a final insult and although I had a farewell drink with a number of the garrison staff I was not even afforded the courtesy of a formal exit interview. All very disappointing.

I was offered the opportunity of a dining out at the sergeants mess but I had reached the point where I just wanted to move on.

The long walk

Leaving Germany was not quite the end of my service life, I still had to make the final journey to the RMP training centre at Chichester for my final clearance.

Once again the insult of nothing more than an administration meeting, no hello or goodbye and not so much as a single word of appreciation or thanks after 23 years.

No bells, no frills and unsurprisingly no thanks.

After the final visit to Chichester I still had a resettlement course and some annual leave at least I was still being paid. I had passed the police entrance exam the previous year however I was in for a bit of a shock when I was informed by the police recruiting team that the 1987 induction quota was closed and that I would have to wait until 1988.

In the meantime I received my final notice of salary and my P45 and that was the end of my career, my Army days were over.

It was at this moment that the full implications of leaving the Army hit me.

Act in haste and repent at leisure.

I now had over six months before I could attempt to join the police, I had never before applied for a job and only now would I realise how poorly prepared I was.

That's another story!!!

ANNEX A
POSTINGS AND HOME LOCATIONS

RMP Training Centre
12 Inf Bde Pro Unit Osnabruck
Single living in Barracks
RMP Training Centre
Single living in barracks
48 Gurrkha Inf Bde Pro unit
Single living in barracks
married
Argyle Street Kowloon
Tak Yuen Villa Fanling
247 Berlin Pro Coy
Walzel Strasse Spandau
Tharauer Allee Charlottenburg
176 Pro Coy
Anson Road Ballykelly
102 Pro Coy
Living in barracks
HQ Brit For Antwerp
Bergen Straat Herentals
110 Pro Coy
Am Wilhelmsburg Schloss Nuehauss
114 Pro Coy

Allandsbusch Hakedahl Detmold
115 Pro Coy
Eullen Platz Hamm Rhynern
RMP Training centre
Living in mess
111 Pro Coy
Memeler Strasse Bergen
HQ Rheindahlen Garrison
Danziger Strasse Windberg MG

ANNEX B

MEDICAL

MEDICAL SERVICES WERE PRETTY MUCH inconsistent most soldiers just carried on even when they feeling unwell mostly because of the unhelpful system in place. My son was born in Berlin and within walking distance of the BMH, this of course meant I was able to visit easily and the care my wife received was first class which included a seven day admission.

What was not so good was the arrangements in Belgium when I had to take my wife on a three hour drive to the maternity wing at RAF hospital Wegberg for the birth of my daughter. This could have been avoided of course if I had either paid into a private arrangement at the local maternity hospital or simply took a chance and waited until the last minute and called for an emergency.

Just a few days after my wife came home from hospital after the birth of our daughter, my son managed to knock himself unconscious when he hit his head on a concrete garden post. Assisted by my neighbour I took him straight to the local Herentals children's hospital where they immediately checked him out, stitched him up and gave him back to me.

The hospital would have sent a bill to the army and I was "rebuked" by the Emblem detachment medical staff for not calling them and requesting an ambulance.

It would have been the case that the ambulance would have taken at least an hour to reach my home and then at least another three hours to reach the nearest military hospital at RAF Wegberg!!!

When I left Sennelager and moved to Detmold less than a year after the birth of my daughter and took my wife to see the SSAFA nurse as it was clear that she was still suffering some level of post natal depression. The very unhelpful and unsympathetic nurse was totally dismissive and not the least bit interested.

In Rheindahlen my son suffered agony for nearly two days before he was admitted to RAF Hospital Wegberg for an emergency appendocectomy. It took a German nurse to convince the doctors that they needed to get their scalpels to work.

There were so many stories circulating about military doctors but my least harmful favourites must be in Hong Kong where the senior garrison medical officer for the RMP was a consultant gynocologist and his standard diagnosis was take two codeine and if you are not better in three days come back. By his own admission he had not practised general medicine for twenty years.

In Emblem Belgium the civilian appointed garrison medical officer to troops and families was in fact a specialist consultant in tropical medicine

In Berlin I took my wife to the ante natal clinic and she fainted whilst lying down on the examination couch, the medical officer rushed out and asked me why she had fainted ? I think that was a very good question but the wrong person was asking it.

In Hamm Germany my daughter was regularly losing weight to the extent that she was missing a week's school every month, the local families medical officer appeared bereft of any ideas. It was not until 1982 when we returned to the UK that she was diagnosed as anaemic, correct medication provided and no more problems.

There were many stories circulating about Military Doctors and some of the strange and bizarre questions that patients were asked. It seemed to me that they were always at their best and most effective when operating under the most trying and difficult conditions. Whilst I had reason to question some of their assessments and treatment I am only too aware of the fact that many soldiers owe their lives to the early treatment they received. I just think that they were more geared up to operating under pressure and not switched on to the seeming trivia of "General Practise"

ANNEX C
ABBREVIATIONS

I HAVE INCLUDED A FEW of the most commonly used abbreviations as a means to assist any non-military reader.

Co	Commanding officer
OC	Officer Commanding
21/2	Second in command
RSM	Regimental Sergeant Major
CSM	Company Sergeant Major
Nco	Non commissioned officer
Ssgt	Staff sergeant
Sgt	Sergeant
Cpl	Corporal
Lcpl	Lance corporal
MT Sgt	Mechanical Transport Sergeant
CQMS	Company Quarter Master Sergeant
QM	Regimental Quartermaster Sergeant
BAOR	British Army Of The Rhine
ACC	Army catering corps
REME	Royal Electrical and Mechanical Engineers
MRS	Medical reception station
BMH	British military hospital
MO	Medical officer
WRAC	Womens royal army corps

COMPO   Composite food rations
QTO   Qualified testing officer =driving test examiner
BFN   British Forces Network
SKC   Services kinomatic corporation
NATO   North Atlantic Treaty Organisation
JHQ   Joint Headquarters
SIB   Special Investigation Branch
GSFG   Group of Soviet Forces Germany
SOXMIS   Soviet Military Mission to Commander in chief BAOR
BRIXMIS   British Military Mission to Soviet Commander in chief
RP COAT   Rubber proofed raincoat
TOTS   Tests of trained soldiers
ASAP   As soon as possible
MFO   Military Forwarding Organisation
DOB   Daily Occurrence Book
DDR   Deutsches Democratic Republic   East Germany
FRG   Federal Republic of Germany   West Germany
USSR   Union of Soviet Socialist Republics
NBC   Nuclear Biological and Chemical
RTA   Road Traffic Act
RTA   Road Traffic Accident
RSA   Road Safety Act
VPP   Village Penetration Patrol
PRI   President Regimental Institute
SSAFA   Soldiers Sailors and Airman's Families Association
NAAFI   Navy Army and Airforce Institute
MSO   Mixed Services Organisation
BFES   British Forces Education Service
AF   Army Form
AA   Army Act
QR's   Queens Regulations for the Army
FTX   Field Training Exercise
TEWT   Training Exercise without Troops
Mat Regs   Material regulations for the Army (The Quartermasters Bible)

REGIMENTAL
Second lieutenant
Lieutenant
Captain
Major
Lieutenant colonel

STAFF OFFICER RANKS
Colonel
Brigadier
Major general
Lieutenant general
General
Field marshal   wartime appointment

ANNEX E
RANK STRUCTURE ENLISTED RANKS

‒ﮨ

DEPENDING ON BRANCH OF SERVICE may have different titles but status unchanged

Private soldier.
Lance corporal
Corporal
Sergeant
Staff sergeant   may be appointed as CQMS
Warrant officer class two   may be appointed as company sergeant major
                                  May be appointed as RQMS
Warrant officer class 1   may be appointed as regimental sergeant major

ANNEX F

KIND AND CRUEL WORDS

—⌒

EDITED EXTRACTS FROM SOME OF my annual confidential reports. I suspect that many readers will have had similar creative and destructive comments written about them, I can laugh now but at the time it was painful.

1964 Training centre   Passed course promoted Lance corporal 2nd
                                     April 1965

1965 1966 1967 1968 Osnabruck
Shy retiring
Useful member of unit
Promoted Cpl
Plenty of common sense
Works well without supervision

1969   Hong Kong

Very immature, no knowledge of job, shows few leadership qualities.

Perhaps should have agreed to play volleyball every lunchtime and drink in the bar with the OC rather than go for lunch in the enlisted men's dining room.

1970   Hong Kong

Shows limited enthusiasm, acts like a disinterested spectator

Bad mistake challenging OC over his right and intention to send me to Singapore because he did not approve of my pending marriage to a Chinese girl.

1971   Hong Kong

Lack of enthusiasm just does the minimum

Perhaps I should have invited OC to my wedding reception along with many others, this omission was justified by the fact that I didn't think he would accept in any case.
He was obviously pissed off.

1971   Berlin

Hangs back from personal contact

Drat the fact that I don't play football.

1972   Berlin

Most reliable and capable but needs to take more interest in unit activities.

Still do not play football, not in the in crowd perhaps I should buy some boots!

1973   Berlin

Mature and hard working. Sets good example to juniors.

Perhaps the new OC is not so interested in sport.?

1974   Londonderry

Strong personality, good leadership uses his own initiative.

Yippee apparently football here is not considered so important.

1975   Londonderry

Good leadership sets excellent example to juniors.

What's football?

1976   Emblem Belgium sergeant

Undoubted ability as detachment commander

No idea of what was about to come

1977   Sennelager Sergeant

Complete lack of knowledge, inability to command by example, acts and be-
haves like a corporal.

Dead man walking in the shadow of a gratuitous and malicious witch hunt
to destroy me.
Very nearly did, down but not quite out.

1978   Detmold corporal

Firm direction and leadership high degree of management skill

Working in the land of sanity

1979   Detmold

Good supervisor leads by example

Continuing sanity

1979   Verl sergeant

MT Expert, sound knowledge of provost operations and police duties.

Reprieved

1980   Verl

Determined powers of leadership would be welcome as platoon commander

It's getting better

1981   Verl

Good supervision leads by example

Was a bit outspoken on this occasion which cost me two points on the report. Learn to keep my mouth shut, some hope.

1982   RMP Training centre

Lack of interest, basic knowledge of job, low grade.

A lesson in being unwilling and reluctant to kiss butts and fall in with the dictates of an inefficient and effectively corrupt and misguided regime.

Report graded at records as ROGUE. Exact comments by Board officer.

Clearly this NCO has been maltreated and his representation adds up to a sorry tale.
I believe this CR should be ignored.

Still cost me a year.

1983   Hohne   SSGT

Loyal and conscientious platoon commander

Not quite at the top but it's a good place to be

1984   Hohne

Very competent strongly recommended for promotion

Just a slim chance to step up one more rung

1985   Hohne

Able and conscientious, excellent ambassador for RMP

Good to know but just wasn't enough

EPILOGUE

IT HAS TAKEN ME THE best part of thirty years to accept that much of my misfortune could have been avoided by a change in my own attitude and to have made better use of the varied opportunities that only came once.

Despite this, the fact is that I did not always (as was the case for many others) get a fair deal and it's a real shame that I was not as lucky as some who were fortunate enough to serve with officers and seniors who were able to recognise and reward talent and hard work. I can still look back with pride at having served with the finest Corps in the British Army and I can hold my head up knowing that I did a better job for the Corps and my colleagues than many and refused to be beaten

The fact is that nothing in the past can be changed or altered, it's all over now and I have survived but only with the support of my wife Jenny to whom i will be for ever indebted and my children Spencer and Sarah for pushing me to write this book.

PAUL'S PICTURES

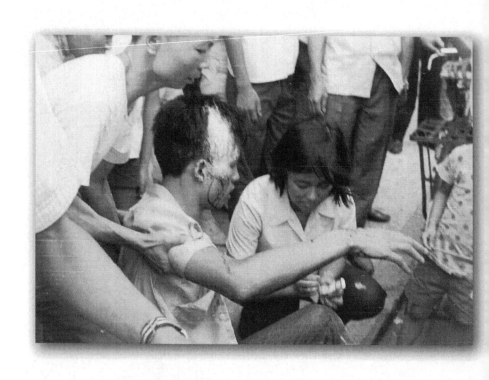

Printed in Great Britain
by Amazon